Shakespeare's Originality

Oxford Wells Shakespeare Lectures

Shakespeare's
Originality

JOHN KERRIGAN

OXFORD
UNIVERSITY PRESS

OXFORD
UNIVERSITY PRESS

Great Clarendon Street, Oxford, OX2 6DP,
United Kingdom

Oxford University Press is a department of the University of Oxford.
It furthers the University's objective of excellence in research, scholarship,
and education by publishing worldwide. Oxford is a registered trade mark of
Oxford University Press in the UK and in certain other countries

© John Kerrigan 2018

The moral rights of the author have been asserted

First Edition published in 2018

Impression: 4

Published in the United States of America by Oxford University Press
198 Madison Avenue, New York, NY 10016, United States of America

British Library Cataloguing in Publication Data
Data available

Library of Congress Control Number: 2017953311

ISBN 978–0–19–879375–5

Printed in Great Britain by
Clays Ltd, Elcograf S.p.A

To Peter Kerrigan

Preface

The extent and nature of Shakespeare's originality have been matters of contention and investigation from the earliest reference that we have to him as a playwright (in 1592) all the way through his elevation to the status of a classic in the eighteenth century and the major phases of source study that went on into the middle of the twentieth. How far, and in what ways, was he a derivative writer? One claim of this book is that, after several decades of relative neglect, it is time to return to this topic, to think again about issues that take us to the heart of Shakespeare's achievement while throwing into relief the contours of his reception.

The Introduction sets out what being 'original' meant and came to mean during and after Shakespeare's lifetime. To prepare the reader for the chapters that follow, it sketches the history of source scholarship and places it in the context of changing views of originality. A brief account is given of developments over the last half century which make a new discussion timely, showing how advances in research and fresh perspectives in criticism allow the matter to be addressed in finer detail and with fuller contexts than was possible for the foundational scholars (Lewis Theobald to Edmond Malone, Karl Simrock to Geoffrey Bullough). Chapters 1–4 then explore contrasting aspects of the topic. The aim is to open up the field with case studies without attempting to be comprehensive. These chapters advance independently but have points of overlap and continuity.

The analysis starts aslant. Chapter 1 moves through Cervantes and Charlotte Lennox to the celebrated attack on Shakespeare as an upstart crow in Robert Greene's *Groatsworth of Witte*. It considers what the passage tells us about originality and derivativeness in both the composition of playscripts and the material culture of performance. Out of this flows a discussion of *Much Ado About Nothing* in which disguise, ambition, and fashion—from modish attire to the fashioning of plays—are foregrounded. This knowing, obscurely sceptical comedy both reflects on and puts to use the author's and the audience's partial awareness of an early modern web of alternative versions of the

Hero-Claudio story. An extrapolation of possible outcomes—not unlike the work of Shakespeare in composition—was creatively engaged in those watching the play.

While Chapter 1 thinks about the narrative and dramatic sources that have been identified for *Much Ado*, its successor looks more radically at how the bases of acting in footwork, in the conventions and practice of performance, became another sort of source for Shakespeare. That an author should follow in the footsteps of earlier writers, should learn from their marks and tracks, was a commonplace of classical and Renaissance writing about the art of imitation (i.e. the lively modelling of texts on already existing works). From the plays discussed in Chapter 2 it is clear that, whether he is following his written originals closely (as in *As You Like It*) or striking out more freely (as in the first act of *Richard III* and various scenes in *Macbeth*), Shakespeare is at least as conscious of how he and other actors in his company follow in other players' footsteps.

This is not to say that classical and early modern ideas about imitation are irrelevant. They bolster, rather dubiously, Greene's denunciation of the upstart crow, and they recur in eighteenth-century contrasts between his supposedly untutored originality and the learned procedures of Jonson and Milton. The growing sophistication of sections of theatrical culture in the decade or so after Greene's attack allowed Shakespeare to become more ambitious in his use of such prestigious originals as Plutarch and in the demands made of actors and audiences. In Chapter 3, I argue that in *King Lear* the practice of imitation is integral to the probing of origins: political, legal, historical, tragic. The resonance of the drama owes much to layers of imitation that go back through Sidney's *Arcadia* (the source of the Gloucester plot) to Seneca, Sophocles, and Euripides. Jonson may have been right when he said in the First Folio that Shakespeare had, by his own erudite standards, 'small *Latine*, and less *Greeke*', but he was also purposeful when he went on to compare the Swan of Avon to the ancient Greek tragedians.

What happens when a Shakespeare play itself becomes a source? In Chapter 4, attention shifts to the originary power of *The Tempest*. Known and neglected sources of the play are reinvestigated, partly to elucidate its textures but primarily to show how it drew out of Virgil and the Virginia and Bermuda pamphlets ecological as well as

theatrical resources that were not just ready for adaptation by
Fletcher, Suckling, and more directly Davenant and Dryden in *The
Tempest: Or, The Enchanted Island* (1667), and for such followers in
alteration as Shadwell and David Garrick, but were available also to
inform and underwrite eighteenth-century and Romantic accounts of
Shakespeare as a poet of Nature, a branching tree, an 'original Poetic
genius' like Homer and Ossian. At this point the book returns to the
means by which such originality became for many the measure of
creative value in the 1740s and '50s—as set out in the Introduction
and Chapter 1; I look more closely at how this promotion of originality was challenged and defended in relation to Shakespeare and at
how arguments in favour of his originality can still have eighteenth-
century overtones in discussions at least of *The Tempest*.

Most of this book consists of a lightly revised version of the Oxford
Wells Shakespeare Lectures that I gave during Michaelmas term
2016. I am grateful to Bart van Es and others who proposed me as
lecturer and to Jacqueline Norton of Oxford University Press who
encouraged me to accept the invitation. My visits to Oxford were
enhanced by conversations with Colin Burrow, John Creaser, Katherine
Duncan-Jones, Paul Edmondson, Antonia and Francis Kerrigan,
Laurie Maguire, Lene Østermark-Johansen, Seamus Perry, Helen
Small, Emma Smith, Robert Stagg, Tiffany Stern, Stanley Wells, and
David Womersley. It was encouraging to see in the audience of the
third lecture Kate Plaisted-Grant and Niamh Kerrigan-Plaisted. To
return to Oxford, several decades after being an undergraduate there,
put me gratefully in mind of those who first got me thinking about
Shakespeare: Anne Barton, John Carey, John Creaser, Barbara Everett,
Emrys Jones, John Jones, Craig Raine, Stephen Wall, and Stanley Wells.

For advice on what to read, ahead of writing the lectures, I am
indebted to Colin Burrow, John Drakakis, Hester Lees-Jeffries,
Willy Maley, and Richard Serjeantson. Theodor Dunkelgrün, Peter
Holland, Micha Lazarus, and Kate Plaisted-Grant generously
supplied material. I value the support I receive from St John's College,
Cambridge and my colleagues in the Cambridge English Faculty.
After Oxford, and an outing in Cambridge, two of the lectures were
tested at the Willson Center for Humanities and Arts, University of
Georgia (where my host was Nicholas Allen and my interlocutor
Sujata Iyengar). At Princeton, later in the process, three chapters

were presented as talks and I benefited from discussion with Bradin
Cormack, Jeff Dolven, Rhodri Lewis and others. The book was read
in typescript by Colin Burrow, Nick de Somogyi (who made the
index), David Hillman, Lorna Hutson, Willy Maley, Subha Mukherji,
and Helen Small. I could not be more grateful to these busy people for
the time and quality of attention that they brought to my arguments.
For help with images, I owe thanks to Clément Chéroux, Manuel
Harlan, Kathryn McKee, Jen Pollard, John Wyver, and staff at the
institutions mentioned in the list of illustrations.

Throughout, I quote from the electronic text of *The Oxford
Shakespeare, Complete Works*, 2nd edn, gen. eds Stanley Wells and
Gary Taylor (Oxford: Oxford University Press, 2005). When citing
early modern books, I have silently corrected misprints, made one or
two adjustments to punctuation, and expanded abbreviations and
contractions ('&' becomes 'and', 'ye' as an article becomes 'the'). Titles
are lightly regularized. A few italics have been added to Shakespeare
quotations to bring out points under discussion. *The Oxford English
Dictionary*, consulted online, is abbreviated to *OED*. With plays
I give, as a rule, the generally accepted date of composition or first
performance, along with the date of print publication where relevant,
though sometimes the latter is close enough to the former to suffice.
With non-dramatic works, I give date of print publication, occasionally qualified. Everything should be clear enough.

Contents

List of Illustrations

Introduction

Most people interested in Shakespeare have wondered about his originality. Is it true that his plays were adapted from other authors' plays, poems, and romances? Are his best-known speeches really lifted out of Montaigne and Plutarch? If so—and it is far from entirely so—does it matter, any more than it does when a classic movie is based on a novel? What distinctions and relationships hold between originality, collaboration, and adaptation? To think adequately about such questions requires a lot of information-gathering and sifting, but the effort is worthwhile because it helps us identify creative decisions made by Shakespeare in the process of composition while it also shows him participating in a larger culture of play-making. We equip ourselves to characterize the techniques by which he managed to achieve the types of originality available during his lifetime.

That is the purpose of this book. It offers four contrasted case studies to cut routes into an enormous topic. The approach is practical—that is, attentive to verbal and theatrical practice—and occasionally conceptual, but also inevitably historical. It has to be historical partly because the dramatist's use of pre-existing material has for so long been an object of investigation that the facts and findings gathered have been used to construct different versions of 'Shakespeare' and reach us coloured by those versions and the arguments that have raged around them; but it must also be historical because early modern ideas about copying, invention, quotation, translation, imitation, plagiarism, and alteration were different from our own and certainly from those that obtained when the word 'originality', which first came into use *c.*1650 to characterize the most essential forces of the universe and ultimately the Divine,[1] was carried over in the 1740s and '50s to define the generative primacy of a writer.[2]

Given the risk of anachronism, why write of 'originality' at all? First, as I note in Chapter 1, the evolving semantics of 'original'—before, during and after Shakespeare's lifetime—from 'The origin or source of something' (1325) and 'a source, cause; an originator, creator' (*c.*1390) through 'the thing . . . from which another is copied or reproduced' (1599) to 'Created, composed, or done by a person directly' (1650) and 'not imitated or copied from another' (1700),[3] anticipate what 'originality' would come to mean in the mid–late eighteenth century and on to the present.[4] Second, as I also indicate in Chapter 1, cultural and conceptual ferment encouraged the implications of 'original' to develop in the late sixteenth century, and a charge of plagiarism figures in the earliest comments that we have about Shakespeare as a playwright—those attributed to Robert Greene, in 1592, which accuse him of profitable derivativeness, an accusation which Leonard Digges felt he had to rebut in a verse tribute that was printed in Shakespeare's *Poems* (1640). Third, the evolving senses of 'originality' are connected not just to what 'original' could imply as an adjective but to that older, related sense of 'the thing, as a document, text, picture, etc., from which another is copied' or more inventively 'reproduced'. If Shakespeare were asked what *King Lear* owed to *King Leir*, he might say that the old play was his 'authority' (though he would more likely have said that of Holinshed); he would not, except metaphorically, say it was his 'source' (on which more below); he would most likely call it his 'original'.

So the word *originality* in my title points to modern ideas about originality that were stirring in the early modern period while reminding us of the then-standard practice of working with originals. Shakespeare does new things with and adds extensively to what he draws from pre-existing texts, but his originality is partly original-ity, a drawing upon originals. The word resonates and diversifies because 'original' during Shakespeare's lifetime could also mean 'going back to origins', to the beginnings or (more confusedly) causes of things—a strong impulse in the culture—but also 'being generative, productive of later texts, recensions, adaptations', which is an attribute of many works, including a number written by Shakespeare. Chapters 3 and 4 of this book explore those aspects of originality in *King Lear* and versions of *The Tempest*. But my title most intently sets parameters for the discussion of what is distinctive in the output. It would be possible to write a book called *Shakespeare's Originality* that explored the peculiar inventiveness of his imagery, his increasingly fluid handling of the verse line, or his singular ways with cross-dressing. My aim is more specifically to reconnect with the long-standing, inter-rupted study of Shakespeare's use of his originals.

We know that members of Shakespeare's audience were alert to the earlier texts on which his plays drew or were based. Sir John Manningham, for example, wrote of a performance at the Middle Temple in 1602: 'At our feast wee had a play called "Twelve night, or what you will"; much like the commedy of errores, or Menechmi in Plautus, but most like and neere to that in Italian called Inganni.'[5] Manningham might be referring to Nicolò Secchi's *Gl'inganni* (1562), in which case his judgement is—like so many in the history of source study—somewhat speculative and off-the-mark. More likely he is referring to a whole class of plays about deceptions (i.e. *inganni*), or is half-remembering *Gl'ingannati* ('The Deceived'), an anonymous play published in 1537 which does feature in the family tree of *Twelfth Night*—both possibilities a reminder that an audience can pick up generic resemblances which shape anticipations even when they do not exactly match the originals from which plays derive.

So the study of Shakespeare's use of originals does not just bring into focus the creative decisions that he makes; it can help us reconstruct the expectations that early audiences would have brought to plays. Those who knew the popular, now-lost *Hamlet*, written (probably by Kyd) in the late 1580s, would respond differ-ently from us to Shakespeare's remake, which capitalizes on the potential of that foreknowledge. Much can be learned about this from John Marston's *Antonio's Revenge* (*c.*1600), which was written independently of *Hamlet* but which correlates at a number of points with the first printed text of that play, the quarto of 1603. Already, originality looks complicated, when two plays end up in parallel without cross-influence because of a lost original. An audience that was familiar with Greene's oft-reprinted prose romance, *Pandosto*, would have expected an outcome much darker than they were shown in *The Winter's Tale*, a play which, for much of its action, follows the prose romance quite closely. They must have been struck by the survival of Leontes (in Greene he goes mad and dies) and even more by the revival of his queen, Hermione, who plays a statue coming to life.

Yet the astrologer Simon Forman, who saw *The Winter's Tale* in 1611, wrote an account of it in a notebook in which the statue scene is not even mentioned.[6] This is another reminder of the complications of derivation: to compare Shakespeare's plays with their originals and highlight what he added is not always to throw into relief what most impressed early auditors, since they might find more satisfaction in what is in the modern sense least original—not just in the play but in its source also: Forman was evidently impressed by the romance and fairy-tale motif of Perdita living as a shepherdess until letters and jewels left with her as a baby prove her to be the daughter of Leontes and an allowable match for Prince Florizel. It is not simply the case, however, that Forman was drawn to those parts of *The Winter's Tale* which figure in Greene. His account of the action is curtailed by an appreciative, self-warning description of the cutpurse and ballad-singer Autolycus, a character added to Greene's storyline by Shakespeare (though derivative in other respects). The relationship between Forman's comments and the originality or otherwise of the plays becomes even more of a cat's cradle when one notices that, in his account of *Macbeth*, what he says he saw on stage has been influenced by his reading of the original on which the tragedy is based. He imports from Holinshed the notion that Macbeth and Banquo enter the action 'Ridinge thorowe a wod' and describes the witches as '3 women feiries or Nimphes'. This reading may have preceded his theatre visit but it just as likely followed it and reshaped what he remembered from performance. Not only authors but audience members drew on originals in their construction of plays.

* * *

The systematic identification of Shakespeare's originals starts with Gerard Langbaine, whose *Momus Triumphans* set out to catalogue (in the words of the title page) *The Plagiaries of the English Stage ... With an Account of the Various Originals ... from whence Most of them have Stole their Plots* (1687). In his preface, Langbaine gives three reasons for putting together his book. The first is catchpenny, though it tells us useful things about publishing and theatre practice: 'to prevent my Readers being impos'd on by crafty Booksellers, whose custom it is as frequently to vent *old* Plays with *new* Titles, as it has been the use of the Theatres to dupe the Town, by acting old Plays under new Names'.

To this he adds a second motive, familiar in source studies to this day: 'By this means the curious Reader may be able to form a Judgment of the Poets ability in working up a *Dramma*, by comparing his *Play* with the *Original* Story.' Finally, he is interested in detecting 'Thefts', where borrowings are unacknowledged. Langbaine's list of plagiaries, extended in his *Account of the English Dramatick Poets* (1691), was evidently appreciated because a further edition, 'improv'd and continued' by another hand, appeared a few years later.[7]

Shakespeare editors from Lewis Theobald (1733) onwards scoured the early modern period for texts behind the plays that would help with points of emendation and explication. Others explored the playwright's learning, trying to reconcile his knowledge of Plautus and Plutarch with the notion that he was instructed only by Nature and 'needed not', in Dryden's words, 'the spectacles of Books'.[8] The study of his 'ability in working up a *Dramma*' (Langbaine) was encouraged by Charlotte Lennox's often pejoratively critical compendium of originals, *Shakespear Illustrated* (1753–4). From the work of the great Shakespeare scholar Edward Capell through that of the antiquarian John Nichols, and again through the later editors of the Shakespeare variorum, George Steevens and Edmond Malone,[9] the investigation went on; it was further substantiated in John Payne Collier's *Shakespeare's Library* (1843), its revision by William Carew Hazlitt (1875) and its offspring, H. R. D. Anders, *Shakespeare's Books* (1904), until it reached a culmination, for now, in Geoffrey Bullough's eight-volume *Narrative and Dramatic Sources of Shakespeare* (1957–75).

Lennox's title, *Shakespear Illustrated*, anticipates what lies beyond her volumes: a move towards collecting materials that 'illustrate' the plays contextually without them necessarily being claimed as sources. Capell's *School of Shakespeare* set a formidable example in gathering poems, songs, histories, masques, and other 'analogous'[10] matter. The research was antiquarian but innovative; it broke out of the point-by-point comparison and contrast of play-text with original that constrained the work of Lennox and demonstrated the interest in its own right of the culture that Shakespeare participated in. From Douce's *Illustrations of Shakspeare, and of Ancient Manners* (1807), with its dissertations on clowns and fools, the *Gesta Romanorum*, and the English morris dance, through Joseph Hunter's *New Illustrations of the Life, Studies, and Writings of Shakespeare* (1845), early nineteenth-century scholarship

opened up enquiry. The development may have been encouraged by
a Romantic-period desire not to make too much of Shakespeare's
borrowing from originals now that originality was regarded as central
to his achievement. There is an undertow of apology and defence,[11]
designed to protect the Bard's reputation even while his list of debts
mounted.

It is striking, from this perspective, that the study of Shakespeare's
use of his originals could be driven by attempts to show that he was not
original even as literate culture was placing a high value on originality.
As I note in Chapter 1, Langbaine's pioneering scholarship was the
product of late seventeenth-century controversies about plagiarism
which scholars have traced back to the assertion of literary property
in the theatre, ahead of the Copyright Act of 1710. Six decades later,
Lennox published her compilation when claims were mounting for
Shakespeare as the ultimate exemplar of originality. Near the end of
this book we shall see how her work encouraged the production
of new accounts—some of them astute, others expedient—of how
Shakespeare was, after all, original. Dominant attitudes to originality are
only ever one part of the story, and counter-currents are always emerging.

Though eighteenth- and nineteenth-century arguments about these
issues often turned on Shakespeare, he was not the only author to
figure: Milton and Jonson were cited as foils. John Dennis anticipated
the mid-century elevation of originality when he declared in 1704 that
'*Milton* was the first, who in the space of almost 4000 Years, resolved,
for his Country's Honour and his own, to present the World with an
Original Poem; that is to say, a Poem that should have his own
Thoughts, his own Images, and his own Spirit.'[12] For some, this was
a challenging claim to make about a poet so knowingly dependent on
Homer, Virgil, the Bible. John Douglas felt moved to defend Milton
by arguing, sagaciously, in 1750: 'as *one* may be what is called an
original Writer, and yet have no Pretensions to *Genius*, so another may
make use of the Labors of others in such a Manner as to satisfy the
World of his own Abilities. There may be such a thing as an *original
Work* without *Invention*, and a Writer may be an Imitator of others
without *Plagiarism*.'[13]

To see what is at stake it is necessary to loop back to classical and
Renaissance ideas about *inventio* and *imitatio*, of importance to this
book as a whole. During the sixteenth and early seventeenth centuries,

the practice of imitation, which required writers to draw on and refashion material from earlier, prestigious texts—with an expectation, in some accounts, that the relationships established would be appreciated by readers—was commended.[14] When imitations were read as following ancient originals, one consequence could be, and often was, a growing sense of the pastness of the past. This generated ideas about backward-looking as well as recreative originality that were both historicizing and transformative; caught up with larger beliefs about cultural and spiritual decline since antiquity (and so with loss, fall, echo), as well as with ideas of renewal, they shaped and developed the ethos of originality in the modern sense that is palpable in Milton.[15] Rhetoricians meanwhile encouraged the view that invention did not entail the generation of storylines and concepts out of thin air but the disposition of inherited elements. Invention, understood in these terms, was the 'finding out or selection of topics to be treated, or arguments to be used' before it came to mean (by about 1638) 'The devising of a subject, idea, or method of treatment, by exercise of the intellect or imagination'.[16]

This model of composition, relevant but by no means entirely applicable to plays written for the public theatre, was well-understood as late as 1700 and beyond. Yet as ideas about invention shifted towards a valuing of the innovative,[17] imitation developed a problematic relationship with originality. The logic of these changes, evident in what John Douglas says about Milton, can be tracked towards Shakespeare in Edward Capell's *Reflections on Originality in Authors* (1766). Capell was no stranger to the classics, but he shows the mutation in sensibility associated with the new valuation of originality when he deprecates the imitation that he is more than capable of recognizing even as he recognizes its elusiveness. Imitation can be undesirable, he says, but he believes it is imputed too often. Sometimes all we have is a coincidence between texts, explicable by the shared experience of writers.[18] In any case, imitation is acceptable as one element in the work of an author who 'forms his descriptions and language, and executes his plan from his own observation' (6). From this springs another defence of Milton, whose writings, 'though he was so great a reader, have as original an aspect as *Shakespear*'s' (56).

In the seventeenth century, Jonson's Art was conventionally contrasted with Shakespeare's Nature. As the cult of originality grew, the

laureate Jonson, who had been virtuosic in exploring the complexities
of *imitatio* in verse epistles, epigrams, and panegyrics,[19] was demoted
against a Bard who 'lower'd his genius by no vapid Imitation'. So
wrote Young in 1759, adding that '*Johnson*, in the serious drama, is as
much an imitator, as *Shakespeare* is an original.'[20] Many knew perfectly
well that *Sejanus* and *Catiline*, which do follow Latin sources closely,
and, in the case of the former, put those authorities on display in the
quarto margins,[21] were not the whole of Jonson; *The Alchemist* is so
brilliantly syncretic and *The Devil is an Ass* so freshly conceived that
both are original by any standards. Others would acknowledge that, if
dependence on classical texts is the measure, Shakespeare in *Coriolanus*
is as much a learned poet as was Jonson following Suetonius.[22] But the
contrast between Art and Nature continued to be inviting, and it
worked to Jonson's disadvantage. Capell concludes that the latter
'seems to have made it his study to cull out others sentiments, and to
place them in his works as from his own mint. This surely is an odd
species of improvement from reading, and savours very little of Invention or Genius: It borders nearly upon, if it is not really plagiarism.'[23]

    The elevation of originality was further heightened during the
Romantic period, as statements in its favour, by Wordsworth, Coleridge, and Hazlitt, and by philosophers and scholars from Kant to
Isaac D'Israeli, show; this enhanced the standing of Shakespeare;
yet the celebration of original genius[24] was often counterpointed
or nuanced and was qualified by literary practice, not least when it
came to the composition of plays in Shakespearean style. As Robert
Macfarlane has shown, peak originality was reached in critical discourse in the 1820s and '30s, a period which, not coincidentally,
generated a further round of the plagiarism-hunting which had
prompted Capell to write his treatise of 1766.[25] A reaction against
the derivativeness of denouncing derivation can most famously be
found in Emerson, who declared that 'Our debt to tradition through
reading and conversation is so massive, . . . that, in a large sense, one
would say, there is no pure originality. All minds quote . . . The originals are not original.'[26] This was not a neoclassical argument in
favour of imitation; it owed more to a Romantic belief that whatever
genius claims, from hills, lakes, and libraries, it makes its own, but
more again to a vision of the embeddedness of major writing that
anticipates modernism. 'Great genial power,' Emerson writes about

Shakespeare, 'consists in not being original at all; in being altogether receptive; in letting the world do all, and suffering the spirit of the hour to pass unobstructed through the mind.'[27]

Emerson cites Edmond Malone on Shakespeare's collaborative and derivative practice. Subsequent work in Britain and America on the originals and diffuse sources of the plays owed much to the gentlemanly scholarship best exemplified by Malone, but greater comprehensiveness and rigour were imported from Germany, where the discipline of *Quellenforschung* sought, with some success, to identify components, drawn from different origins, in classical and Biblical texts and in folk tales.[28] The approach was extended to Shakespeare by Karl Simrock, the translator of the *Nibelungenlied* into modern German and of Shakespeare's poems and some of his plays, in his *Quellen des Shakspeare in Novellen, Märchen und Sagen* (1831), a work that was brought into English 'with notes and additions' by J. O. Halliwell in 1850.[29] During a century much given, in England and America, to evolutionary interpretations of words and texts (etymology, stemmata), and increasingly systematic in its tabulation and reproduction of Shakespeare's sources,[30] the influence of Simrock was considerable. Perceptive and culturally attuned, he was more interested in Shakespeare's development than in breaking up the plays into modules; yet the reputation of *Quellenforschung* for ignoring the integrity of literary works in its desire to isolate pieces in the jigsaw was not entirely undeserved. The condescension of such critics as Saintsbury echoes as late as Bullough.[31]

That Shakespeare was known to have made extensive use of pre-existing texts made him valuable to those Victorian commentators who argued for the worth of reinvention as well as creation. Shakespeare, Pater observes, 'refashioned . . . materials already at hand, so that the relics of other men's poetry are incorporated'. 'The originality . . . which we ask from the artist,' wrote his disciple Oscar Wilde, in 1885, 'is originality of treatment, not of subject', adding with a twist of wit, 'It is only the unimaginative who ever invents.'[32] This was the moment of the Berne Convention, which protected the intellectual property of authors (1883); but the critics who immediately precede T. S. Eliot's 'Tradition and the Individual Talent' do not typically promote self-generating talent. Already, the 'prating about originality' which characterized the mid-eighteenth century was giving way to

'the ceaseless prating about unoriginality which would characterize
the twentieth'.[33] What of the twenty-first? Uncreative writing and
pseudo-modernism are not the only aesthetics, but in key manifest-
ations they go with copying, sampling, mashing—the disciplines of the
internet. Most of us are in tune with 'unoriginal genius'.[34]

One side effect of the changes just outlined was the replacement
during the Romantic period of 'original' (as a noun) by 'source'.
'Origin' itself originates in Latin *oriri*, 'to rise', but its connotations of
flow were hardened by the legal and scholarly uses of 'original' to
mean the exemplar from which copies were made. 'Source' by contrast comes from Old French *sors*, and it kept for longer than 'original'
the associations of *sourdre* ('to rise or spring'). From the medieval
period to the present 'source' has meant 'The fountain-head or origin
of a river or stream', and figuratively 'The chief or prime cause *of*
something of a non-material or abstract character; the quarter
whence something of this kind originates'.[35] That it could also
mean, during Shakespeare's lifetime, 'The act of rising on the
wing, on the part of a hawk or other bird',[36] underlines its lack of
attachment to texts. During the sixteenth century, the word's meta-
phorical application to literary production, affiliation, and descent
began, in English as in French,[37] and spring-like and fluvial sources
flow into learned poetry from Book IV of Virgil's *Georgics* and the
Book of Genesis.[38] With Milton, we might indeed think more use-
fully of sources than originals, given his mingling of imitation and
echo to achieve the sort of originality[39] that owes as much to
Protestant commitment to the autonomous conscience[40] as it does
to the practice of the eristic, classically derived form of imitation
known as *aemulatio*.[41] Certainly the word 'source' emerges in Milton
commentary slightly ahead of its use in Shakespeare studies.
Dr Johnson wrote in 1750, of Grotius' *Adamus exul*, that he 'doubted
not but, in finding the original of that tragedy, I should disclose the
genuine source of *Paradise Lost*'.[42]

Because 'source' is so readily used in a figurative way, it is difficult to
judge precisely when the same shift began in Shakespeare scholarship.
When Richard Farmer, for instance, writes as follows in 1767, he is
probably using 'source' as Johnson does: 'whence have we the Plot of
Timon, except from the *Greek* of *Lucian*? . . . the source of a Tale hath
been often in vain sought abroad, which might easily have been found

at home'.[43] We can say with assurance, however, that by 1778 the word 'source' was being used (by Steevens) where 'original' would once have appeared.[44] The following year, Capell observed that the blinding of Gloucester in *King Lear* is 'a part of the story that was the source of this episode' (i.e. in Sidney's *Arcadia*).[45] Elsewhere, he prefers 'original'—not just of etymologies but source-texts—and it is not until Douce's *Illustrations* three decades later that 'source' becomes truly current, remaining so from Skottowe's *Life of Shakespeare* (1824) through Dowden's *Shakespeare* (1875) and Hazlitt's revision of Collier. By the early twentieth century, 'original' had become quaint, as in the 1907 reprint of a source discussed in Chapter 2 of this book: *Lodge's 'Rosalynde', Being the Original of Shakespeare's 'As You Like It'*, edited by W. W. Greg.

It looks as though the modern meaning of 'originality' could only emerge and lead to the suppression of 'original' as a noun once the new implications of 'originality' had depleted its earlier associations. Further reasons can be found, though, for the growing incidence of 'sources'. First, it could evoke those widely diffused beliefs—about ghosts, for instance, or devils—that belong to what William Duff, in his *Essay on Original Genius* (1767), calls 'the same source, that of traditionary relation'.[46] 'Source' is more applicable than 'original' (a word that Duff still uses for source-texts) in the contextual fields of cultural history that were being unpacked by illustration. A second, related point is that sources can be multiple and messy while originals tend to be fixed. The source of a river might be a muddy field, and the main current would be fed by tributaries—other sources—or lead off into channels that produce those streams or texts that resemble but are not generative originals (i.e. those texts that nineteenth-century scholars following the scientists called 'analogues').[47] This riverine model of textual production maps well onto Shakespeare, given his tendency to draw on tales that had tangled lines of descent and his distinctive though not unique impulse to consult multiple works even when basing his play on a single original (working from Plutarch, he draws on Seneca and Livy). Third, and again relatedly, 'source' can be used to characterize a more organic, communal process than 'original', one which potentially embraces what Emerson called 'the world ... the spirit of the hour'. Despite these sophistications, however, there remains a line of descent from Lennox's and even

Langbaine's cataloguing of 'originals' to Bullough's massive compilation of Shakespeare's narrative and dramatic 'sources'.

*   *   *

The limitations of Bullough's compendium are so familiar to Shakespeareans that they need only be lightly touched on: the exclusion of discursive material even when debts are obvious (e.g. the Montaigne passage given to Gonzalo, in *The Tempest*, as discussed in Chapter 4); the related lack of attention to how Shakespeare picked up, and countered, ideas, in the absence of verbal echoes, as though he only latched onto words and stories;[48] a fuzziness about the rationale for including illustrative texts and analogues. Of greater significance for *Shakespeare's Originality* is the irony that, just as Bullough brought his eight volumes to completion, in 1975, interest in sources fell away. The scale of his achievement might itself have contributed to this. It must have been easy to feel, when confronted with his *summa*, that the main discoveries had been made. Kenneth Muir, symptomatically, delayed and truncated his survey of *Shakespeare's Sources* as Bullough published his volumes.[49] More potently, though, poststructuralism was at that date putting in doubt the authorial subject as an origin of meaning and dispersing 'source' and 'influence' into proliferating and receding textuality. 'Alongside each utterance', Roland Barthes observed, 'off-stage voices (whose origin is "lost" in the vast perspective of the *already-written*) de-originate the utterance.'[50] The concept of 'intertextuality', drawn out of Saussure and Bakhtin by Julia Kristeva, advanced a valuable critique of lineal derivation from originals: 'any text is constructed as a mosaic of quotations; ... The notion of *intertextuality* replaces that of intersubjectivity.'[51] Reconceived in this way, the analysis of interaction between plays and their textual environment[52] could avoid imputing intention and encourage attention to the retrospective influence of later texts on precursors.

Intertextual criticism had roots in modernism and its nineteenth-century genealogy but it was well-adapted to illuminate an early modern environment in which originals could be plastic: the semantics of 'copy' at the time include the adaptative and generative because source-texts were often rephrased when quoted, apothegms and commonplaces cited, works translated (to correct their values, or in emulation), and even when poems and plays were transcribed from one manuscript into another.[53] For all its promise, however, 'intertextuality' did more for Joyce studies than it ever did for Shakespeare criticism. It lacked a Renaissance psychology of purpose. New Historicism, and the revived older historicisms that followed it, promoted social forces and topicality over the analysis of textual derivation,[54] while identity politics and queer theory had little incentive to isolate what is original in Shakespeare's use of his originals.

This is not to say that attention ceased entirely. The custom of reprinting sources at the back of major editions often fell into abeyance, but some editors, rethinking the issues, distributed such material through their commentary, or, in an introduction, widened the focus beyond originals in graduated stages to the ambient contexts and culture that earlier scholars would call illustrative.[55] Assiduous critics still adduced sources, and a few impressive books—notably Emrys Jones's *The Origins of Shakespeare*—returned to the field.[56] Micro-studies of indebtedness continued to make their mark in the journals. Notwithstanding exceptions, however, the potent claim, which Bullough makes but does not fulfil, that to investigate the use of sources is 'the best, and often the only, way open to us of watching Shakespeare the craftsman in his workshop',[57] faded before the material assembled and briefly discussed in the *Narrative and Dramatic Sources* could be explored in a receptive climate.

Stirrings of attention can now be detected. Janet Clare's *Shakespeare's Stage Traffic* (2014) investigates how the dramatist drew on pre-existing plays. Raphael Lyne invokes cognitive psychology to reconstruct Shakespeare's experiences as a reader and rewriter.[58] Stuart Gillespie has revised and reissued *Shakespeare's Books: A Dictionary of Shakespeare's Sources* (2001, 2016). Folk tales, usually ignored, though revisited in a stimulating essay by Linda Woodbridge (1993), have been reassessed by Charlotte Artese in *Shakespeare's Folktale Sources* (2015).[59] A volume of *Shakespeare Survey* entitled 'Shakespeare, Origins and Originality', which includes several valuable contributions, appeared while I was writing this book.[60] Digital work on Shakespearean collaboration already overlaps with, and shows a potential future for, computer-assisted analyses[61] of debts, echoes, allusions, data, borrowings, stimuli, heritage, hauntings, and all the other critical terms[62] that now define source/text relations in discussion. Early English Books Online and the Text Creation Partnership are changing the questions and methodology used for investigating intertextual relations on the largest scale, but they also facilitate the identification of specific points of contact. The long neglect of the topic, combined with these developments, suggests that the time is ripe to reconsider Shakespeare's originality.

In three respects, at least, we are better informed than the many cataloguers of sources from Langbaine to Bullough. First, we have a fuller sense of the landscape of oral and literate culture, popular as well as educated, within which the plays took shape—among ballads, rumours, proverbs, newsletters, and sermons as well as printed texts. Shakespeare's creativity was fed by the sung and spoken as well as by the handwritten and printed, and these spheres of verbal production were interactive, not distinct.[63] Within that bigger picture, three decades' research into early modern 'used books' and reading has elaborated and distanced our understanding of how the written word was consumed and redeployed. The modern, everyday experience of passive reading tells us relatively little about the active early modern engagement with texts, often underlined and marginally annotated. 'Renaissance readers were not only *allowed* to write notes in and on their books, they were *taught* to do so in school.'[64] The marginalia printed in so many books of the time[65] should more often than not be regarded as aids towards the customizing of these volumes for use.

Histories, romances, and playbooks were then as now read for the plot, for character (simply put) and as whole arguments;[66] but the more usual, legible aims were knowledge, policy, precept, and example, all of which privileged selection. There are instances of this in Shakespeare's plays, as when Lavinia in *Titus Andronicus* looks for and finds a version of her rape and mutilation in the example offered by Ovid's Philomel, in an onstage copy of the *Metamorphoses*, which prompts knowledge in other readers (her family) and leads to action (4.1); or when Imogen, in *Cymbeline*, reading the same section of Ovid, before Iachimo climbs out of the trunk in her bedchamber and subjects her to a visual rape, asks her maid to customize the book: 'Fold down the leaf where I have left' (2.2.4). At these moments, Shakespeare's sources are not just drawn on, or even (more artfully) drawn on and allowed to comment on the action for the better awareness of the audience: they are put to use by characters looking for examples to live and act by within a dramatic design that puts book and reader to employment.

Folding, marking, and annotation readily extended into the writing down of *sententiae*, curious lore, or rhetorical ornament. People did this in their 'tables' or notebooks like Hamlet (1.5.107–9), or in the more substantial commonplace books which survive in large numbers from the period, both in manuscript and (as in the case of Jonson's *Discoveries*) transferred into print. Commonplacing and extracting was more than a filing system; the product, often enough, of repeated reading and meditation, 'practised', 'incorporated', and 'digested',[67] it could be textually generative. Compilation was tessellated with what was, by modern standards, astonishing directness into new compositions. A number of the books that we classify as Shakespeare's sources— Montaigne's *Essais*, for example, or Holinshed's *Chronicles*—are themselves compilations, on different scales, just as Shakespeare's own works were put into commonplace books and published in formats which adapted, mixed and supplemented them.[68] 'For writers in the Renaissance, compiling was fundamentally entwined with textual production.'[69] At this date, 'to compile' could mean 'to compose',[70] as it does in Shakespeare's sonnet 85. Thanks to such procedures, inculcated in the schoolroom, 'composition' was held to be 'centred on intertextuality',[71] which enhanced the prestige of *imitatio*. 'In imitation', as Terence Cave notes, 'the activities of reading and writing become virtually identified',[72] though this highlights only one part of the spectrum across which reading and writing could be experienced as continuous.

When we write about 'Shakespeare's reading', therefore, we are designating a practice as much as all the books he consulted. It was a practice in which he was caught up, involving many more agents than he, but one which also—whether or not it was done pen in hand (and much of the time it probably was)—led readily into writing. The imbrication of major sources in his plays and poems with other extracts, *sententiae*, and borrowed figures, once categorized by scholars as 'echoes' or 'allusions', should be thought of as strands of matter derived and compiled, probably in hard copy but certainly through mental operations encouraged at grammar school. The often-heard explanation for the appearance in Shakespeare's plays of disjected phrases from his reading, that his memory was peculiarly retentive, probably overlooks—though memories were indeed well-trained, especially among actors, for obvious reasons—the 'material intertextuality'[73] of marked-up books and commonplacing that went with the cognitive training. His reading of Sidney's *Arcadia*, for example, ahead of writing *King Lear*, shows a keen eye for an episode and within it phrases that bear on the main action of the tragedy. Among early modern books, prose romances were relatively less often annotated and compiled. The *Arcadia*, with its affairs of state and the high status of its author, was something of an exception.[74] The book was extracted by readers alert to (for instance) passages modelled on the *Aeneid*[75]—much as, I argue in Chapter 3, Shakespeare noticed Sidney's imitation of Seneca and Sophocles.

It need not become our ambition as students of Shakespeare's originality to project back from the plays and poems all the evidences of his reading into the lost underlinings, sigla, notes, cross-references, and compilations that we can reasonably imagine him creating. His procedures are unlikely to have been as systematic as those of Jonson, or of another early seventeenth-century compiler, who read a number of the same romances as he did and drew from them scores of pages of extracts in which the *Arcadia* was dominant[76] and narrative order was followed even when passages were decontextualized.[77] No doubt Shakespeare also indulged in that 'reading for pleasure' which, as others have wisely noted, was part of Sidney's vision of reading even though he found it hard to accommodate it to his theoretical justifications.[78] Along with many early modern readers, however—especially the male ones[79]—his reading would have been purposeful because there were things that he wanted to do with books in the theatre. He will not have 'studied for action' as politically as Gabriel Harvey, reading Livy with noble patrons interested in applying Roman to Elizabethan politics,[80] but he will still have 'studied for' (i.e. to extract) the 'action' of plays, and for the acting opportunities provided by that action.

A second important way in which we can think more accurately about Shakespeare's use of his sources than scholars of an older vintage is that we have a better picture of how play-texts went from working papers through scribal copying and preparation of the prompt-book,[81] licensing (with or without censorship)[82] to authorial revision (which may have been recurrent),[83] and adaptation post-performance. The manuscript *Book of Sir Thomas More*, to which Shakespeare in my view contributed, shows us several hands at work, with various obligations and (one can infer) intentions, overlapping and not always converging, the 'authorial' being a discontinuous role since authors could act like scribes and book-keepers like authors.[84] *More* is an extreme case, because difficulties with the Master of the Revels induced an extra round of rewriting which affected the use of source material. Even so, it encourages vigilance about textual detail in relation to the alteration of sources, and reminds us of the many steps that lie between a playwright's reading and the playscript.

Greater awareness of the latter has also made it easier to recognize how, in the course of writing and revision, Shakespeare moved away from his originals. The treatment of Rosencrantz and Guildenstern, for instance, comparing Belleforest's prose version of *Hamlet*, in which they figure as the king's faithful ministers, with quarto and Folio texts of the tragedy, shows increasing ambiguity about their involvement with the Claudius figure and a growing unease around their deaths.[85] The energies of composition are complex, however, and sources can exert a backwards pull. *King Lear*, discussed in Chapter 3 of this book, is a case in point. Work on its textual history has thrown into relief how Quarto (1608) and Folio (1623) texts show a progression in the depiction of characters away from both *King Leir* and the play's other major 'original', used for the Gloucester, Edgar, and Edmund plot: *The Countesse of Pembrokes Arcadia*. Authorial revision, mixed up with scribal and book-keeping changes and, more extensively, adaptation by the company, can be inferred.[86] Yet we should be wary of assuming too single a line of development. In the Quarto, probably written with a court performance in view, the crown of Britain is eventually taken by the Duke of Albany (one of the titles held by James VI and I). In the Folio it goes to Edgar, who bears the name of an Anglo-Saxon king who laid claim to Britain. This would satisfy the geopolitical bias of a London, public theatre audience not by pushing beyond the sources but by reverting to Sidney, where Edgar's equivalent becomes King of Paphlagonia. The stories caught up in the play have some of the properties of a matrix.[87]

A third and final reason for thinking that we are better placed to think about Shakespeare's originality than scholars once were is that we now know more, and more accessibly, about the levels of reliance on source material among other early modern playwrights. This allows a keener assessment than was possible for the likes of Lennox because we can see that overall his borrowing resembles that of his contemporaries. Robert Greene, for example, who complained about Shakespeare's derivativeness, drew on *The Famous History of Frier Bacon* (a prose work) for his *Frier Bacon, and Frier Bongay*, on Ariosto for his *Orlando*, and so on. Marlowe, whose sources have been assembled in a volume that takes Bullough as its model,[88] has the same sort of profile as Shakespeare in his use of lives and chronicles for *Tamburlaine*, chapbook narrative for *Doctor Faustus*, eclectic invention for *The Jew of Malta*. A full account of the kinds of originality that are probed in the case studies that make up this book would have to be comparative as well as huge, and it would throw up contrasts between, for example, the fabric of Shakespearean dialogue and the vermiculate borrowings of Webster;[89] but we can briefly say that Shakespeare was not unusual in the extent of his dependence on sources. It is the originality with which he uses those originals that this book aims to explore.

1
Upstarts and *Much Ado*

In the sixth chapter of *Don Quixote*, the curate is urged by the niece to burn the huge collection of romances—more than a hundred of them—which have so deluded the Don that he takes peasant girls to be fine ladies and mistakes windmills for giants. Though the barber and the curate, in a satirical glance at the Inquisition, condemn dozens of books to the flames, including *The Adventures of Splandian*, *Amadis of Greece*, and other derivatives of *Amadis of Gaule*, they pause over a romance about the Lord Raynald of Montalban because, as Cervantes writes, it 'containe[s] some part of the famous Poet *Matthew Boyardo* his inuention. Out of which the Christian Poet *Lodouicke Ariosto* did likewise weaue his worke'.[1] All this knowingly reflects on the status of *Don Quixote* as imitation and parody. The Don's library reminds us that what is often called the first European novel is a late text.

One instance of this lateness takes us back to Shakespeare. We are routinely told that *Don Quixote* is the source of the lost play *Cardenio*. Up to a point, this must be so. Shakespeare and Fletcher will have worked from Thomas Shelton's translation of Part I, which he published in 1612. But Cervantes' account of Cardenio derives from Ariosto, whose *Orlando furioso* was influential in the stories it spread across Europe, one of them going straight into the play that I shall focus on in a moment: *Much Ado About Nothing*. Beyond that, Ariosto's tale of Genevra and Polynesso, on which Shakespeare's plot about Hero and Claudio is based, was itself derived from a fifteenth-century Spanish romance called *Tirant lo Blanc*. It is worth establishing at once that, during Shakespeare's lifetime, to base your work on an original was not at odds with being an *auctor*. Cervantes plays with this model of authority when he claims, through his narrator, to have taken the story of Quixote from a Moorish source.[2]

That *Don Quixote* was the first-ever novel must, of course, be doubted. Many would argue for *Robinson Crusoe* (1719), while others look back to Hellenistic romance, the earliest example of which, Chariton's *Chaereas and Callirhoe*, is a version of what became the Hero and Claudio story. That this first-century AD tale was not published until 1750, in Greek, brings out the paradox latent in the case of *Tirant lo Blanc*, that the sources of Shakespeare's plays were often unknown to Shakespeare. Whatever we decide, however, about the slightly futile argument about when the novel as a genre began, *Don Quixote* became original in the sense originary as it fed into subsequent texts. Think of its influence on Fielding and Sterne, but also, more directly, on another mid-eighteenth-century author of importance to this study: Charlotte Lennox, who published, under the title *Shakespear Illustrated* (1753–4), the first critical selection of Shakespeare's sources, a few months after the appearance of her novel, *The Female Quixote*.

The Quixote of Lennox's title is a naive, intense young woman, who constantly interprets her life through the situations and attitudes she finds in the romances of Madeleine de Scudéry and others. Exacting and fanciful, Arabella develops a haughtiness which is inhibiting as well as self-deceiving. At one point she becomes so insufferable that, in a rerun of *Don Quixote*, her father decides to burn all the romances in her library. As in Cervantes, however, those who hope to bring a quixotic character to reason are also prudently reluctant to commit good books to the fire. This does not mean that the romances win out; Arabella is eventually persuaded by a suitor that she should abandon them. Lennox's conclusion is droll in the way it follows the template of *Don Quixote*, where the knight of the doleful countenance denounces on his deathbed—in a scene that I shall revisit—all the fanciful romances he has been reading.

The piles of books in Quixote's study and web of stories in Arabella's head give us a better picture of how books were read and lived with in the world that we have lost than do the ranks of sources set out in modern Shakespeare editions. In its compilation of what were known in the eighteenth century as 'originals' (i.e. immediate source-texts), however, *Shakespear Illustrated* marks almost the beginning of the process of gathering and ordering that would culminate in Geoffrey Bullough's still-standard, eight-volume *Narrative and Dramatic Sources of*

Shakespeare (1957–75). As scholarship, it leaves much to be desired.
Lennox did not work out, for instance—as Edward Capell did after
her[3]—that *Much Ado* owes almost as much to Bandello's twenty-
second novella, the tale of Timbreo and Fenicia, as it does to Ariosto.[4]
Yet although her selection and discussion are limited, they are also
shrewdly slanted to challenge Shakespeare's reputation. The dramatist, she sets out to show, is not just not original but often garbles his
originals to produce improbable plots.

This emphasis on plotting follows from Lennox's priorities as a
novelist, but it also owes something to a neoclassical, and so Aristotelian, strain in her thinking[5] which encouraged her, in 1759, to
translate *The Greek Theatre of Father Brumoy*, a work, now largely forgot-
ten, which conveyed a lot of serious matter from classical antiquity
into the vernacular. Dr Johnson consequently found himself in a
dilemma when writing the dedication of *Shakespear Illustrated*. Willing
to agree that the ability to invent—that is, design—a plot is the
primary power of a poet, and that the creation and development of
an entirely 'new Fable' requires 'the utmost Effort of the human
Mind', he takes the sting out of Lennox's work—almost rebuts it—
by declaring that Shakespeare's excellence lay not in 'the naked Plot,
or Story of his Plays' but in a fuller form of *mimesis*: 'the Representation of life'. His plots might well be faulty, since (like Quixote) he 'lived
in an Age when the Books of Chivalry were yet popular, and when
therefore the minds of his Auditors were not accustomed to balance
Probabilities'.[6]

One reason for Johnson's discomfiture is that Lennox was questioning Shakespeare's achievement at a time when he was becoming—
courtesy of Garrick and others—a national icon, and was becoming so
not least because his claims to greatness could be secured by an
enhanced valuation of originality. The 1750s constitute a watershed
in the history of sensibility because during that decade 'originality'
began to assume the primacy that is familiar to us from the Romantic
period.[7] As we saw in the Introduction, this is when the word itself,
which comes into English in the mid-seventeenth century to describe
the most basic and essential forces of the universe, and ultimately the
Divine creator, began to be extended to the originating mind of
the author. By the time we get to Hazlitt, 'originality' is identified
as the genius of Shakespeare,[8] though the word is not even there

about mere novelty but the capacity to see for the first time something that is and has been true in nature and the world of man.[9]

The prevailing view among scholars is that the origins of this privileging of originality as it plays out in attitudes to drama can be found in the competitiveness of Restoration theatre. 'During the theatre wars of the 1670s,' Brean Hammond writes, 'in the battles between professional playwrights and gentlemen-amateurs, and the internecine contests between professionals...accusations of plagiarism hail down...When a conception of literary *property* thickens up,...attitudes towards plagiarism also harden.'[10] To this prehistory of the 1710 Copyright Act we can add what Paulina Kewes highlights in *Authorship and Appropriation*: the beginnings of scholarly attention to the sources of drama that provided ammunition in these contests. Gerard Langbaine's *Account of the English Dramatick Poets* (1691), most often now remembered for its accusations of plagiarism against Dryden, gives us the first account of the origins of *Much Ado* in Ariosto and Spenser. It provides, in that sense, the raw material for Lennox's *Shakespear Illustrated*, a study that is itself less original than it claims.

After the Restoration, Kewes argues, 'there was a growing tendency to condemn both appropriation and collaboration, practices which in the Renaissance had been habitual and mostly unremarked, as evidence of artistic insufficiency. Imitation was now denounced as plagiarism.'[11] This would be more entirely true if, a century earlier, the lines had been clearly drawn between the virtuous, classically grounded art of imitation and accusations of theft. As I shall briefly show, before pursuing what emerges into a discussion of *Much Ado About Nothing*, the question of whatever it is that 'originality' came to signify was a live one in Shakespeare's England. One indicator of this is the appearance of the pejorative 'plagiary' (from Latin) in the late 1590s,[12] with 'plagiarism' following in 1621.[13] Another is the growing belief that 'invention' should include innovation.[14] A third, more tangential, is the diversification of 'discover' to mean 'find in the course of a search or investigation' as well as the older 'make known, divulge, disclose';[15] Jonson's commonplace book, *Timber: Or, Discoveries*, edges out in this way from classical, rhetorical sources.

It was noted in the Introduction that the semantics of 'original' itself—as the precursor of 'originality'—were multiple in the late sixteenth and seventeenth centuries, from 'document, text, picture, etc., from which another is copied' to 'being generative, productive', and they included strands that by 1700 could polarize the word against 'plagiarist'. The grounds of this were long-standing; medieval Latin *origo*, *originalis*, and vernacular *original* could mean 'original document' or 'writ', 'The origin or source . . . an originator, creator';[16] but changes were in process, cultural as much as linguistic, and they were shaped by the kinds of originality sought in literary and dramatic works. Fortunately, there is no need to establish the absolute, receding moment where arguments about originality originate. The next section of this chapter aims only to show that the link between such arguments and competition over status, profit, and literary property that has been dated to the Restoration can be found in the 1590s.

* * *

The first mention that we have of Shakespeare as a dramatist comes in *Greenes Groatsworth of Witte* (1592), a posthumously published work by the playwright, romance-writer, and pamphleteer Robert Greene that was seen into print and possibly part-written by the printer and writer Henry Chettle. Warning other, university-educated writers not to sell their wares to the actors, 'those Puppets', as he calls them, 'those Anticks garnisht in our colours, . . . Yes trust them not', Greene adds,

> for there is an vpstart Crow, beautified with our feathers, that with his *Tygers hart wrapt in a Players hyde*, supposes he is as well able to bombast out a blanke verse as the best of you: and beeing an absolute *Iohannes fac totum*, is in his owne conceit the onely Shake-scene in a countrey. O that I might intreat your rare wits to be imploied in more profitable courses: and let those Apes imitate your past excellence, and neuer more acquaint them with your admired inuentions.[17]

Briefly put, the passage runs together the crow-like, ape-like imitativeness of actors with an insinuation of literary theft against a Shake-scene who, as a Jack-of-all-trades, is both a stage player and a writer. The allusion to a speech in *3 Henry VI*, where York accuses Queen Margaret of having a 'tiger's heart wrapped in a woman's hide' (1.4.138) most likely indicates that Greene is having a stab at Shakespeare for gaining more credit for the *Henry VI* plays than he deserves, since the hands of other writers—Nashe, Marlowe, Peele, and Greene—have often been detected in them, and with good reason, according to recent computer analysis.[18]

What has been called 'artiginality'[19] needs to be factored into our understanding of the creative activity to which 'originality' would later become attached. The artisan-like production of playscripts for an avid, commercial theatre, which set aside plays almost as quickly as it staged them, required piecemeal collaboration, recycling, and adaptation. Co-authorship, in other words, was mixed up with the fabrication of scripts from pre-existing texts. Yet artiginality, as surely as originality, was competitive as well as interactive, so collaboration could give rise to charges of plagiarism and appropriation—the more readily for an out-of-luck writer who saw the 'vpstart Crow' enjoying the applause and profit that came to the actors rather than the (other) authors of the first tetralogy.[20] Hence Greene's assertively educated but accessible allusion to Horace's *Epistles* I.iii, where the crow in the Aesopian canon, who competed with other, more colourful birds by borrowing their feathers, only to be stripped of these plumes and laughed at, is invoked to discourage Celsus from publishing, as his own, poetry filched from other writers.

Greene's lack of originality in charging Shakespeare with lack of originality runs back to his earlier works. In the dedicatory address to *The Myrrour of Modestie* (1584), a work which retells the story of Susanna from the Bible, he writes 'But your honor may thinke I play like *Ezops* Crowe, which deckt hir selfe with others feathers'. Again, in *Francescos Fortunes* (1590), he compares Roscius the actor to 'Esops Crow... pranct with the glorie of others feathers'.[21] Almost as relevant to the *Groatsworth* is Nashe's preface to Greene's *Menaphon* (1589), in which, after rebuking other scholars for writing for the players, he praises Greene's extemporal inventiveness. Down with the orators, he declares, ahead of *Much Ado*, that 'must borow inuention of *Ariosto*', and those 'shifting companions' (again, like Shakespeare) that lift *sententiae* from English Seneca while writing English *Hamlet*s. Given Greene's notable imitativeness of Sidney, Spenser, and others—his willingness, as Gabriel Harvey complained, to put on, in pursuit of sales, the 'borrowed and filched plumes of some little Italianated brauery'[22]—Nashe, it might be thought, protests too much. 'Sundrie other sweete Gentlemen I know', he writes, 'that haue ... trickt vp a companie of taffata fooles with their feathers.'[23]

It has been argued that the *Groatsworth* should be read in the light of what Greene says about Roscius, and Nashe about the taffeta fooles (i.e. that it complains only about the way actors profit from the scholar playwrights whose scripts give them their plumage). This is hard to reconcile not just with *The Myrrour of Modestie* but with the many other Elizabethan uses of Aesop's fable that follow Horace in being about plagiarism.[24] Even if one insisted on a narrow construction of Greene's intentions,[25] the passage in the *Epistles* I.iii was so well-known at first or second hand that a large proportion of readers would have taken from the *Groatsworth* a smearing implication of literary derivativeness—especially given its attribution to Shake-scene of a style of writing that shows no great individuality ('to bombast out a blanke verse').[26]

Greene's denunciation of the 'vpstart Crow' is often used to supplement what little we know about Shakespeare's working life at the start of his career.[27] The larger value of the passage lies in its raising the question of how far and in what ways derivativeness was acceptable in a theatre in which so much was eclectically fabricated. Does the *Groatsworth* wilfully misapply criteria appropriate to Horace's Celsus to a playhouse whose procedures did not match the learned ideas about originality and imitation set out in Horace's *Art of Poetry*?[28] Greene apparently fell out with the players when he sold the Queen's Men his *Historie of Orlando Furioso* 'for twenty Nobles', and then, when they were on tour, 'sold the same Play to the Lord Admirals men for as much more'.[29] Given that his *Orlando* derives so extensively from Ariosto, we might ask whether Greene outstripped the dishonesty of the upstart crow when he sold stolen goods twice over. But then, *As You Like It* (discussed in Chapter 2) recycles material from Greene's play, or, with his prompting, from Ariosto's poem, in the sequence where Orlando hangs poems about Rosalind on trees in the forest.[30]

Of course, the Shake-scene passage *is* also about acting. Greene mocks the actors as puppets, antics, apes, and painted monsters smeared with cosmetics. They are what Nashe calls 'counterfeits',[31] taffeta fools tricked out with false hair and feathers in their hats—a satirical gibe about the players reiterated by Hamlet.[32] The emphasis on deception is obvious, but so is the focus on clothing, not just as an instrument of counterfeiting but with an implication, often heard in the period, that actors are both effeminate and dress above their station. Feathers, at this date, were shifting from a masculine to a feminine semiotic; they were also fairly expensive.[33] These 'rude groomes', as the *Groatsworth* calls them, 'buckram Gentlemen', and 'peasants',[34] are not just low in status but in their lucrative attire are upstarts.

'Vpstart Crow' comes awkwardly from Greene, who was probably the son of a saddler (as Chettle was the son of a dyer) and thus not a mile away, socially, from Shakespeare's upbringing as the child of a glover and leather worker. '*Wrapt in a Players hyde*' is telling, beyond John Shakespeare's employment, as though even an actor's skin is not his own but another layer of costume. The hide on Shakespeare's back should be no grander than a buff jerkin, but by association with the plumes he might be wearing finely worked leather. The context for this satire lies in the widely flouted sumptuary laws,[35] which, for the sake of the indigenous cloth industry, and to reinforce social hier-archy, promulgated the view that, like the feathers grown by birds, clothes should spring from the God-given nature of those they clad: russet coats for the lowly, silk for noblemen. Statutes and proclam-ations instilled these principles. A homily was read in churches 'against Excesse of apparell'.[36] Greene latched on to the orthodoxy, and satirized 'vpstart changelings'—the 'proud peacockes' with their 'beautious feathers', who extravagantly overspent on clothes—in his dialogue between velvet and cloth breeches, *A Quip for an Vpstart Courtier* (1592).[37] The title page, which features a woodcut that says much about finery and feathers, is reproduced as Fig. 1.

Actors were an affront to these rules. Playing allowed the son of a commoner to come on stage dressed as a lord. Worse, it encouraged the actors to break the sumptuary laws outside the theatre. As Stephen Gosson complained, 'the very hyerlings of some of our Players . . . iet vnder Gentlemens noses in sutes of silke, . . . when they come abrode'.[38] According to John Earle,

> *A Player* . . . is like our painting Gentle-women, seldome in his owne face, seldomer in his cloathes, and he pleases, the better hee counter-feits, except onely when he is disguis'd with straw for gold lace. Hee do's not only personate on the Stage, but sometime in the Street, for he is mask'd still in the habit of a Gentleman.[39]

The actor is a conjunction of cosmetics and the habit of a gentleman, the more counterfeit when he wears truly rich clothes and not the

A

QVIP FOR AN VP-
ſtart Courtier:

Or,

**A quaint diſpute betvveen Veluet breeches
and Clothbreeches.**

*Wherein is plainely ſet downe the diſorders
in all Eſtates and Trades.*

LONDON
**Imprinted by Iohn Wolfe, and are to bee ſold at his
ſhop at Poules chayne. 1 5 9 2.**

Fig. 1. Velvet and cloth breeches on the title page of Robert Greene, *A Quip for an Vpstart Courtier* (1592). Reproduced by permission of the Huntington Library.

straw (or copper) that was sometimes substituted for gold lace on stage. I shall get to a couple of upstart crows in *Much Ado About Nothing* shortly. One is called Margaret, a gentlewoman not always in her own clothes; the other is a thief called Deformed, who masks himself in the habit of a gentleman.

* * *

About a score of versions of the Hero and Claudio story were published before or during Shakespeare's lifetime. No audience would have known all these poems, prose romances, and plays, but the loose ends, staggered reports, and misconstructions in *Much Ado* that have tempted generations of scholars to posit imperfect adaptation or revision often hook up with this array of narratives. Despite this dense variation, from Spenser through Belleforest to Della Porta, the 'sources and analogues' of *Much Ado* have traditionally been divided into two families, like the Montagues and the Capulets. In both, deriving respectively from the *Orlando furioso* and Bandello, the key turn in the plot is provided by a scene of mistaking in which the Claudio-figure, accompanied by a friend or brother, is deceived by a rival who arranges for someone to get access to the window of his mistress, the Hero-figure, the night before their wedding. Bandello makes Timbreo seem the more gullible—before he becomes reflective and doubting—because he simply sees a man climb up a ladder and through the window.[40] There is no more elaborate masquerade. In Ariosto, by contrast, Ariodant sees Dalinda, disguised as Genevra her mistress, entertaining her own lover Polynesso, who wants to marry Genevra.

Charlotte Lennox complained that the motivation of this episode made little sense in Shakespeare. In Ariosto, Dalinda is seduced into disguising herself by Polynesso. He plausibly tells her that, if she puts on her mistress's finery and indulges his sick fancy for Genevra, it will die. In *Much Ado*, Margaret's assignation with the gallant or ruffian Borachio, played out at her mistress's window, where she is dressed (we learn late on) in Hero's clothes, is encouraged, of course, by Don John. He has fallen out with his brother, Don Pedro, and decides in his melancholy to frustrate the match that Pedro has sponsored and in the process to get back at Claudio for his success in winning Pedro's favour. In Ariosto, Lennox notes, the plot is cogently driven by Polynesso's desire both to win Genevra and to revenge himself on his successful rival in love. Shakespeare motivated the plot by making Don John 'a Villain merely through the Love of Villainy',[41] then compounded this by adding the obscurely bad Borachio. Her unhappiness goes back to Margaret. How did Borachio persuade her, she wonders, to put on her mistress's garments, and dally with him out of her window? 'It was not likely she would engage in a Plot that seemed to have a Tendency to ruin Hero's Reputation, unless she had been imposed on by some very plausible Pretences, what those Pretences were we are left to guess' (III, 263).

Lennox writes about Margaret as though the audience sees the scene at the window. This is wrong, but obliquely right, because Shakespeare—as we shall discover—presents a displaced version of it, which adumbrates Margaret's motives. In Ariosto, Dalinda the waiting woman is the narrator of the entire Genevra/Ariodant story. From this source, likely enough, sprang the play's interest in report. Is Dalinda telling the whole truth, imperfectly remembering or justifying herself? Part of Shakespeare's originality, in a play which strikingly diverges from the procedures of earlier, Elizabethan comedies, with their impulse to self-explication and forensic connection, was to refract that centrality by giving her a socially ambiguous, opaque presence, moving between different levels and groups, and no more telling us what motivates her than people do in life.

By inference and visible action, Margaret's interests are 'fashion-mongering' (to use a phrase of Leonato's) and being what Don John calls Claudio: a 'start-up', that is, an upstart, aspirational in a society not open to such mobility.[42] In Ariosto fashion is latent in the attention given by Dalinda to the 'head attire', 'gorgets', and 'iewels rich' that Polynesso told her to wear.[43] Shakespeare works this into a play about the ambitions of a waiting gentlewoman who is, on the one hand, treated like a servant, but who, on the other, mixes with the high-born, joins in the masked dance (2.1), flirts with Benedick, asking him to write a sonnet in praise of her beauty, and jokes about deserving better: 'why, shall I always keep below stairs?' (5.2.1–23). Aspiration is implicit in Ariosto,[44] but in his long poem *Ariodanto and Ieneura* (1575), which the dramatist probably knew, Peter Beverley describes how Dalinda was tempted by the prospect of not being 'subiect . . . to beck and to obey' yet rather to 'beare the sway'.[45] Shakespeare's account of her 'vile ambition' (in Beverley's phrase) is, by contrast, while not uncritical, as sympathetic as would be expected from an upstart crow.

To elucidate the Margaret-as-Hero episode, I want to glance at three consecutive scenes that are thematically, as in line-count, central to *Much Ado*. The middle one of the three, Act 3 Scene 3, shows us Borachio telling Conrad about the intrigue as the Watch eavesdrop on his 'tale' (99). After promising that he will, 'like a true drunkard, utter all to thee' (his name means 'leather wine bottle'), Borachio appears to wander:

> Thou knowest that the fashion of a doublet, or a hat, or a cloak, is nothing to a man.
> CONRAD Yes, it is apparel.
> BORACHIO I mean the fashion.
> CONRAD Yes, the fashion is the fashion.   (101, 113–18)

Conrad is rightly unwilling to admit that fashion is nothing. But what sort of something is it? Borachio has a point to make:

> BORACHIO Tush, I may as well say the fool's the fool. But seest thou not what a deformed thief this fashion is?
> A WATCHMAN (*aside*) I know that Deformed. A has been a vile thief this seven year. A goes up and down like a gentleman. I remember his name.   (119–23)

Discounting this bizarre but, as we shall see, perceptive, half-heard comment as the noise of 'the vane on the house', Conrad is ready for more, and Borachio repeats, with a drunken insistence that is also a prompt to the audience,

> Seest thou not, *I say*, what a deformed thief this fashion is, how giddily a turns about all the hot-bloods between fourteen and five-and-thirty, sometimes fashioning them like Pharaoh's soldiers in the reechy painting, sometime like god Bel's priests in the old church window, sometime like the shaven Hercules in the smirched, worm-eaten tapestry, where his codpiece seems as massy as his club?
> CONRAD All this I see, and I see that the fashion wears out more apparel than the man. But art not thou thyself giddy with the fashion, too, that thou hast shifted out of thy tale into telling me of the fashion?   (126–37)

Conrad is less acute than the Watch, but he sees his way beyond intractable confusion between fashion as how clothes are made and fashion as the modishly ephemeral (shifts of meaning in the 1590s)

once Borachio explicates with examples. Fashion is a thief because it
turns young men about (idiomatically, a deceitful manoeuvre) but also
because it lifts ideas about attire from several places—from several
stories, put another way—rotating what people wear in a merry-go-
round or weathervane of clothes. It is now, in the context of fashion
and the exchange of clothes, that Borachio relates his nocturnal
encounter with Margaret:

> know that I have tonight wooed Margaret, the Lady Hero's gentle-
> woman, by the name of Hero. She leans me out at her mistress'
> chamber window, bids me a thousand times good night—I tell this
> tale vilely, I should first tell thee how the Prince, Claudio, and my
> master, planted and placed and possessed by my master, Don John, saw
> afar off in the orchard this amiable encounter.   (138–45)

He tells this tale vilely not least because he forgets to tell Conrad what
his diversion about fashion has shown to be at the front of his drink-
sozzled mind, that Margaret was wearing her mistress's fashionable,
fine-lady attire. Rather strikingly, as we have noted, the audience is
not explicitly told that until Borachio confesses to Don Pedro and
Claudio in 5.1.

Lennox complains that the Watchmen are idiots not to understand
what Borachio is admitting. This is true enough, and necessary for the
plot of the play, though they are no more incompetent in their
eavesdropping than is the Prince's person, whom they represent,
observing Hero's window.[46] In any case, they have a perverse insight
into the nature of the thief Deformed. On arresting Borachio and
Conrad, the First Watchman decides that they are only part of a gang:
'one Deformed is one of them. I know him—a wears a lock' (162–3).
This lock is a piece of long, often curled, sometimes interpolated hair
that hangs by the ear (as mocked by Greene and Nashe).[47] For an
example, see Hilliard's portrait miniature of Shakespeare's patron, the
3rd Earl of Southampton (Fig. 2). Locks of this sort were often said to
be *deforming*. In *The Vnlouelinesse of Loue-lockes* (1628), for instance,
William Prynne condemns 'long Haire, and Loue-lockes, . . . as Vnna-
turall, Womannish, Hatefull, and Vndecent vanities; which more
deforme Men, then adorne them'.[48]

For Prynne, as for others, locks are only one type of fashionable
deformity. Clothes can be just as bad. According to Stubbes, 'new

Fig. 2. Henry Wriothesley, 3rd Earl of Southampton, by Nicholas Hilliard, with dangling lovelock (1594). Reproduced by permission of the Fitzwilliam Museum, Cambridge.

fangled fashions, rather deforme vs then adorne vs: disguise vs, then become vs'.[49] They deform because they are singular as well as body-distorting; they diverge from the norm and are immoderate.[50] After writing against feathers, Stubbes denounces 'monsterous ruffes' as 'deformed'.[51] Not only puritans objected: Drayton wrote against 'Deformed fashions'; John Taylor the Water Poet deplored 'fashions new deform'd'.[52] Fashion as deformity was contrary to those passages in scripture that are quoted in the Homily on Apparel. To put on such attire was socially unsettling, the mode of an 'vpstart changeling' (in Greene's memorable jibe). Simply to wear fashionable clothes was to be disguised, as Stubbes orthodoxly complains; how much the more so when worn by a thief or actor pretending to be his better. As the Watch well know, Deformed passes himself off as a gentleman by wearing fashionable clothes.

Though Deformed is a virtual figure, his followers fill the fore-ground of the play. In the scene just before 3.3, Benedick is teased about his turn to fashion, after he falls in love with Beatrice. He has taken, Don Pedro says, to 'strange disguises' (3.2.30). His clothes are a gallimaufry—a familiar point in satire[53]—Dutch today, French tomorrow, German slops with Spanish doublet. He brushes his hat in the mornings. His hair, that site of deformity, has been tended by a barber. His beard has been shaved off, he rubs himself with civet; they even say that he paints, applying—like the actor playing him?—the cosmetics so often said to 'defourme and mysshape'.[54] How much we see of this transformation is up to the director, but there must be something changed when Benedick enters the scene.

Deformed gets lodged in the minds of the Watch—and conse-quently those of the audience—because he represents what the citi-zenry have heard against gallants like Borachio.[55] There is what used to be called a discourse, a set of linked assumptions. This is how Dogberry fills out his report to Leonato, Claudio, and Don Pedro, after Borachio has confessed:

> the watch heard them talk of one Deformed. They say he wears a key in
> his ear and a lock hanging by it, and borrows money in God's name,
> the which he hath used so long and never paid that now men grow
> hard-hearted and will lend nothing for God's sake.   (5.1. 299–304)

This comically represents how report is elaborated by mistaking, adding a key to the lock, but also how mistaking is conditioned by what people believe. Dogberry gives us the civic view of fashionable deformity, that it wastes the general purse, drives people to ruin, and blocks up the flow of credit. Men are so eager to borrow money with a divinely sealed oath, in order to buy fashionable clothes, and then cannot pay their loans back, that those who have money to lend will not give credit any more. This is where Shylock comes in: Dogberry shows us that, for Shakespeare, there was a set of associations around his Jewish *lock*, meaning both the lock on the usurer's cashbox, about which he is *shy* in the sense of 'wary', and the unshorn sidelocks or *pe'ot* that, as the dramatist clearly knew, early modern Jews wore as a sort of Old Testament lovelock.[56]

This is not just about men. From 1576, the sumptuary laws applied to women, and anti-fashion writing is often about female apparel.

Women were just as likely to be deformed by their attire, as Barnabe Riche, among others, noted: 'our *Ladies* and *Gentlewomen* in these daies are so exceeding in their *attires,* and so deformed in their fashions, that all the *Ladies* and *Gentlewomen* that be in *hell,* did neuer weare nor see the like.' As in Stubbes, so in Riche, fashionable attire is disguise. 'I haue many times beene hartily sorry', he writes, 'to see some women . . . that haue disguised themselues . . . with the deformities of fashions, that of amiable and louely creatures, they haue transformed themselues to be most deformed and loathsome monsters.'[57] One of the subtleties of *Much Ado* is that Hero disguises herself in fashionable attire (and not just twice with masks) as surely as Margaret disguises herself as Hero.

Hence the drama of 3.4. The scene that follows Borachio on Deformed is just as concerned with fashion as the one before it. We are shown Margaret at a levée with Hero, about to dress her mistress. It is a scene in which fashion is used as a ground on which an upstart can compete with her mistress. 'Troth, I think your other rebato'—your ruff or collar-support made of wire[58]—'were better', is Margaret's opening line, which Hero rather tartly resists: 'No, pray thee, good Meg, I'll wear this' (6–7). The waiting gentlewoman does not give up ('By my troth, 's not so good') and she goes on to display her credentials by showing niceness of judgement and by advertising her acquaintance with fashion: 'I like the new tire within excellently, if the hair were a thought browner.[59] And your gown's a most rare fashion, i' faith. I saw the Duchess of Milan's gown that they praise so' (12–15). Margaret secures some social cachet while proving herself (we might realistically add) the more serviceable because of what she knows about apparel. She has seen the Duchess's gown that others merely talk of. Milan is far from Messina, the setting of the play. The competition to have the finest gown operates across large distances, in the hyper-connected world of the elite, but Margaret has travelled and learned. Now Hero has to find out from her gentlewoman what the gown was like. She has at least *heard* of the gown, she takes care to impart, and in doing so she shows her awareness that fashion involves keeping up with and outdoing others, not merely indulging in the sumptuary 'excess' warned against in the Elizabethan homily: 'O, that *exceeds*, they say' (16).

Margaret's reply is fascinating, and not just for the gallants and ladies who, we know, came to the theatre to look at fashionable clothes and to be seen in them. Evidently, the *Vogue* gossip has to be properly informed. Margaret shows her competence by knowing exactly how to describe the exquisite clothes that we never see—like the clothes she has worn at the window, for Borachio; which means knowing how they are put together as an eclectic ensemble. Meanwhile she shows her skill by accenting her ability to keep her mistress abreast of fashion and by judicious flattery:

> By my troth, 's but a night-gown in respect of yours—cloth o' gold, and cuts, and laced with silver, set with pearls, down sleeves, side sleeves, and skirts, round underborne with a bluish tinsel. But for a fine, quaint, graceful, and excellent fashion, yours is worth ten on 't.   (17–22)

Compare the gown brought onstage to Katherine in *The Taming of the Shrew* (4.3.59–166). Snipped, slashed, and fashionable. The one described by Margaret is almost as present for the audience, but like so much in the play it is all a matter of report. Shakespeare, like others in the theatre, would have seen images of gowns from Milan in the fashion books that circulated through Europe—Cesare Vecellio's most notably (Fig. 3).[60]

You could see Hero as competing with the Duchess by having a gown that exceeds even hers. Like Margaret the night before, she dresses (in both senses) up. The governor's daughter moves higher than a Duchess, but this is also known as deformity. She has a rebato for a monstrous ruff, and the sort of hair piece (which should be browner) that is the female equivalent of a lovelock. Even if Hero is not competing, Margaret can frame her as such because that is how the fashion system operates. And if Margaret trumps her mistress, Hero puts down Beatrice for being 'so odd and from all fashions' (3.1.72). Excess leads to following trends, stealing ideas, and the literal theft of clothes. 'The Crowe in the fable was sharply taxed for her borrowed feathers', writes Richard Brathwait in *The English Gentle-woman*: 'The *fable*', he adds, 'though it spoke of a *Crowe*', is really about '*Habit*'.[61] Margaret, like her mistress, puts on what Brathwait calls 'vailes of deformity' (23). She envies and filches from a fashionable, deformed wardrobe. When she dresses and presents herself to Borachio in Hero's clothes, she is (in his words to Conrad) a 'deformed thief'.

How far does the dressing scene recapitulate what Claudio and Don Pedro saw at the window? If I were directing the play, I'd have

MILA.   NESE.

Fig. 3. Milanese lady with monstrous ruff and feathers, in Cesare Vecellio, *De gli habiti antichi et moderni di diversi parti del mondo* (1590). Reproduced by permission of the British Library.

the gown held up by Margaret against herself, as a way of alluding to, or enacting, what the audience has not been told, that she was dressed up in Hero's clothes the night before. Equally, it could be on a mannequin, the dress with nothing inside it projecting an eery, deformed identity. Early in the play, Benedick is called a stuffed man by Beatrice—the usual composition of mannequins—and Beatrice will herself, a few lines after this, be said to be stuffed (1.1.56, 3.4.60). Either way or otherwise, the drama of travesty goes further. Whether the clothes are held up against Margaret or Margaret moves to dress Hero, the gown is put onto a boy. This is ripe for queering, given that satirists liked to quip, 'If [a player] marries, hee mistakes the Woman for the Boy in Womans attire, . . . he is but a shifting compan- ion; for he liues effectually by putting on, and putting off.'[62] What the scene immediately transmits, however, is femininity constructed out of

clothing, with the boy actor's limbs as armature,[63] femininity as integral
to the masquerade played out by Borachio and Margaret.

That Margaret's dressing up is contrary to the Homily on Apparel
goes without saying. More interestingly, it is contrary to the advice
that is given to waiting gentlewomen in Renaissance conduct books.
No account of Shakespeare's originality would be complete without a
claim to have found a new source, or at least a new angle on an old
one. Castiglione's *Book of the Courtier* has long been fingered as one
origin of the wit combats between Beatrice and Benedick,[64] but it is
also worth wondering why Dalinda is renamed Margaret. There is a
whole book in *The Courtier* on the qualities and duties of a waiting
gentlewoman addressed to a Lady Margaret. According to Hoby's
1561 translation, such a gentlewoman should 'be wittie and foreseing'
but not 'yltunged, lyght, contentious nor untowardlye'.[65] Occasionally
the presence of a source can be felt by its *inversion*. Margaret is utterly
light-tongued, as in the banter that she throws at Beatrice in the
dressing scene, but also, more uncomfortably, when she jests bawdily
with Benedick after Hero's disgrace in the chapel (5.2.1–23), for which
the audience knows she is responsible. Further down Hoby's list one
finds more that she pointedly lacks: 'To take hede that she giue none
accasion to bee yll reported of'. She should 'apparaile her self so, that
she seeme not fonde and fantasticall'. The 'meete garmentes' of a
waiting woman should be fit for her person and station, and free, of
course, from deformity.

* * *

On his deathbed, Don Quixote leaves money to his maid to buy
clothes.[66] Shakespeare bequeathed his apparel to his sister Joan.[67]
Greene, according to Nashe, did not die in poverty but left a gown of
goose-turd green with sleeves, silk stockings, and a doublet worth
thirty shillings.[68] These legacies are indicative of the high value of
clothes, but also in an extreme way their capacity to be recycled.
Fashion these days is mostly off the peg. You put on your Versace and
go. During the early modern period, tailoring involved assemblage,
piecing, patching, and slashing—as in the Duchess of Milan's dress—
and the recirculation of fabric. Queen Elizabeth often gave her
apparel to gentlewomen in waiting.[69] We can imagine Margaret
saying to herself, as she flirts with Borachio at the window, 'Hero

will one day give me this outfit, I'm not stealing it but trying it out in advance.' Recycling was certainly the way that clothes moved in the theatre, not just because costumes went round actors playing different roles in various plays, but because the costumes themselves were cut up and redeployed as they became physically worn out or familiar to the audience, cloth of silver migrating from the lining of German slops to fishermen's bodices to the costume of torchbearers for a masque of Turks.[70]

It was all a matter of craft. The process of making the clothes was continuous with putting them on—often on someone else, since the cut could be imperfect and getting yourself into fashionable clothes (which might fit Margaret better than Hero) required the skill of a waiting gentlewoman, someone more your equal than a maid up from the country. You were laced, pinned, your bum roll was arranged. Clothes had to be matched, gartered, retied with points. In this hand-made society, the making and putting on of clothes was not just metaphorically like other skills involving art and judgement but metonymically, synecdochally, so. The root of 'fashion' is, of course, *facere*, 'to make'.[71] Plays were fashioned from the putting on of clothes by actors—king, soldier, princess, all with recognizable outfits—but also from the piecing together of lines, speeches, parts (pinned or stitched into a roll for the actor to learn).[72] Jonson was not unusual in thinking of such language as a fabric, the habit of thought. 'Nothing is fashionable,' he complained, using an adjective that is now familiar, 'till it bee deform'd; and this is to write like a *Gentleman*. All must bee as affected, and preposterous as our Gallants cloathes.'[73]

So it went with plays more largely. Dekker and Middleton note that 'The fashion of play-making can properly compare to nothing, so naturally, as the alteration in apparell: For in the time of the Great-crop-doublet, your huge bombasted plaies'—in the style of Marlowe's *Tamburlaine* (1587–8)—'quilted with mighty words to leane purpose was onely then in fashion. And as the doublet fell, neater inuentions beganne to set vp. Now in the time of sprucenes, our plaies followe the nicenes of our Garments, single plots, quaint conceits, letcherous iests, drest vp in hanging sleeues'.[74] Within *Much Ado*, the scripting of inset, contrived situations similarly depends on fashion. After Don Pedro tells Claudio that he will 'fashion' a plot to bring Beatrice and

Benedick together, Borachio assures Don John that he will put on a
little playlet by having Margaret call him Claudio, as he will call her
Hero, and 'so fashion the matter that Hero shall be absent'.[75] It is
partly because the word 'fashion' is extended in this way—from 'the
fashion of the world' (as things are habitually done) to Benedick's
fashioning a sonnet (1.1.92, 5.4.88)—that it is so plentiful, used
nineteen times in *Much Ado*, more than three times its nearest rival
(*Love's Labour's Lost*).[76] The whole comedy, however, is pieced and
patched and recycled. Its originality is real because the assemblage
is unique, edged with uncertainty as to origins. If it is plumed
with many birds' feathers, it is so for an artful purpose. Cloned out
of its own materials, as in the sub-plot of Beatrice and Benedick,
which is added to Ariosto and Bandello to show that eavesdropping, report, and mistaking can enable as well as disrupt love,[77] it
is also, to echo Dekker and Middleton, 'drest vp in hanging
sleeues', with redundancies that lead nowhere but are trailed in
the variant co-texts.

This could be shown in many particulars, all converging on the
point that, as compared with the transparent functionality and
contrapuntal elegance of multiple plotting in early Shakespeare,
Much Ado initiates his maturity in being more interested in creating
opacity. To take a final instance: there is no precedent in Ariosto or
Bandello for the masked ball in which Don Pedro woos Hero for
Claudio but is taken by others, including Hero, who does not seem
to resist, to be wooing her for himself. That Hero *could* be false when
masked in fashionable disguise is not just a pre-shock of the scene at
her window. It is anticipated by Luigi Pasqualigo's *Il fedele*, in which
the Hero figure *is* unfaithful. Yet in Anthony Munday's translation
(or alteration) of *Il fedele*,[78] the Hero figure is *not*. The duplicity and
uncertainty seem integral to the intertext. Each version shadows the
other. Such ramifications go beyond the question of intention and
the extent of Shakespeare's reading into the matrix of stories in
which *Much Ado* is caught up,[79] and the ability of audiences (not
unlike playwrights) to produce, suspend, or abandon extrapolations
from events in performance. Hence Giambattista della Porta's *Gli
duoi fratelli rivali*, a play which Shakespeare evidently did not
know when writing the Claudio–Hero action yet which has generated from the inherited narratives (especially Bandello) features so

distinctively found elsewhere only in *Much Ado* that a lost common source has been posited.[80] The point of this parting shot is not to cast aspersions on Hero—the comedy already does that—but to suggest how originality can stem from the creative, piecemeal superflux that so often gives Shakespearean drama depth and perspective.

2

Shakespeare Afoot

Something original happens at the start of *Richard III*. I don't just have
in mind the astonishing immediacy of the opening line, with its boldly
turned first foot, '*Now* is the winter of our discontent'; nor am
I thinking only of Richard's usurpation of the role of prologue—
telescoping it into his soliloquy—an innovation that galvanizes what
Hazlitt called 'the fine abrupt introduction of the character'.[1] Even
before he speaks, an audience will be seized by the shape of his
deformity, his outline as bunch-backed toad. Yet the fact that he or
the actor is, in the words of *The True Tragedie of Richard the Third*—a play
on which Shakespeare drew—'ill shaped, crooked backed, lame
armed',[2] is not in itself novel. Those disabilities go back through the
chronicles to Thomas More's *History* (*c*.1513).[3] What is not found in
the play's sources, or anywhere else in the record, is Richard's further,
peculiar feature, his trailing, erratic, provocative limp.[4]

Tamburlaine means 'Timur the lame' but Marlowe did not show
this on stage. The Jew of Malta was played by Edward Alleyn with a
large, false nose, but although this marked out Barabas as an ethnic
outsider it did not skew his every movement. Shakespeare's originality
lay in extrapolating from what the sources say about Richard having
one shoulder higher than the other a disability that betrays him as he
acts and by looping this back psychologically into resentment and
compensating energy. 'But I', he bitterly reflects,

> But I, that am not shaped for sportive tricks
> Nor made to court an amorous looking-glass,
> I that am rudely stamped and want love's majesty
> To strut before a wanton ambling nymph,
> I that am curtailed of this fair proportion,
> Cheated of feature by dissembling nature,
> Deformed, unfinished, sent before my time

> Into this breathing world scarce half made up—
> And that so lamely and unfashionable
> That dogs bark at me as I halt by them ...   (1.1.14–23)

Like the early modern moralists, from Gosson to Richard Brathwait, who write incisively about the abuses of walking, Richard satirizes the postures struck in gendered perambulation, but his mockery also vents his contempt at being so 'lamely' fashioned that such options are unavailable to him. That 'lamely' means 'poorly, inadequately', yet also plays on and with his limp, shows him, as so often, insinuating his deformity with an aggressive edge. As for the last, halting line, a prompt to any actor, it is almost impossible to scan, given the disruptive anapaest of 'bark at me' and tripping stall at 'halt' before the wrong-footing trochaic, '*by* them'. Antony Sher wrote, while working at the role, 'when you look at someone who is disabled: they have a different *rhythm*.'[5] Richard knows this so well that he can use limping feet to command his limp. As in the reversed foot that he opens the play with, mastery springs from a driven distortion turned back against cheating nature.

I'm hooking back at this point to the deformity discussed in Chapter 1. This time, however, the motif and associated anxiety do not involve fashionable dress but the imperfect 'garments of flesh' that early modern commentators[6] would see in Richard's mortal body. Nothing that I have written so far would particularly surprise them. Francis Bacon noted that 'Deformed persons are commonly euen with nature: for as Nature hath done ill by them, so do they by nature; ... Therefore it is good to consider of deformity, not as a signe, which is more deceiuable; but as a cause, which seldome faileth of the effect.'[7] That Richard feels cheated licenses his vindictiveness (getting even with the world) but also his deceit, using the deformity which is a cause as a sign of vulnerability or malevolence. Though he must go with the singular limp, he embraces ambition, not having what you want—the crown, love, anything—because those hinderings make him more like others. We can extend this by recalling Freud's helpfully obvious suggestion that Richard appeals to everyone in the audience who feels disadvantaged by life in some way (bad hair, big ears, dull job).[8]

Perhaps it ultimately goes down to what Georges Bataille calls 'Man's secret horror of his foot'.[9] You can see what he meant from

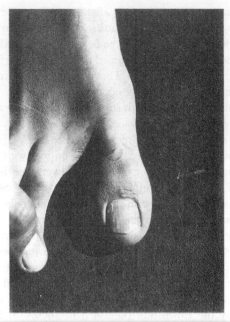

Fig. 4. Horror of the foot. Photograph by Jacques-André Boiffard (1929). Collection Lucien Treillard.

Fig. 4, a physically grainy photograph by the surrealist Jacques-André Boiffard that was cropped and published with Bataille's essay on the big toe. It may be incidental, though I doubt it, that Shakespeare added to Plutarch, in Menenius' fable of the belly in *Coriolanus*, his debasement of the First Citizen as the 'great toe' of the assembly.[10] We all have feet of clay, and as frail, lame creatures a connection with Richard. Most of us know what it is to be 'made lame by fortune's dearest spite'. 'Speak of my lameness, and I straight will halt.' I quote from Shakespeare's Sonnets (37, 89) to suggest that the dramatist—who presumably did not limp, though the claim has been made[11]—must have found something of himself in the crookedness of Richard. This need not lead to the notion that he wrote out of his affliction, a creative version of Philoctetes, like the writers psychoanalysed in Edmund Wilson's *The Wound and the Bow*.[12] The point might rather be that he was an actor, who knew what it meant to hide and project the lameness of his humanity by putting on another man's limp.

Early modern actors walked. Even before they strutted and fretted their hour upon the stage they tramped the roads looking for work like the travelling players in *Hamlet*. They were open to prosecution as vagrants unless they had the protection of a noble patron.[13] Out there with the disabled, as well as with sturdy beggars putting on an act of lameness, like Simpcox in *2 Henry VI* (2.1.137–59), they went about with fardels on their backs (as Greene says when mocking the players), like hunchbacks, you might say.[14] Touring on foot with pack horses did not die out with the building of theatres.[15] Even after their elevation to the royal household in 1603, the King's Men—Shakespeare's company—went into the provinces. Dekker reminds Jonson how he ambled in a leather pilch by a play-wagon in the highway, while Jonson has Tucca, in *Poetaster*, spell out what it meant 'to travaile, with . . . pumps full of gravell, . . . after a blind jade and a hamper: and stalke upon boords, and barrell-heads, to an old crackt trumpet'.[16]

Even when 'footing' the highways was not itself a kind of performance, as it was in Kemp's morris dance from London to Norwich, written up by the clown and published in 1600,[17] it led directly, indeed metonymically, into walking onstage, where the actors did not just walk but acted walking. Alleyn, in his major roles, was given to strutting and stalking.[18] Jonson recalls, in *Discoveries*, 'the *Tamerlanes*, and *Tamer-Chams* of the late Age, which had nothing in them but the *scenicall* strutting, and furious vociferation'.[19] Hamlet, similarly, complains about those players who, 'neither having the accent of Christians, nor the gait of . . . no man, have so strutted and bellowed' (3.2.29–32). The conjunction of walking and talking is something to return to. But when Richard disparages the art of strutting before an ambling nymph, he does more than deprecate a performance of manhood that he cannot emulate.[20] Burbage, who played the part, was capable of feats of footwork, as when, in a celebrated *coup*, he leapt into Ophelia's grave (i.e. the stage trap),[21] but he was less stylized than Alleyn.[22] To judge from an early seventeenth-century poem, he did, as Richard, swagger;[23] but it was the limp that gave him the look-at-me profile of an Alleyn without the out-of-date strut.

When an actor walks or limpingly dances through a role, the body is their medium. If a Richard achieves physical mastery, like Antony

Sher on his crutches, he shows what it is to be 'differently abled'. Audiences were struck by Olivier's 'gymnastic grace' in the part.[24] Of course, limping along, especially with élan, can *create* disability in an actor. As Sher notes more than once, playing Richard can be crippling.[25] Olivier tore his knee cartilage on stage and got shot in the leg with an arrow on the film set—fortunately the very leg with which he was wont to limp.[26] Yet the secret of Richard's attraction is that the actor limping does not fuse with the role but represents the Duke's ability to dally and threaten with his limp as though himself putting it on (as he must most wish he were). Those adapters and actors from Colley Cibber to Ralph Fiennes who import into *Richard III* the passage in *3 Henry VI* where the Duke says that he can 'Change shapes with Proteus for advantages' (3.2.192) catch at something vital in both the artifice of the actor (Burbage was praised as a Proteus)[27] and the desire of the character to change shape by being histrionic, to be enabled by disability. This dynamic is integral to Shakespeare's realization of the role and one source of its originality.

Actors did not just strut. They jigged, they ran, they jetted and tripped, they wore leg irons and danced the galliard. The dramatist Thomas Heywood characterizes the pleasures of the theatre in pedestrian terms: 'to see a souldier shap'd like a souldier, walke, . . . to see a Hector . . . trampling'.[28] Nor should we forget the feet of the audience. For if early modern actors were walkers, so were those who watched them. The theatre was a confluence of perambulators, the stage a labyrinthine space in which footwork was folded and opened up. Audiences walked to the theatre, across the bridge to Southwark. As Gosson put it disapprovingly: 'if we flocke to Theaters to gase vpon playes, wee walke in the Counsell of the vngodly'.[29] The audience made its way through crowded, uneven streets, which can only have made them podiatrically self-conscious. Montaigne, who was not lame, catches the experience: 'My foote is so staggering and vnstable, and I finde it so readie to trip, and so easie to stumble', 'Going afoote, I shall durtie my selfe vp to the waste: and little men, going alongst our streetes, are subject . . . to be justled or elbowed.'[30] The stage, we tend to forget, was at eye level for the groundlings; they looked straight at legs and feet.[31] The action was choreographed for the galleries. That groundlings walked about, to make sure they could see the action, is a truth universally acknowledged. Tiffany Stern has persuasively argued that this was true in the galleries also,[32] where even the eyes follow the actors in a kind of 'walking' (says Dekker).[33] When people went to see *Richard III* they found themselves, in more ways than we might anticipate, in a theatre of walking.

This is a running motif in the play. It compels our attention even as we wonder whether like Richard, troubled by Richard, we have become paranoid about feet. We notice how he inverts his blazon of King Edward's mistress—'Shore's wife hath a pretty foot', he starts, then up towards her head—and what he says of Clarence, tricked into execution, 'Go, tread the path that thou shalt ne'er return' (1.1.93, 118). As Lady Anne comes onstage in Act 1 Scene 2, with the body of Henry VI, he calls for the coffin to be put down and defies a gentleman: 'by Saint Paul, I'll strike thee to my foot | And spurn upon thee, beggar' (41–2). The foot is used to bully even though, and because, it is incapable of roundly spurning (i.e. kicking).[34] Is this why Anne is seduced? That she cannot allow herself to register the deformity that repels her? Or is it the eroticism of Richard's status, ambition, evil, or the threat projected by his deformity, or some bizarre early modern idea that the crippled make good lovers? Montaigne reports a belief that '*The crooked man doeth it best.*'[35] In an epigram from the 1590s that draws extensively on Richard's opening soliloquy, one Ignoto boasts, 'harke in thine eare, zounds I can ( ) thee soundly.'[36]

Clarence's dream, which is not in the chronicles, shows how deftly Shakespeare could add in footwork. The Duke tells Brackenbury that he dreamt he was on a boat, when his brother, Richard, 'tempted' him 'to walk | Upon the hatches', and

> As we paced along
> Upon the giddy footing of the hatches,
> Methought that Gloucester stumbled, and in falling
> Struck me—that thought to stay him—overboard
> Into the tumbling billows of the main.   (1.4.12–20)

'Paced . . . giddy footing . . . stumbled': barely suppressed anxiety about Gloucester's disability (about being caught up in it, giddily knocked into death by it) is palpable. 'Tempted' alerts the audience to a suspicion that Clarence will not admit to. In the dream what looks like an accident was an assault, and one that goes down to Richard's aggressive limp. The power of the unacknowledgeable foot repeatedly makes itself felt. When the news is broken of Clarence's death, King Edward protests that 'the order was reversed', and Gloucester (who has prevented the reprieve) replies: 'Some tardy cripple bore the countermand' (2.1.87, 90). The black joke is hidden in plain sight, blanked by characters who sense the growing threat to themselves.

Where does this leave originality? In Chapter 1, I discussed how Shakespeare was accused, after the composition of the *Henry VI* plays, of beautifying himself with others' feathers. Given how little of the first act of *Richard III* can be found in Holinshed, or the *True Tragedie*, or even the Latin history play *Richardus Tertius*, by the aptly named Thomas Legge,[37] it is easy to warm to Geoffrey Bullough's suggestion that, having 'recently been accused of plagiarism by Robert Greene', Shakespeare 'wished to prove his independence.... a resolve to make *Richard III* different from either *Richardus Tertius* or the *True Tragedy* may have been in part responsible for some features of the play's *ordonnance*'.[38] The critical implications are subtle—that the presence of sources might be felt not when they are followed but when they are reacted against; and the case is the more intriguing, given the early modern generic assumption that history plays will be secured by sources when comedies or sonnets need not. Yet the characterization is incomplete. Acts 2 to 5 of *Richard III* are much closer to the chronicles, and they manifest the originality that can be achieved when the same material is transposed from one medium or mode to another (prose to verse, page to stage, chronicle history to Kydian tragedy). As the Roman plays often show, when following North's Plutarch word for word, adherence to an original can be innovative in stage effect. This is a thought that I want to pursue from *Richard III* to *As You Like It*. In the final section of the chapter I shall look again at what Shakespeare adds, by heeding the footfalls of *Macbeth*.

* * *

The art and practice of footwork were widely discussed in antiquity. Shakespeare would have picked this up from classical drama and such rhetoricians as Quintilian, who writes at length about the placing of the feet in orations[39] and notes that 'In plays, young men, old men, soldiers, and married ladies advance sedately; slaves, slave girls, parasites, and fishermen move with more speed.'[40] The rudiments go back to Aristotle, who said that the frantic are hasty and the great-souled measured.[41] Walking was status- and gender-inflected: if servants ran, like the Dromios in *The Comedy of Errors*, which is based on Plautus' *Menaechmi* and *Amphitruo*, patricians strolled at leisure, like Antipholus of Syracuse, 'up and down to view the city' (1.2.31); women and gay men waggled their hips, declared the ancient experts, while the furious, like Seneca's Medea, dashed about: 'Why trotst thou fysking in and out so rash from place to place?', the nurse asks her mistress in the 1566 translation.[42]

Renaissance treatises and conduct books inherited much of this lore. An educated observer of *Richard III* would know from a literature that went back to Galen that, 'The feete crooked, and hauing the soles verye hollow, and wrinckled: are persons to be shunned, for that such are craftie, and wicked in their dooinges.'[43] Yet although inward qualities were believed to show themselves in the actions of the feet,[44] a pedestrian style could also be cultivated. 'Yee must take very good heed vnto your feete', wrote James Cleland in 1607, 'and consider with what grace and countenance yee walke, that yee go not softly, tripping like a wanton maide, nor yet striding with great long paces, like those Rhodomonts and Kings in Stage-plaies.'[45] For Cleland, as for others, the theatre sets a bad example, encouraging in those who walk to it an affected body language. Pistol is one such, swaggering with his scraps of *Tamburlaine*.[46] Scripture added its guidance. 'We were not borne to glory in our feet,' Richard Brathwait warns, 'but to walke as *children* of *light*.'[47] He deplores any woman who goes 'mincing and measuring her pace, tinkling with her feet'.[48] Such females 'demeane themselues more like *Actors* than ciuill Professants'.[49] 'With what *Apish* gestures they walke, … How *phantastically* those, as if their walke were a theatrall action?'[50] It matters to such plays as *A Midsummer Night's Dream* that wandering feet lead women astray. Barnabe Riche is orthodox when he writes of harlots (out of Solomon): 'shee is euer more wandring; her feete are wandring, her eies are wandring, her wits are wandring.'[51]

It would be naive to transfer the taxonomies and glosses of treatises directly to the streets of London. But Shakespeare and his contemporaries were at least as alert as we are to the semiotics of other walkers, male or female, young and old. That we can make judgements about identity fairly accurately—are psychologically predisposed to do so—within a few paces of someone swinging into view[52] is part of how theatre works. Burbage cannot have taken many steps from the back of the stage before showing the audience what he was. 'It is no hard thing', wrote Brathwait, 'to gather the *disposition* of our *heart*, by the *dimension* of our *gate*.'[53] The early modern playhouse had no need for the extended entrances and exits that take Kabuki actors along the *hanamichi* or 'flower path' that runs through the audience.[54] To look at the foundations of the Rose theatre, and read the plans for the Fortune, is to be struck by how small the stages were, how very few feet lay (the foot was then the measure of all things)—as few as fifteen and a half—between the doors in the tiring house and the audience.[55]

Academic drama seems to have been different. It is likely that the actors in *Richardus Tertius*, performed with huge resources at St John's College, Cambridge in 1580, had lengthy entrances and exits. Lengthy and dull. In the *Parnassus* plays, also written for St John's, *c*.1599, the character of Kemp, talking to Burbage, mocks the conventions of university theatre: 'tis good sporte in a part, to see them neuer speake in their walke, but at the end of the stage, iust as though in walking with a fellow we should neuer speake but at a stile, a gate, or a ditch, where a man can go no further.'[56] Players in the public theatre, by contrast, had learned the art of talking while walking—a banal point of major significance, as we shall see. Olivier limped all the way down stage before launching into 'Now is the winter of our discontent', but it is likely that Burbage mixed limping with language. A few lines further on in the *Parnassus* plays, a student called Philomusus asks for an audition. Burbage says, 'I like your face and the proportion of your body for *Richard* the 3., . . . let me see you act a little of it.' 'Now is the winter of our discontent | Made glorious summer by the sun of York, [&c.]' declaims the student, no doubt as badly as he limped. 'Very well I assure you', says Burbage, 'walke with vs to our fellows, . . . ' (4.4 [lines 1835–42]). *Exeunt*, conceivably down the full length of the college hall.

In the public theatre, the effect was more often one of compression, of jump-cut shifts to location and switches between inside and outside created *by* short walks. The actors' paths crissed and crossed on the planks and rushes of the stage, like a fractal version of the road plan that reticulated across England. To wander here is to wonder, through surprising, even deranging encounters, where a maze creates amazement (both bits of wordplay are routine). In a society where almost all journeys were taken, exhaustingly and even lamingly, by foot, this was the magic of theatre, traversing and transforming space. 'On foot', writes Rebecca Solnit, 'everything stays connected'[57]—true of the large, walked world, but on stage walking can leap. Sidney captures this while complaining about the absurdity of the Tudor stage: 'you shall have Asia of the one side, and Afric of the other,… Now ye shall have three ladies walk to gather flowers, and then we must believe the stage to be a garden.'[58]

This is the modality of *A Midsummer Night's Dream*, where dancing footwork and quick-change prosody along with walking, wandering, and dashing about rather mobilize than fantasize the conditions of existence. As the poet Henry King put it, 'Life is a crooked Labyrinth, and wee | Are daily lost in that Obliquity.'[59] The lovers leave Athens with a sense of direction that is quickly deranged, led astray by tracks. The roaming Helena and Hermia must almost prudishly guard their virtue, for fear of attracting blame from the readers of Riche and Brathwait. The mechanicals, like Rosalind and Celia on tour with Touchstone, the clown, in *As You Like It*, present a version of the vagrancy to which the company performing the play was accustomed, ready to put a show on anywhere: 'This green plot shall be our stage,' says Quince, alluding to those rushes on the scaffold, 'this hawthorn brake our tiring-house' (3.1.3–4). Scholars have overlooked the innovativeness of the sequence that follows in which Bottom, given an ass's head and abandoned by his companions, decides to 'walk up and down', then sing to cheer himself up (116). The catalogue of early modern stage directions lists a number of similar actions: '*walk about, off, apart, aside … walks up and down musing … seems amazed, and walks so up and down*';[60] but Bottom's unwitnessed, mere walk sets a default for acting in the play—how to make nothing happen—that is both new in Shakespeare and unusual. We shall return to this in *Macbeth*.

*   *   *

Let me reboot with another limp. In Thomas Lodge's *Rosalynde*, the heroine and her friend Alinda make their way into the Forest of Arden via a circuitous, romance-style route, passing along vineyards 'and many by-waies' until they come to a fountain in a cypress grove.[61] Rosader, the equivalent of Orlando in the play, and old Adam, trying to find a short cut to Lyons, wander among the trees and end up hungry and weak (F4r). Shakespeare follows Lodge closely, but at both points he cuts out the details and implies distance by having the actors walk on as though worn out. 'O Jupiter, how weary are my spirits!' Rosalind cries, to which Touchstone tartly responds, 'I care not for my spirits, if my legs were not weary' (2.4.1–2). Adam then enters with Orlando for a tiny scene designed to show that he 'can go no further' (2.6.1). The old man, Orlando tells Duke Senior, 'hath many a weary step | Limped in pure love', and needs to be carried on stage (2.7.131). Whether Adam limped from the outset is a point worth consideration as we try to diversify casts. And perhaps on biographical grounds. It was said in the late seventeenth century that Shakespeare 'appeared' in the role of Adam 'weak and drooping and unable to walk'.[62] Made lame by fortune's blows?

These points of adjustment show both the economies available to Shakespeare when he translated narrative into action and the shift that this brought into the physicality of walking. Yet the footwork already in *Rosalynde* must have been a factor in attracting him to the source. He will have noted at the start of the romance that Rosader, denied his patrimony by his older brother, Saladyne, was made his 'foote boy' (B3v). Also that he decided to rebel while 'walkyng in the Garden' (B3v). The sequence in which Rosader wrestles with the Duke's champion encouraged him to show Orlando barefoot, tripping up the wrestler's heels.[63] Rosader's life in Arden, where he woos the 'wandring' Rosalynde (D3r, E4r–v), peaks when he is put in charge of those 'walkes' which, in early modern forestry, were cut through the wild and wooded (K2r). When the repentant Saladyne turns up, confused by the 'by pathes' and 'wearie with wandring' (K1r), he is given a tour of these walks.[64] Just as walking brings Rosader and Rosalynde together, so the sibling relationship is advanced by feet that, in the theatre, cry out to be choreographed.

Shakespeare finds all sorts of ways to add in fancy footwork, from Orlando's 'Run, run' to hang verses on trees in the forest, through Audrey's rustic 'Trip . . . trip', to the dance at the end of the play which is not left to the discretion of the company as a jig after the action but incorporated before the epilogue.[65] This is a play in which Rosalind's transformation into Ganymede requires not just a change of clothes but 'a swashing and a martial' gait (1.3.119). How the boy actor walked as a woman when she was playing a youth must have been a beguiling point of complexity. One recalls the worry of puritans that boy players trained to walk like women would become effeminate.[66] Phoebe, played by a boy, takes a fancy to Ganymede's shapely 'leg' (3.5.120). In the eighteenth and nineteenth centuries, the exposure of the legs of actresses who performed the breeches part gave men in the audience a thrill. This attraction was enhanced and kinked when Rosalind was played by women, able to show off their pins as Ganymede. Georgian and Victorian reviewers, accustomed to seeing little more than ladies' ankles on stage, dotingly remark on Dora Jordan's 'shapely leg' and Mary Anderson's 'nether limbs'.[67]

More interesting to the likes of us is how, in *As You Like It*, walking finds expression figuratively and in displaced forms. Shakespeare may have learned from *Every Man Out of His Humour* the satirical possibilities of a comedy in which characters do not follow plotting conventions derived from Plautus and Terence but drift around chatting and jibing. Jonson's play is footloose, and its characters often comment on walking, notably in a long, satirical sequence set in Paul's Walk— that is, the cathedral, where (according to John Earle) all the world's business was 'stirring and a foot'.[68] Whether or not *As You Like It* is the play in which Shakespeare (according to the *Parnassus* plays) gave Jonson 'a purge',[69] by satirizing him in the figure of Jaques, who is added to Lodge, the Duke derives the malcontent's misanthropy from the 'licence of free foot' that he indulged as a libertine (2.7.68). Touchstone is a milder satirist, but he shares with the Jaques of 'All the world's a stage' a liking for divagatory set pieces. 'How now, wit: whither *wander* you?' is Celia's apt question, prompting him to detour through a routine about swearing, pancakes, and mustard (1.2.53–83).[70] The most strikingly errant set piece is Rosalind's on 'the lazy foot of time', which wanders away from an exchange with Orlando to list what sorts of people, from priest to lawyer, Time ambles, gallops, trots, and stands still withal (3.2.298–324). Her idle jokes almost run on the spot, but they have thematic work to do about the relationship between time and feet—ambling, trotting, or just going: something that recurs in Shakespeare all the way to Macbeth's great monologue on the death of his wife.

Before I turn to the Scottish play, I ought to probe a little further the connection between wandering, feet, and language. That walking is semiotic, a point well made in the classical sources, is still a claim widely current, whether in the abstruse disquisitions of Michel de Certeau[71] or in more popular, accessible studies. 'Walking is talking', says Joseph Amato in *On Foot*: 'It can be understood as a language, having its own vernacular, dialects, and idioms. Expressing intentionality, walking conveys a wealth of information about the walker's identity, importance, condition, and destination.'[72] This is so, as far as it steps. It prompts one to reflect, however, on the more compressed ways in which the walking choices of an actor counterpoint or echo the words that are given them by a script. In performance, language educes the sign-idiom of the walk but also points up what is temporospatial and incomplete in stage dialogue.

This would not grip us if it were simply the product of artifice. It is grounded in our condition as walking, talking animals, whose perambulations can be a source of originality—as through encounter and wonder in Arden—precisely because they reach before and after any origin. 'When did our walk begin?', the anthropologists Tim Ingold and Jo Lee Vergunst ask, 'When will it ever end? We cannot remember, and will never know.'[73] So far, so Richard III, born out of sync with time, both an 'indigested lump' or 'chaos'—premature and potentialized, like the origins of everything in Ovid[74]—'sent before my time' yet coming late into the world, with teeth and 'legs forward', as he tells Henry VI, the better to 'make haste',[75] always already walking. But the anthropologists go further:

> We are already talking by the time we realize that this is what we are doing; and only those who remain after we are gone will know which words will have been our last. So it is, too, with our first and last steps. Life itself is as much a long walk as it is a long conversation, and the ways along which we walk are those along which we live.... every step faces both ways: it is both the ending, or tip, of a trail that leads back through our past life, and a new beginning that moves us forward towards future destinations unknown. (1)

I want to explore, in Chapter 3, what the connections were for Shakespeare between origins and originality, and I shall start with a scene of walking. What can be said for now is that walking is one powerful way in which *As You Like It* achieves the originality apparently denied by its debts to Lodge. It matters that, as Kemp reminded Burbage, actors walked onstage talking, often (in mature Shakespeare) caught in mid-conversation, making entrances a continuation as exits were not often an ending.

The radical point is not so much that walking has its semiotics, or that walking elides with and answers the talking that accompanies it, but that walking has a rhythm, and that, since antiquity, verse (and prose) has been said, more than airily, to have feet. Shakespeare digs into metrical footing in the dialogue about Orlando's arboreal love poetry. Touchstone pointedly mocks the 'false gallop' of his verses.[76] Dr Johnson would be just as scornful when glossing his comparison of Rosalind's charms to 'Atalanta's better part' (3.2.144). 'I know not well', he pontificates, 'what could be the better part of *Atalanta* here ascribed to *Rosalind*. Of the *Atalanta* most celebrated, . . . the *better part* seems to have been her heels.'[77] He regards the line as a mistake; but in this play of footwork, not so. Rosalind is being complimented on having feet as fleet and feat as Atalanta, the virgin huntress of antiquity, who outran her suitors in races, as Jaques will praise Orlando's 'nimble wit; I think 'twas made of Atalanta's heels' (270).

At this point, Rosalind's cleverness returns us to Richard III. Celia says to her friend, of Orlando's poems, 'Didst thou hear these verses?' 'O yes,' she wryly replies,

> I heard them all, and more, too, for some of them had in them more feet than the verses would bear.
> CELIA That's no matter; the feet might bear the verses.
> ROSALIND Ay, but the feet were lame, and could not bear themselves without the verse, and therefore stood lamely in the verse. (160–7)

Some Renaissance theorists doubted that accentual, vernacular poetry, as against the classical variety, based on quantity, went on feet.[78] You would have to be deaf, however, to miss the da-dum iambic of everyday footsteps. Isidore of Seville is in the classical and medieval mainstream when he says that verses have feet because 'In each foot there occurs . . . a raising and lowering of the voice—for the feet would not be able to follow a road unless they were alternately raised and lowered.'[79] Such feet would run into trouble if, as is sometimes the way in Elizabethan writing—see Ascham on the Earl of Surrey, Gabriel Harvey on Spenser—they are 'deformed'.[80] Then, in Hamlet's words, 'the blank verse shall halt for't' (2.2.327). This is the logic, at once bodily and prosodic,[81] of Richard's ungainly, nimble gait as it warps and propels his verse line.

* * *

Did *Macbeth*, at the Globe or at court, start, like *Richard III*, with limping? On balance, it is more than likely. That witches were lame was widely believed. Recall the Belvoir witches, in the celebrated woodcut, recycled on a 1619 ballad sheet, with their sticks and crutches (Fig. 5). Reginald Scot, in *The Discouerie of Witchcraft*, describes how 'One sort of such as are said to bee witches, are women which be commonly old, lame, bleare-eied'; 'Sometimes they are called witches...that are old, lame, curst.'[82] Sceptical about witchcraft, Scot jests that such 'heauie, and commonlie lame' women are 'vnapt to flie in the aire' (219). But that is the magic of magic, as when the witches of *Macbeth* heavily enjoin themselves to hover (1.1.11). There is a theatrical tradition of presenting them as halt and so antic in their dances. In Charles Kean's production of 1853, for example, just before the protagonist's first entrance, 'the three witches joined their crutches and went round in a circle, then stood still, pointing to Macbeth'.[83]

Yet it needs no witches to show us that walking is at issue in this play. It is full of flagged-up steps, paces, rounds, and struts, and the theatrical record shows a more than usual elaboration of footwork. Take the sequence in which Macbeth makes towards Duncan's chamber to murder him:

> Is this a dagger which I see before me,
> The handle toward my hand? Come, let me clutch thee.
> I have thee not, and yet I see thee still ....
> Thou marshall'st me the way that I was going, ...   (2.1.33–42)

'Going' in Jacobean English means 'walking'. As Macbeth walks, his going is dramatized because every step takes him closer to committing regicide. Some unsteadiness would be understandable. Garrick said that '*Come let me clutch thee!* is not to be done by *one* Motion only, but by several *successive Catches* at it, ... preserving the same Motion, at the same Time, with his Feet, like a Man, ... out of his Depth.'[84] Edmund Kean traversed the stage with such wary indecision that Hawkins, his early biographer, described him 'slowly guiding his halting footsteps to the door of Duncan's chamber'.[85]

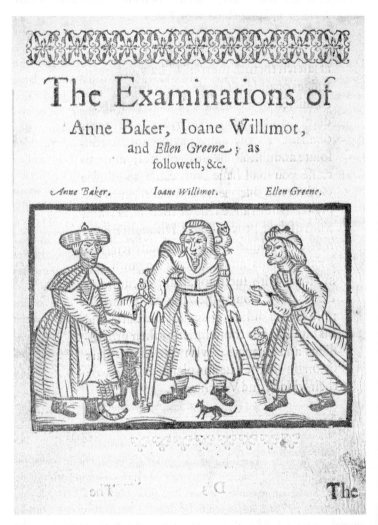

Fig. 5. Old, lame, curst witches. Woodcut in *The Wonderful Discouerie of the Witchcrafts of Margaret and Phillip Flower* (1619). Reproduced by permission of the British Library.

However the actor walks, the audience will be prompted by his lines to notice:

> and withered murder,
> Alarumed by his sentinel the wolf,
> Whose howl's his watch, thus with his stealthy pace,
> With Tarquin's ravishing strides, towards his design
> Moves like a ghost. (2.1.52–6)

Alec Guinness once said, about getting into roles, 'I try to get the feet right first'.[86] We know that, as Macbeth, he went 'Slithering forward at great and sinister speed on the word "stealthy"',[87] but it is possible to counterpoint what is said, with Macbeth urging himself to stride while he visibly drags his feet. In Olivier's performance, almost as with his Richard III, 'Tarquin's strides were only dimly reflected in his dragging pace'.[88]

It needs to be remembered at this point that the stage was a sounding board. The wooden O was a drum. Ulysses, in *Troilus and Cressida*, describes an actor exploiting this when he compares Patroclus to

> a strutting player, whose conceit
> Lies in his hamstring and doth think it rich
> To hear the wooden dialogue and sound
> 'Twixt his stretched footing and the scaffoldage,... (1.3.153–6)

Macbeth is at the other extreme. In his guilt and anxiety, he wants to muffle the sound of the steps that, along with horses' hooves, bells, knocking at the gate, marching troops, and drums, mesh the sound-scape of the play with pacing, passing time until they echo into meaningless repetition. 'Thou sure and firm-set earth,' he continues,

> Hear not my steps which way they walk, for fear
> Thy very stones prate of my whereabout,
> And take the present horror from the time,... (56–9)

In the TV version of Rupert Goold's *Macbeth*, Patrick Stewart is seen walking down a long corridor towards the murder; his steps are dismally articulate; the sense of alienation is as palpable as the determination required by ambition. The confined space of the stage has to find other ways of dramatizing the protagonist's impeding doubts. The great Victorian actor Macready stepped towards the murder with 'ghastly and impalpable tread';[89] but in a grotesque, stilted gesture, 'when his body was actually off the stage, his left foot and leg remained trembling in sight, it seemed, fully half a minute'.[90] This 'point' was admired and imitated, though it was also, understandably, satirized by Dickens and others.[91] At 'Hear not my steps' Irving was unstable, like Clarence in his dream, 'his feet, as it were,' feeling 'for the ground', according to the *Fortnightly Review*, 'as if he were walking with difficulty a step at a time on a reeling deck'.[92] None of this, needless to say, is in Holinshed. It springs from an originality which is grounded, we might hazard—and I shall come back to this later—on the bases of performance in getting the feet right.

Macbeth 'Moves like a ghost', lost to the murder he has not yet committed. How do the dead walk, both the actual and the proleptic? It may be that Banquo's ghost had the same sort of 'martial stalk' as the old king's spirit in *Hamlet* (1.1.65). A poem by Henry Higden suggests that, in Davenant's version of *Macbeth*, the actor still conducted himself like Alleyn, the more portentous for being dated: 'Like *Bancoe*'s Ghost, his ugly Sin, | To marr his Jollity, stalks in.'[93] One of the strengths of the Goold theatre production was to contrive a mighty shock by having the ghost enter back-centre stage, then step up onto and stalk the length of the dinner table towards Macbeth and the audience. A Shakespearean violation of order (Fig. 6). At that point, the stage lights were cut for the interval, and when the action was resumed the sequence was rerun without the actor playing Banquo present, so that the king was felt to be hallucinating what we had been shown minutes before. The screen version was even more potently fixated on Banquo's feet, tracking them along the table as they tread relentlessly towards Macbeth (Fig. 7).

There is, of course, another ghost scene, which the King's Men must have played for contrast: Lady Macbeth's sleepwalking. Jacobean dramatists, such as Tomkis, who recycled this episode in *Lingua* (1607), could be interested in physiological explanations for sleepwalking, but more often, as in Lavater's *Of Ghostes and Spirites Walking by Nyght* (1572), it was discussed in conjunction with the supernatural.[94] Lady Macbeth, in performance, has often walked like a revenant. Mrs Siddons 'glided on and off the stage like an apparition'.[95] The Lady is not just haunting but is haunted by what she has done. Many in the role have re-enacted their actions around

Fig. 6. The ghost of Banquo, walking. Rupert Goold production of *Macbeth*, Headlong Theatre Company (2007). Reproduced by permission of Manuel Harlan.

Fig. 7. Further horror of the foot. From the TV version of Rupert Goold's *Macbeth* (2010). Courtesy Illuminations.

the murder of Duncan—walking to and from the king's chamber with the daggers, washing their hands of blood. The Lady's words are fragmented, her identity given continuity by her feet, pacing back and forth, like the traumatized, consoling steps of Amy in Beckett's *Footfalls*, which owes so much to *Macbeth*. Harriet Walter says of Lady Macbeth: 'Her sleepwalking is her release—her soliloquy, if you like—though sleep itself removes her from self-understanding.'[96] Driven by what she has done, and what cannot be undone, she becomes her own ghost. The tread or flit of her feet—usually visible, often naked[97]—becomes a way of spelling this out, ringing through the repetitions of 'One, two' and 'O, O, O!' to her parting words, 'To bed, to bed, to bed' (5.1.33, 49–50, 65), that echo into that later monologue of ghostly walking, 'Tomorrow, and tomorrow, and tomorrow', which is where I want to end.

We hear it after the cry of women, with the announcement of Lady's Macbeth's death:

> She should have died hereafter.
> There would have been a time for such a word.
> Tomorrow, and tomorrow, and tomorrow
> Creeps in this petty pace from day to day
> To the last syllable of recorded time,
> And all our yesterdays have lighted fools
> The way to dusty death. Out, out, brief candle.
> Life's but a walking shadow, a poor player
> That struts and frets his hour upon the stage,
> And then is heard no more. It is a tale
> Told by an idiot, full of sound and fury,
> Signifying nothing.   (5.5.16–27)

Now time itself does the pacing. The monologue gives us the most compressed version, like the seven or nine repeated steps in *Footfalls*, of what the walking artist Hamish Fulton says: 'Walking is about an investment of time, the time of your life.'[98] Tomorrow and its repetitions take tiny, trivial steps, in a movement (pace) which has hardly any speed (pace). It paces and so passes (the quibble is audible) like the *not* which is a *pas*, or footfall, in Beckett. One reason why the stage business of a nineteenth-century *Macbeth* like Edwin Forrest must always have been a distraction at this point ('he stalked about the stage rattling his truncheon')[99] is that walking is now in the voice or the head. The verse feet do the walking—echoes of the play's soundscape, talking of a walk without choice or purpose. When we get to the end of time it is already spoken for (a syllable, recorded).

Dissociative in despair, Macbeth is the performance of himself, like an actor (a shadow) that walks. In one way the passage goes back to Hamlet on the bad actor ('poor player' means 'incompetent', as well as 'pitiable') who struts and bellows. Again the actor struts, frets, and then shouts out speeches full of sound and fury. It signifies nothing, among other reasons, because the tale is *tolled* like the ringing of the bell that triggered the murder of Duncan. Scholars have noticed a debt to Studley's translation of Seneca's *Agamemnon*, 'To morow shall wee rule, as we haue don to daye. | One clod of croked care another bryngeth in.'[100] As in the sleepwalking scene, however, the play recycles its materials, becomes *its own source*—a recurrent feature of Shakespeare's originality—as an element of its fatalism. Macbeth says to the ghost of Banquo in material added to Holinshed: 'Hence, horrible shadow' (3.4.105). As Banquo stalks about the stage he is indeed a 'walking shadow'. Moreover, if Simon Forman's account of seeing Shakespeare's company at the Globe can be trusted, Banquo triggered sound and fury in Burbage's Macbeth: 'he fell into a great passion of fear and fury'.[101] Consider too the eight kings shown to Macbeth in procession by the witches after the feast: 'Come like shadows, so depart' (4.1.127). As they form a line they are like a single walker stretched through time, as in an Eadweard Muybridge photograph. 'What', Macbeth asks, 'will the line stretch out to th' crack of doom?' (133). To the last syllable of recorded time. Lady Macbeth, another walking shadow, is part of this sequence too. The brief candle might be the one she carries, or keeps lit by her bedside (5.1.22–3), until she dies.

All of which may be true without quite catching the originality of Macbeth's tissue of commonplaces. At which point, we return to acting, and the sense that it was for Shakespeare already—and to the end which lies beyond death—pedestrian. Peter Brook famously wrote, at the start of *The Empty Space*: 'I can take any empty space and call it a bare stage. A man walks across this empty space whilst someone else is watching him, and this is all that is needed for an act of theatre to be engaged.'[102] The claim has been contested with all the political rectitude that comes from asking why a man rather than a woman—he could so easily be describing the sleepwalking scene—and why not a man whose walk is a disabled, asymmetrical activity, dragging a lot of psychology with it. More drastically, it can be challenged by Declan Donnellan's claim that 'For the actor the space is never empty, the space is always charged with meaning.... otherwise the actor would become neutral and lose energy.'[103] There is some truth in this, but only some. To ask (as Donnellan does) of Juliet, 'Will the floor let her pace on it? | Or make her run on it?' (126) would strike the protean Burbage as verging on the precious. Shakespeare and his fellow actors *made* places with paces, whether they were in the Globe theatre, the Inns of Court, or under some greenwood tree, and they put their feet into their mouths whenever they had lines to speak.

3

King Lear and its Origins

An old man, blinded and bereft, shuffles across the stage, led by his disguised and estranged son. The stage is flat or gently raked, but Gloucester's senses are uncertain. 'When shall we come to th' top of that same hill?' he asks, meaning the brow of Dover Cliff, from which he plans to fling himself. 'You do climb up it now', Edgar replies, half-confusing the audience:

> EDGAR   Look how we labour.
> GLOUCESTER Methinks the ground is even.
> EDGAR   Horrible steep.
> Hark, do you hear the sea?
> GLOUCESTER   No, truly.[1]

Gloucester's senses do not deceive him, though his son does, to save him (he tells us) from despair. Whatever his mix of motives, some of them obscure to himself, Edgar leads his father to the brink of the imaginary cliff, from which 'The crows and choughs that wing the midway air | Show scarce so gross as beetles', and everything dwindles and fades until 'The murmuring surge ... Cannot be heard so high' (13–22). By now he has forgotten to pretend to hear the sea.

What is the source of this extraordinary sequence? It cannot be found in the anonymous play *The True Chronicle History of King Leir*, written in the 1580s and published in 1605, though Shakespeare drew extensively on its capable, affecting account of an ageing king who divides his realm between two uncaring daughters after rejecting his third and youngest for not flattering him in a love-trial.[2] As Charlotte Lennox noted,[3] the Gloucester plot derives from the *Arcadia*, in which we are told of 'an aged man, and a young'—the King of Paphlagonia and his son, Leonatus—'both poorely arayed, ... the olde man blinde, the young man leading him'. This king, usurped and disabled by his wicked, illegitimate son, 'hath bin', Leonatus explains, 'driuen to such griefe, as euen now he would haue had me to haue led him to the toppe of this rocke, thence to cast himselfe headlong to death'.[4]

That this story of thwarted suicide is not in Heliodorus' *Æthiopian Historie*, Sidney's own source at this point, and a romance known to Shakespeare,[5] might seem to secure the received idea that the *Arcadia* gave the dramatist all he needed to invent Dover Cliff. One of my contentions in this chapter, however, is that the model still taken for granted in the study of Shakespeare's sources, despite much talk of intertextuality—that a source is left behind in the generation of a text—is, in some contexts, and genres, anachronistic and misleading. In *Lear*, as in *Arcadia*, layers of imitation resonate back to antiquity, to something like symphonic effect. Just as Sidney grafted into the Paphlagonian tale in Heliodorus what he called, in the *Apology for Poetry*, 'the remorse of conscience in Oedipus'—self-blinded and led by Antigone—and 'the violence of ambition in the two Theban brothers' (i.e. Eteocles and Polynices, who become rivals for their father, Oedipus' crown),[6] so Shakespeare found his way back in *Lear* through Seneca's *Oedipus* and *Thebais* to ancient Greek beginnings. The tragedy is original in the early modern sense of going back to origins.

Seneca's *Thebais* (or *Phoenissae*) starts with Oedipus being led into the action by Antigone. 'Plungde in misery', in Newton's 1581 translation, he wants to fling himself 'in breaknecke tumbling plight' from any convenient precipice.[7] Yet the places of death that he calls to mind are loaded with the problems of origin: the 'hill | Of craggy stiepe Cytheron', where, as a baby, he was abandoned (41); 'Bring me that am dispos'd to dye,' he cries, 'where *Sphinx* that Monster fell' (43). That Shakespeare knew this play, and in Latin, is indicated by Antigone telling Oedipus that she will lead him across even ground ('in plana tendis') or up steep slopes ('praerupta')—'rough and smoth' in Newton[8]—alternatives that are conflated for Gloucester, who thinks, as we have seen, that he walks on level ground though Edgar tells him the contrary. To which Antigone adds:

> Here is an huyge Promontory that elboes into Sea
> Let vs from thence throw downe our selues, . . .
>   Heere beaten with the tyde
> Bee craggy Cliffes, let's goe to them: . . .   (42)

There is no reason to doubt that those cliffs are there in Seneca's play world. In making Dover Cliff virtual, Shakespeare innovates by drawing on a passage in Montaigne's *Essayes* about the vertiginous effect of hearing (even if you are a blinded philosopher) about slopes and precipices.[9] Shakespeare, you could say, heard about cliffs from Seneca, and put them dizzyingly (for blind Gloucester) into *King Lear*. Meanwhile, in the shaping of Edgar, the art of imitation is evident. Antigone offers to precipitate herself from the cliffs to dissuade Oedipus from despair. Like Edgar, she encourages her father by imparting stoical counsel.

The text of Seneca's *Thebais* is anomalous and fragmentary. Quite likely it is unfinished. It reaches us without choruses and before the conflict between Polynices and Eteocles is resolved. Treated as marginal by classicists today, it engaged early modern readers preoccupied with the dangers of contested succession. A century ago, when most Shakespeare scholars had a classical education, it was taken for granted that Elizabethan drama was saturated in Seneca. John W. Cunliffe showed, for instance, that another tragedy about ancient Britain, *The Misfortunes of Arthur* (1588), is larded with quotations from the *Thebais*.[10] As critical fashions moved on, Shakespeare's awareness of classical drama was neglected.[11] There is nothing about the *Thebais* in Bullough's *Narrative and Dramatic Sources* or in current editions of *King Lear*. Impressive books by Gordon Braden, Robert Miola, and Colin Burrow have done much over the last few years to bring Seneca back into view,[12] but none of them discusses the *Thebais*. Beyond a few words by Kenneth Muir and hardly more by Michael Stapleton,[13] the link has been ignored, and even those accounts miss Shakespeare's imitation of the latter parts of the *Thebais* (i.e. the war between Polynices and Eteocles), which I shall get to in due course. They also leave unexplored the connection between Shakespeare's drive back to tragic origins and *King Lear*'s seeking out of the origins of nature and culture, in the divided, the atomistic, the aetiological, the surgical, and the metaphysical. That, roughly speaking, is the scope of this chapter.

* * *

Among the origins of *King Lear*, and among the origins that interest the play, are, as I have suggested, the tragedies of Greek antiquity. We need not go to the treatises written in Renaissance Italy to find the

works discussed in Aristotle's *Poetics* being treated as originary. Puttenham's *Arte of English Poesie*, which we know that Shakespeare read, and
probably reread while engaged with *King Lear*, and the *Apology for Actors*
written by his fellow dramatist Heywood, say as much out of Horace,
Evanthius, and Donatus.[14] Greek tragedy was 'widely recognized' as
being the genre of tragedy's 'origin'.[15] It is unlikely that an ambitious
dramatist, conscious of his growing powers, would have been aware of
this without trying to access the ancient plays. You could limit his
knowledge of Greek tragedy to what he divined from Seneca—taken
by educated readers to be an imitator of Sophocles and Euripides.[16]
But what happens if we look beyond Jonson's reference in the Folio to
Shakespeare's 'small *Latine*, and less *Greeke*' (which is all that I shall
claim for him—several years of classics at grammar school) and take
seriously Jonson's comparison between his friend and thundering
Aeschylus, Sophocles, and Euripides?[17]

    Over the last couple of decades, a number of scholars have argued
for the influence of Euripides, mediated by Latin-Greek bilingual
editions, in such plays as *The Winter's Tale*, adding, I believe convin-
cingly, to the case made by Louise Schleiner for the presence of Latin
Aeschylus in *Hamlet*.[18] As it happens, Euripides' *Phoenissae* is an obvious tragedy to invoke in relation to *Lear*, because Shakespeare had
ready access to its representation of Oedipus and Antigone and the
war between Eteocles and Polynices in Gascoigne and Kinwelmarsh's
Iocasta: A Tragedie Written in Greke by Euripides.[19] Staged at Gray's Inn in
1566, this version of Euripides via Latin and the Italian of Dolce was
published in 1573, 1575, and again in 1587. I shall return to the
Greek *Phoenissae* later. But Sophocles awaits his moment, and I want to
make that claim now.

    The challenging but then inevitable thought that *King Lear* forma-
tively draws on the *Oedipus Tyrannus* and *Oedipus at Colonus* has not been
pursued, except in a brief 'Note' published forty years ago by John
Harvey.[20] With its riddles, stumbling age, incestuous undercurrents,
irascible protagonist, the child leading a blind man into exile, con-
cealed identity, and civil strife, *Lear* shares much of the matter and
outline of Sophocles' Theban plays. Elements of the story were dis-
persed in England, beyond Seneca, with hints of Greek, from Erasmus'
Apophthegmes through Cooper's *Thesaurus* and beyond.[21] The ancient
hero even puts in an appearance in one acknowledged source of *King*

Lear, Samuel Harsnett's *Declaration of Egregious Popish Impostures*, where mention of an authority on the expulsion of devils, Thyraeus, leads via Tiresias the riddle solver—which is not what he does in Seneca—to Oedipus: '*Oedipo opus est*, I am at a full point. And if I send you to *Thyraeus*, to vnridle the ridle, I doubt you will laughe at him.'[22] Yet these traces are patchy, and thin on Oedipus' death at Colonos[23]—particularly relevant, as we shall see, to Dover Cliff—which Shakespeare could have accessed directly in one of the Latin versions of Sophocles found in the widely distributed bilingual editions of his works.[24] It was probably from such an edition that Ascham quotes *Oedipus at Colonus* in Greek in his preface to *The Scholemaster* (1570). Ben Jonson had a Greek/Latin Sophocles in his library. Everyone agrees that Milton imitates *Oedipus at Colonus* in *Samson Agonistes*: 'A Little onward lend thy guiding hand' says the blinded hero, led by a boy.[25]

Let me repeat the question I started from, uttered by Gloucester to Edgar: 'When shall we come to th' top of that same hill?' Why a hill as well as a cliff? This is not in Seneca, and Sidney's Leonatus refuses to lead his father to the top of a rock. When Sophocles' Oedipus is brought on stage by Antigone, he is coming to a place at the edge of Athens—riven with hidden ways, ledges, and falling paths—whose name *means* hill (*colōnē, colōnos*). Dedicated to Colonus, hero of horses, and site of a temple devoted to Poseidon, the sea god, it is also, as reported by Cicero,[26] the birthplace of Sophocles himself. Like the white cliffs of Dover—supposed source of the name Albion, from *albus*, 'white', and site of the chronicled throwing of Gogmagog over '*The fall of Douer*'[27]—Colonos is a sacred locus whose significance for Athens is enhanced by being a point of origin that is also an edge. Resting on 'unhewn rock', Sophocles' Oedipus prays to the Eumenides, like Gloucester praying at the brink of what he takes to be a cliff. Again like Edgar, Antigone leads her father to a ledge at the limit of the site where his position is precarious. 'Here!', the Chorus warn, 'Do not incline your steps beyond this ledge [ἔξω πόδα κλίνῃς] of native rock!'[28]

This is even more like Dover Cliff than the equivalent situation in Seneca's *Thebais* because there Oedipus is not, and does not believe that he is, on the edge of anything, and in Sophocles the tragic point is that, as in *Lear*, the ledge is not high. This is a psychological drop, on the edge of mysterious space. At this extreme, individual as well as collective origins are in question: 'δεινὰ φύσις', Oedipus tells the chorus at line 202, 'Calamitosum genus' at the same point in Winsheim's—or Melanchthon's—Latin (i.e. line 210; see Fig. 8).[29] 'Terrible was my birth' says the Loeb translation, but 'terrible my origin' would be closer, because *phusis* means 'origin' as well as 'nature' (much as in Acts 3 and 4 of *Lear*). 'Who are you?' the Chorus demand. 'Tell us, seeing that you are driven to the brink!' In a line that early modern editions attribute to Antigone, the Greek word for 'brink' is *eschata*, as in 'eschatology', here meaning 'extreme'. Winsheim's Latin reads: 'Dic, iam enim *extrema* sustines [you are held up by only the extreme].' Compare Edgar's guidance to Gloucester, anxious about tiny movements.

> Give me your hand. You are now within a foot
> Of th'extreme verge. For all beneath the moon
> Would I not leap upright.   (4.5.25–7)

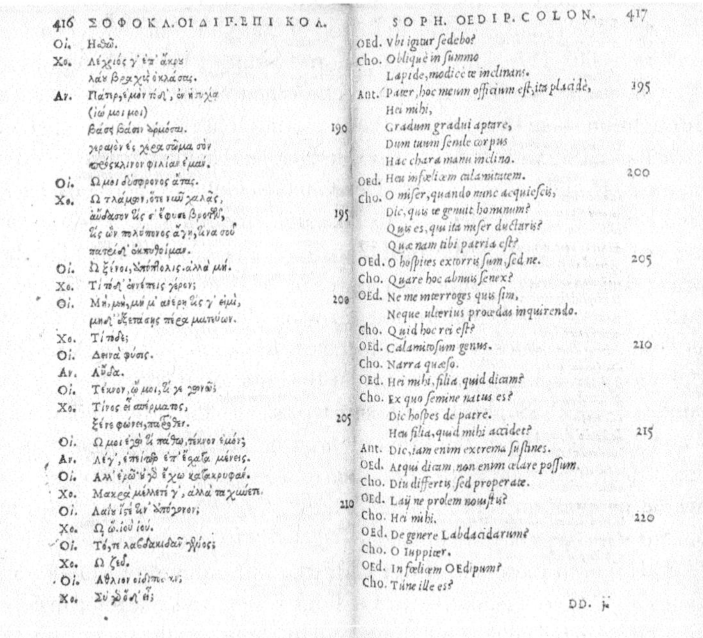

Fig. 8. Parallel texts of Sophocles, *Oedipus at Colonus*, in a 1597 edition. Reproduced by permission of the Wren Library, Trinity College, Cambridge.

This extreme verge will turn out to be eschatological as well as geographical—as we shall see at the end of this chapter; but it is also, like the 'final bourne' of Sophocles' Oedipus, 'the goal of my long-suffering life' (lines 87–92), an end-of-life location. 'Nature in you', Regan tells Lear, 'stands on the very *verge* | Of his *confine*' (3.2.220). The cliff, when Gloucester firsts mentions it, looks out over 'the *confinèd* deep' (4.1.68).

What would the author of *King Lear* have known *about* the *Oedipus at Colonus*? It is generally agreed that Edgar's advice to Gloucester, 'Ripeness is all' (5.2.11), derives from the standard authority about old age, widely read in Elizabethan grammar schools, Cicero's *De senectute* (XIX [71]).[30] What has been neglected is the firmness of Cicero's opinion that old men should hang on to power. Even when blind, they can sway the senate. The elderly should never abdicate, 'For old age is honoured only on condition that it defends itself, maintains its rights, is subservient to no one, and to the last breath rules over its own domain.' Sophocles, he notes,

> composed tragedies to extreme old age [*ad summam senectutem*]; and when, because of his absorption in literary work, he was thought to be neglecting his business affairs, his sons haled him into court in order to secure a verdict removing him from the control of his property on the ground of imbecility, . . . Thereupon . . . the old man read to the jury his play, *Oedipus at Colonus*, which he had just written and was revising, and inquired: 'Does that poem seem to you to be the work of an imbecile [*desipientis*—old and foolish]?' When he had finished he was acquitted by the verdict of the jury.[31]

Life story and tragedy are so close as to suggest some feedback. In the *Oedipus at Colonus*, as in Seneca's *Thebais*, the protagonist resigns his property to his sons—as Sophocles wisely does not—with disastrous consequences. In *King Lear*, abdication in favour of two daughters is recapitulated in the ousting of Gloucester by his two sons (viciously by Edmond, benignly but in the end killingly[32] by Edgar). Reading Cicero would have helped Shakespeare see how plots from Holinshed and Sidney could combine and resonate with Greek tragedy.

* * *

I want to go back to the beginning of *King Lear*, the better to understand Dover Cliff as itself a search for origins. Scholars used to be of

Cicero's mind, viewing Lear's abdication as 'crass folly'[33] and his division of Britain as worse. Precedents can be found. In *Gorboduc* (perf. 1561), for example, we see how a king of Britain 'deuided his Realme in his lyfe time to his Sonnes, *Ferrex* and *Porrex*. The Sonnes fell to dyuision...The people...fell to Ciuill warre'.[34] Yet Shakespeare is never that simple: not Sophocles and Cicero, never mind *Gorboduc*, could deflect his unerring ambivalence. Without a male heir, what was Lear to do? Why not distribute his inheritance, keeping the 'name and all th'addition to a king'—like Seneca's Oedipus, 'retain[ing] vpon my selfe the entyre Soueraygntye'[35]—to preserve in some measure the authority to resolve disputes (1.1.136)? The politics of 1605 differed from those of Elizabethan England. With succession to the throne assured, the great issue of the day was union between England/Wales and Scotland. Remember the Quarto/Folio variant, 'the division of the kingdoms/kingdom' (1.1.3–4). Given the refusal of the House of Commons to accede to the policy of union, Lear could be seen as reinstating ancient realms as much as splitting Britain up.

This is often now noticed, given the present, tottering state of the union and the currency of archipelagic approaches. But we can find deeper arguments for division, or at least divisions about division, in the play's reversion to origins. When Lear demands 'Give me the map there', and declares 'that we have divided | In three our kingdom', when he tells Goneril 'Of all these bounds even from this line to this...We make thee lady', the king initiates something—tragic but creative—that goes back to the beginning of all (1.1.37–63). The opening of the Book of Genesis, as heard by Shakespeare in church, reads:

> In the beginnyng GOD created the heauen and the earth.... God deuided the lyght from the darknesse...And God said, Let there be a firmament betweene the waters, and let it make a diuision...And God made the firmament, and set the diuision betweene the waters...[36]

The Bible starts from divisions between day and night, water and earth, earth and sky, separated into bounds that, for such early modern commentators as Lancelot Andrewes, allowed for causation, places, times, uses.[37]

The repeated, traumatic division of Britain after Brut is often cited as evidence that Shakespeare's Lear gets it wrong. Yet the first chapter of Holinshed is entitled 'Of the diuision of the whole earth' and it begins:

> We read that the earth hath beene diuided into three parts, euen
> sithens the generall floud. And the common opinion is, that *Noah*
> limited and bestowed it vpon his three sons, *Iaphet*, *Cham*, and *Sem*,...
> giuing vnto each of them such portions thereof as to him seemed good,
> and neuerthelesse reteining the souereigntie of the whole still vnto
> himselfe: albeit as yet it be left vncertaine how those seuerall parts
> were bounded,...[38]

It is probably coincidental that the bounds marked out on the map by Lear's dividing finger—even while 'retaining' a part of 'the souereigntie of the whole'—are unspecified, and usually not visible to the audience. Yet we see from the relations between France and Burgundy, great rivals for Cordelia's love, yet not discernibly in conflict, that the division of an old country like Gallia, whether into Caesar's three parts or the multiple kingdoms mentioned by Holinshed,[39] need not lead to disaster.

Put the map next to Dover Cliff and we see division going all the way down. Within the bounds marked out by Lear are 'shadowy forests and . . . champains riched, . . . plenteous rivers and wide-skirted meads' (64–5), natural and cultivated borders constituting a mosaic. Edgar's astonishing description is a chorography, similarly taking in land use, fishing, and ships; the view is full of fractions, and division goes even deeper:

> The crows and choughs that wing the midway air
> Show scarce so gross as beetles. Halfway down
> Hangs one that gathers samphire, dreadful trade!
> Methinks he seems no bigger than his head.
> The fishermen that walk upon the beach
> Appear like mice, and yon tall anchoring barque
> Diminished to her cock, her cock a buoy
> Almost too small for sight. The murmuring surge
> That on th'unnumbered idle pebble chafes
> Cannot be heard so high.   (4.5.13–22)

It is not just that every thing is compared to something smaller but that things are *gone into* by synecdoche: the man no bigger than his head; the bark reduced to its cock-boat. We pass into the atomized 'Almost too small for sight', until we could not see the pebbles on the beach, even if we were there, as Edgar is not.

Whether we invoke corpuscular theory out of Aristotle, or a more fashionable debt to Lucretius, Edgar's reaching into the seeds of life has an atomistic aspect. That Shakespeare knew the *De rerum natura* is indisputable, because Montaigne quotes so much of it,[40] and we do get at Dover Cliff Lucretius' leading preoccupations: with the void, the declension of matter into what Lear calls nature's 'germens' (3.2.8), borders (Lucretius finds them everywhere), yet everything bound up with what bounds it since there is matter in every direction.[41] We also get his remarkable, experimental view of mass and gravity. When Edgar says to Gloucester, after he falls onto the stage,

> Hadst thou been aught but gossamer, feathers, air,
> So many fathom down precipitating
> Thou'dst shivered like an egg. But thou dost breathe,
> Hast heavy substance,...   (4.5.49–52)

his lines can I believe be traced to a celebrated passage in which Lucretius talks about the creation of the world from swerving atoms and the thesis (that was tested by Leonardo da Vinci, Galileo, and others)[42] that falling bodies would all descend at the same speed regardless of mass if they passed through an unresisting medium (II.62–250). Early modern atomism found a correlation between falling and division. 'If of two bodies one be more dense than the other', wrote Kenelm Digby, 'that which is so, will cutt the ayre more powerfully, and will descend faster then the other: for in this case, density may be compared to the knifes edge, since in it consisteth the power of diuiding.'[43]

The point is not to simplify *Lear* by following Edgar into natural philosophy. Dover Cliff is prismatic. One of the origins of Gloucester's falling flat on the stage must be a jest-book pratfall. Editors have overlooked a couple of late Stuart pamphlets that allude to a well-known joke—while not evidently echoing Shakespeare—about how easily people can be deceived: 'you may perswade them upon *New-Market-Heath*, that they are Tumbling down *Dover Cliff*'.[44] Yet the sequence also invokes the testing of Jesus in the Bible when Satan urges him to fling himself from the top of the temple because if he is the Son of God angels will bear him up (Matthew 4:5–7)—much as

Edgar tells Gloucester that he has fallen almost weightlessly, and describes a previous version of himself, glimpsed on the clifftop, as a fiend with horns. This is a fall of princes that reprises the fall of man and aims at atonement. Guilt-stricken about rejecting Edgar, after both were deceived by Edmond, but also about the sins of the flesh which brought his bad son into the world, Gloucester asks 'Have I fall'n, or no?' (56). The answer cannot be that he has not, yet not in the way he means. A more tractable question is how Shakespeare gets us from Dover Cliff to the death of Lear, where another guilty father looks to 'Fall and cease' (5.3.239), and for that we need more Greek tragedy.

* * *

I had better reassure any doubters that Shakespeare had read some Sophocles. In Plutarch's life of Antony, which he drew on for *Julius Caesar* and *Antony and Cleopatra*, he will have found the following passage, describing Antony's journey into Asia Minor:

> euery one gaue them selues to riot and excesse, when they saw he delighted in it: and all Asia was like to the citie *Sophocles* speaketh of in one of his tragedies:
>
> > *Was full of sweete perfumes, and pleasant songs,*
> > *With woefull weping mingled there amongs.*
>
> For in the citie of Ephesus, women attyred as they goe in the feastes and sacrifice of *Bacchus*, came out to meete him with such solemnities and ceremonies, as are then vsed: with men and children disguised like Fawnes and Satyres.[45]

This tells us almost everything that we still know about what Nietzsche calls the birth of tragedy: the feasts, the sacrifices, the satyrs. But if Plutarch is setting out what Aristotle says is the *archē*, or 'origin', of tragedy, his quotation from *Oedipus Tyrannus* represents the origin of a tragic plot, that articulation of the *muthos* which is also for Aristotle an *archē*.[46]

The lines come into North's Plutarch from the opening speech of Sophocles' tragedy, where Oedipus speaks of Thebes as a city afflicted by the plague. Actually, he poses a question: 'why is the city filled at the same time with incense, and with the sound of paeans and lamentations?'[47] The answer, as the audience knows, is that Thebes has been afflicted because of the king's parricide and incest. The play is driven by his questions, searching out the causes of the plague, as in the stichomythic exchanges with Creon about the murder of Laius and with the Shepherd as he probes his own birth. He needs to know where the action comes from, though the irony is, of course, that the quest back to his origins will lead him to the womb which is both his source and his crime scene. From this recursive and expansive drive to know emerge the great questions of the play about the gods, prophecy, what has to be, and whether Oedipus' culpability is not the cause but the effect of a curse put upon the house of Labdacus. That this is a drama about knowledge is one reason why the *Oedipus Tyrannus* was exemplary for Aristotle.

Causation in Aristotle is not mechanical. But the commentators are broadly correct when they say that he 'made much of cause and effect and their psychological vagaries in drama' and that in Seneca such ligatures are pulled more tightly and correlate with a fatalistic view of nature.[48] The latter is nowhere clearer than in Seneca's Oedipus plays. From the pattern of the plot spin out questions about Fate and the relationship between prophecy and event, brought out with peculiar force in the passage about the haruspication of sacrificed animals in which the disease and disorder of organs show something awry in nature that is also awry in Oedipus' life. The irony is again that while Oedipus searches out the causes of the plague, he is himself, though the Chorus resists it, 'the cause of these great hazards'.[49] Oedipus is determined to dig back into origins, 'even about shameful blood ties; . . . I am resolved to know'.[50] The need to know, in this play, composed, of course, by a philosopher, is in excess of the needs of the action. The Chorus ends up with an orthodox Stoic account of the workings of the universe which goes back to a mesh of causes more powerful even than Jupiter; 'Not even a god can change events | which run in a woven series of causes [. . . quae nexa suis currunt causis]' (lines 989–90).

It would be relevant, if there were room at this point, to trace Oedipus' role in post-Reformation arguments about foreknowledge, predestination, and causation. Peter Martyr Vermigli, for instance, cites his story to show that a 'sure connexion of causes' can be known by God not just in nature but in the will of man.[51] It is more pressing to ask how far the drama of knowledge and causation that Aristotle and Seneca respond to in Sophocles gets into Shakespearean tragedy. Any plot is open to cause-and-effect interpretation even when not written to an Aristotelian recipe; but *Oedipus Tyrannus* had become, by the 1570s, the 'master text' in humanist accounts of tragedy.[52] Emrys Jones was on track when he wrote of Shakespeare as 'a writer of modified neo-classical sympathies' who aimed at 'a lucid sequence which illustrated cause and effect'[53]—which does not preclude, of course, the testing and questioning of ideas about causation.

It was a commonplace in Renaissance logic that, 'although by effects and other arguments wee may haue a probable gesse and make sensible coniectures at thinges: yet no true science or knowledge is had but from the causes'.[54] In rhetoric, by the same token, what were known as causes or cases—the stuff of persuasion in drama— often had a causal infrastructure.[55] Puttenham explicitly recommends this. 'In many cases', he observes,

> we are driuen for better perswasion to tell the cause that mooues vs to say thus or thus: or els when we would fortifie our allegations by rendring reasons to euery one; this assignation of cause the Greekes called *Etiologia*, which if we might without scorne of a new inuented terme call *Tellcause* it were right according to the Greeke originall: ... (191)

What is original in this word-formation goes back to cultural origins. But Puttenham has already established, more radically and relatedly, that the origins of poetry lay in finding out the causes of things:

> Then forasmuch as [poets] were the first obseruers of all naturall causes and effects in the things generable and corruptible, and from thence mounted vp to search after the celestiall courses and influences, and yet penetrated further to know the diuine essences and substances separate, ... they were the first Astronomers and Philosophists and Metaphisicks. (6)

Knowledge in this passage is elevated from natural to metaphysical causes; from that flows moral insight. For those of a Christian and Stoic disposition, to understand 'originally' how things come to be (i.e. originatingly, essentially) gives judgement a firmer basis than being 'led by euents' and repeating the most recent outcomes of life.[56]

To origins of this sort *King Lear* repeatedly recurs. The king obsesses, Oedipus-like,[57] about the organs of generation, the sulphurous pit, and riddles with the Fool about the stars.[58] His question to Tom is as ancient as Aristophanes though associated with Lucretius:[59] 'What is the cause of thunder?' (3.4.145). Given what has been said about Oedipus and Greek tragedy, I need not stop to explain why Lear within a few lines calls Tom a 'learnèd Theban' and 'good Athenian' (147, 169). The play interrogates the early modern 'pursuit of origins as a basic philosophical activity' that was meant to subdue scepticism.[60] The role of Tom challenges the notion of a 'determining origin' as it relates to law, for example, or 'original' sin.[61] But life-crises push Lear like Oedipus to ask bigger, aetiological questions: 'Then let them anatomize Regan; see what breeds about her heart. Is there any cause in nature that makes these hard-hearts?' (3.6.34–6). The conundrum now seems as distant as haruspication in Seneca, cut off by modern surgery and psychology, yet we do know what it means. In Edward Bond's *Lear*, an autopsy is actually performed on Fontanelle. All the investigation shows is how beautiful the human machine is. For Bond an inward search for the origins of evil will fail: 'the causes of human misery and the sources of human strength'[62] lie in the social order. Would that strength and misery were so readily found and fixable. In *Lear*, the question about Regan leads to Cordelia's words in the recognition scene, where, like Gloucester at Dover Cliff, the king looks to be punished for rejecting his good child and favouring the bad: 'You have some cause', he says; 'No cause, no cause', she replies (4.6.68).[63]

While characters look for causes, *King Lear* is sceptical about aetiology. Montaigne was famously so, and we can add to the usual claims made for the influence of the *Essayes* on *Lear* this element in his outlook. He notes that imputed causes often do not explain effects and that we are drawn to causal explanations not when they are true but when they show 'inuention and beautie'.[64] 'In naturall things', he writes, 'the effects doe but halfe referre their causes.' The initiating principles are too far up to be known, and it can be foolish, even blasphemous, to seek them. No good will come of such 'crazed curiositie', even though philosophers (like Oedipus) have sought out '*hidden and great causes*' at the cost of their lives.[65] 'The extreamities of our curious search', he writes in a wonderful passage, turne to a glimmering and all to a dazeling.... The end and beginning of learning are equally accoumpted foolish.... by what simplicitie did the Epicurians first imagine, that the Atomes or Mothes, which they termed to be bodies, having some weight and a naturall mooving downeward, had framed the world;...Why should we not likewise believe that an infinit number of greek Letters confusedly scattred in some open place, might one day meet and joine together to the contexture of th'Iliads?[66]

* * *

What are the origins of what happens to Gloucester? For the unhappy father, betrayed, as he thinks, by Edgar, the cause is in the stars. 'These late eclipses in the sun and moon portend no good to us', he tells Edmond; 'nature finds itself scourged by the sequent effects. Love cools, friendship falls off, brothers divide' (1.2.101–5). Montaigne was not the only contemporary of Shakespeare's to be sceptical about astrology, but it is striking how often he denounces 'Prognosticators, Fortune-tellers, Palmesters,...presuming to finde out the causes of every accident'.[67] We could be sceptical about scepticism by noticing that what Gloucester divines from the sky is not false about how things turn out. Yet we doubt his talk of 'sequent effects' when the bastard son derides his lines in soliloquy. For Montaigne, it is not just folly 'to search in heaven the causes...of...ill-lucke':[68] the stars distract us from questioning the truth of what is alleged. Gloucester looks to astrology to explain how things have gone wrong between himself and Edgar instead of asking whether they have. 'I ordinarily see,' says Montaigne,

> that men,...leave things, and runne to causes. Oh conceited discour-
> sers! The knowledge of causes doth onely concerne him, who hath the
> conduct of things [that is, God]: Not vs, that have but the sufferance of
> them.... They commonly beginne thus: *How is such a thing done?*
> Whereas they should say: *Is such a thing done?*...
>
> I finde, that we should say most times: *There is no such thing.*[69]

When Edmund, in Quarto *Lear*, entertains and troubles the audience by repeating in the deception of his brother much of what Gloucester has said to him about eclipses, discord, and 'divisions in state'[70]—in lines added to Sidney that are cut back again in the Folio—he leaves out the phrase 'brothers divide' so as not to alert Edgar to a danger.

The two plots of the tragedy are almost duplicates along this axis. It is not just that the older sisters oppose Cordelia, then one another. Albany and Cornwall, brothers by marriage, are at odds: 'There is division,' Kent tells a Gentleman, "twixt Albany and Cornwall' (3.1.10–12); 'There's a division betwixt the Dukes' (3.3.8–9) echoes Gloucester. Such divisions can be found in the *Arcadia*. Yet the rivalry between Leonatus and Plexirtus is protracted way beyond the death of their father. If division between the brothers with an abrupt and bloody outcome does not come from the stars, and not fully from Sidney and Seneca either, where should we look? Back to Greek tragedy.

For in Plutarch's life of Pyrrhus, we read,

> one of his sonnes beinge but a boy, asked him one day to which of them he would leaue his kingdome: *Pyrrus* aunswered the boy, to him that hath the sharpest sworde. That was much like the tragicall curse wherewith *Oedipus* cursed his children.
>
> *Let them (for me) deuide, both goodes, yea rentes and lande:*
> *With trenchaunt sword, and bloody blowes, by force of mighty hande.*[71]

This is an accurate dilation of Euripides' *Phoenissae*, 'that they should divide [διαλαχεῖν] this house with the whetted sword'.[72] The Latin translation likely to be behind Dolce and Gascoigne reads: 'ut diuidant hanc'.[73] In Euripides, then, from North's Plutarch as read by Shakespeare back through Latin and Greek, it is division all the way down, and in the *Phoenissae*, as in *Lear*, there is a culminating duel.[74] The suicidal condition of Euripides' old, blind Oedipus as he laments the curse he has imposed on his sons—looking for a sword, a hanging noose[75]—may be felt in the death wish of Gloucester after his estrangement from Edgar and Edmond, but the formal, extended sequence of combat between the brothers, though medieval in style, is more clearly indebted to antiquity. There are many Renaissance versions of the fight between Eteocles and Polynices figures, from Jean Robelin's *La Thébaïde* (1584) to Jean Rotrou's *Antigone* (1637). Just as it helps us understand the return to Greek tragedy in *King Lear* by putting it next to *Samson Agonistes* as another imitation of *Oedipus at Colonus*, so the rivalry of Edgar and Edmond is more clearly imitative of antiquity when compared with Racine's *La Thébaïde, ou les frères ennemis*.

Yet we are not quite done with Sophocles, and not just because *Oedipus at Colonus* is the only major version of the Eteocles/Polynices story—even taking account of Statius—in which the younger son is the one who, as in *Lear*, seizes power from the older after they agree to divide the kingdom by taking turns to rule. Sophocles' Eteocles is a schemer who outmanoeuvres his brother and drives him into beggarly exile before he returns with a foreign army—like Edgar fighting alongside the French. More intriguing is the death of Gloucester. Sidney is routinely paradoxical when the Paphlagonian king crowns his son and dies 'with many teares (both of ioy and sorrow)'.[76] In *King Lear*, with more troubling irony, Edgar tells us, after the duel, that, when he revealed himself to his father,

> his flawed heart—
> Alack, too weak the conflict to support—
> 'Twixt two extremes of passion, joy and grief,
> Burst smilingly.   (5.3.188–91)

Dramaturgically, it could be argued, this has to happen off stage because so much must go on before us: Goneril and Regan competing over Edmond, Albany's assumption of authority, the entrance of the ailing Kent, the deaths of Cordelia and Lear. Double-plotting may be the most creative act of division in *Lear*, but it is not without its difficulties. Yet if the congestion of the denouement encouraged the use of report, Edgar's big speech does nothing to simplify the audience's experience: almost unparalleled in mature Shakespeare for length and elaboration, it is so hard to bring off in performance that it is not surprising to find it cut by about a third between Quarto and Folio. Formally, and deliberately, it follows the pattern of a classical, messenger speech, like the one that reports the death of Oedipus at 'the threshold that plunges down' in Sophocles (lines 1590–1), though it might not be coincidental either that, in *Oedipus at Colonus* as well as *Lear*, the good child is also a messenger: 'neither the war god nor the sea came against him,' Antigone reports, 'but the immeasurable plains took him, carried away in a mysterious end' (lines 1679–82).

Lear also dies caught between emotions, joy and grief, as the actor projects them, hoping Cordelia to be alive. What should we make of the fact that Oedipus exits to death, in the most Lear-like way, wavering in his sanity (lines 1486–7)? The sureness of Edgar's narrative contrasts with the uncertainties of Lear's passing. The tragic etiolation is such that we do not know what is going on. The closer

the audience is taken to bare, comfortless event, the less clear we are
about what it is. These difficulties start, of course, with Lear's devas-
tating entry '*with Cordelia in his armes*'. That is the Q/F direction. When
Rowe emended it to read 'Cordelia *dead in his Arms*'[77] he closed off the
possibility of revival which the play so often anticipates: Lear, in sharp
decline, brought out of the grave by Cordelia; Kent, whose 'strings of
life | Began to crack'[78] when reunited with Gloucester, but who
returns to the stage. Lear does have some reason to hope that Cordelia
is alive. Most importantly, given our theme, so does the audience,
because in the chronicle sources and in the old *Leir* play both she and
the king survive.

The great precedent for these revivals is, of course—to revert to my
beginning—Gloucester, after his fall from Dover Cliff. It is a real as
well as a joke revival. When his father drops onto the stage, Edgar
worries, not unreasonably, that the stress of the imaginary fall might
kill him. Leaning over the body, 'Alive or dead?', he asks (4.5.45). 'Look
up a-height', he urges, 'Do but look up' (58–9). In a sequence equally
taken up with demands to look and see, we get this exchange, which
is like a heightened, abstracted, even choric version of Dover Cliff:

KENT   Is this the promised end?
EDGAR Or image of that horror?
ALBANY   Fall and cease.
LEAR This feather stirs. She lives. If it be so,
It is a chance which does redeem all sorrows
That ever I have felt.   (238–42)

Gloucester has been promised death but it is denied him. He stands
at the extreme, the eschatological point, in Greek, where the end is
apocalyptic and a matter of judgement (the fall and redemption). Yet
'promised end' might more modestly yet metadramatically point to
a question about how the story turns out, for the audience as well as
the actors. Is this how it was always going to end? 'Promised' by which
causes?

It is not the end anticipated by any audience aware of the sources.
The tragedy reacts against the providentialism of the 1580s *King Leir*.
'Fall and cease' is what Gloucester wanted, but Edgar showed him
what Lear now endures, that life and death are not for us to choose.
'Hadst thou been aught but ... feathers, air ... Thou'dst shiver'd like

an egg', Edgar says to his crumpled-up father on the planks, 'But thou
dost breathe' (4.5.49–52). The feather between Lear's fingers could be
that of a crow or chough, that wings the midway air. It hangs between
life and death, a falling body that might float up. Lear crouches over
Cordelia like Edgar over Gloucester, or rather the actor in the role of
Gloucester, who is only playing maybe-dead: the uncertainties of life
and death educe the limits of representation, as with the boy actor
playing the breathing statue of a woman in *The Winter's Tale*. This is
the originality of the cliff sequence, and with it the death of Lear, that
the problem of what is real and what is not allows the audience to
participate in the experience of the ending as a death or the illusion of
it, a growing acceptance that what looks like death *is* death, as it was
not at Dover Cliff. 'Look up', Edgar said to his father, and he did
(4.5.58–9). 'Look up' he says to Lear (5.3.288), and he does not.

The American poet C. D. Wright, who died not long ago, once
wrote about 'the genesis of an ending':

> It's not how we leave one's life. How go off
> the air. You never know do you. You think you're ready
> for anything; then it happens, and you're not.[79]

The gradualness of death at the end of *King Lear* is partly about
this perplex. The 'promised end' is unavoidable but it refuses to be
punctual or explicit—there is no thunder from the gods—and its
uncertainty puts origins in doubt. We are not sure whether the
beginning of the end came when Cordelia's head was put in a
noose, or back in the love trial, or the unseen years of friction with
her sisters, or in the stars. Wright's phrase can be tilted to reflect how
the play's drive to origins problematizes beginnings. The end that is
promised hangs between acting and action in the deaths of Cordelia
and Lear, but Shakespeare restates it, in another key, in the lines that
Albany delivers between the former and the latter. 'All friends shall
taste', he promises, with teleological naivety, 'The wages of their
virtue, and all foes | The cup of their deservings' (5.3.278–80). The
de facto ruler of Britain declares his intention of abdicating on behalf of
the frail, incapable Lear, then compounds the problem by saying to
Kent and Edgar—proposing another division of the kingdom—
'Friends of my soul, you twain | Rule in this realm, and the gored
state sustain' (295–6).

The conclusion of the *Oedipus at Colonus* used to be taken as harmonious, even redemptive. We are now more likely to reflect that the death-escape of the protagonist is offset by impending war and the destruction of Antigone. How Shakespeare's ending has been understood has parallels with the reception of the ancient tragedy and draws us back to it. Many, encouraged by Bradley—though his account of Lear's death is far more riven than we tend to remember[80]—have argued for transcendental affirmation. If we are in tune with the play's originality, its resonance with classical antiquity, such accounts will not suffice. The ending of *Oedipus at Colonus* is the genesis of the *Seven Against Thebes*. The division of the kingdom between Polynices and Eteocles initiates civil strife. Whether Britain falls to Albany by default, as in Quarto *Lear*, or to Edgar by decision, in the Folio, the resolution pursued by Albany is ominous. The ending of the action takes us back to its origins, which cannot just mean the division of the kingdom/s in Act 1 but those layers of articulate imitation that go back through Sidney to Sophocles.

4

The Tempest to 1756

'It was originally *Shakespear*'s'. So writes Dryden in his preface to *The Enchanted Island*, the adaptation of *The Tempest* that he co-wrote with Sir William Davenant.[1] What does 'originally' mean here? Dryden is admitting defensively, but also to his advantage, that the main design of the play and much of its dialogue are taken from Shakespeare. By 1670, the Restoration controversies about literary property and plagiarism discussed in the Introduction and Chapter 1 had become noisy enough to make it prudent for him to be explicit on this point, and, over the next few years, he would develop arguments to justify the arts of derivation and alteration.[2] Already in the late 1660s a name to conjure with, Shakespeare, Dryden would contend in 1679, had the same status for his generation as Aeschylus had had for his adapters in antiquity, who won prizes for altering his work.[3] For a play to be 'originally *Shakespear*'s' gives 'originally' more weight and value than it would have if *The Enchanted Island* were (for example) 'originally *Dekker*'s'.

Yet Dryden still feels the need to compensate for the play being 'originally *Shakespear*'s' by highlighting what is 'original'—in a second, emergent sense, that is, fresh and innovative—about Davenant's additions. Though the Restoration Prospero is, like Shakespeare's, a Duke usurped by his brother, cast away on an island, Davenant gives his daughter Miranda a sister, and adds a well-born young man, Hippolito, even more ignorant of the opposite sex than the sisters, while Caliban is coupled (in every way) with a sister called Sycorax. Shakespeare had earlier cloned situations and characters out of narrative and dramatic sources in much the same way in such multi-plotted works as *The Comedy of Errors* and *Hamlet*. Even in *The Tempest*, there is a reference to the usurper, Antonio, having a 'brave son' (1.2.441), the stub of a character once intended to parallel Ferdinand,

the son of Alonso, King of Naples. But Davenant's original prolifera-
tions are almost as surprising as Dryden claims. Always 'remote
and new', Dryden says of his collaborator, 'He borrowed not of any
other' (A3r).

By 1670 the travel narratives that described the wreck of the *Sea
Venture* off Bermuda in 1609, identified by Malone in 1808 as the
major source-matrix for *The Tempest*,[4] had slipped out of literary memory. When Dryden calls *The Enchanted Island* 'originally *Shakespear's*'
he means—another sense of the word—that the play originated with
Shakespeare, who did not in this case borrow of any other. Yet the
notion that *The Tempest* is ultimately Shakespeare's swings around,
courtesy of 'was', to tell us that although the play '*was* originally' his
property it is now Dryden's (after the death of Davenant). Having
mixed his labour in the text—to invoke Locke[5]—or having inherited
it from the king-progenitor, Shakespeare—to think of Filmer[6]—the
ownership of this play about an island the ownership of which is in
question (is it Prospero's, Caliban's, or the butler Stephano's?), now
falls to its adapter.

That said, the means by which the play falls to Dryden complicates
possession. For *The Tempest*—in a fourth meaning of 'originally', of
signal importance to this chapter—has been *originary*, generating later
plays. 'Our excellent *Fletcher* had so great a value for it', Dryden writes,
with some tactical simplification, 'that he thought fit to make use of the
same Design' (A3r). Not only was Fletcher's *Sea Voyage* 'a Copy of
Shakespear's Tempest', he declares, but 'Sir *John Suckling*... has follow'd
his footsteps in his *Goblins*' (A2v). Originality in this sense is something
that a play can only achieve over time, as *The Tempest* spectacularly
has, beyond Dryden and the Garrick opera of 1756—which is roughly
where I shall end my account—through Browning and Aimé Césaire
to Margaret Atwood.

Dryden's description of *The Tempest* in the prologue to *The Enchanted
Island* is prescient about its ability to originate and regenerate:

> As when a Tree's cut down the secret root
> Lives under ground, and thence new Branches shoot
> So, from old *Shakespear's* honour'd dust, this day
> Springs up and buds a new reviving Play.
> *Shakespear*, who (taught by none) did first impart

> To *Fletcher* Wit, to labouring *Johnson* Art,
> He Monarch-like gave those his subjects law,
> And is that Nature which they paint and draw....
> But *Shakespear*'s Magick could not copy'd be,
> Within that Circle none durst walk but he.   (A4v)

This witty, magisterial writing touches on several of the topics that
will emerge as my argument moves into the eighteenth century.
Nature, magic, Shakespeare as Prospero. But notice, less expectedly,
Dryden's crypto-ecological opening. *The Enchanted Island* was written
shortly after John Evelyn's *Sylva* (1664), the best known of the early
modern tracts that lament the deforestation of England, due to iron
manufacture, domestic firewood (priced out by sulphurous sea coal),
and the need to build ships for the navy. Evelyn, like others, proposes
replanting and the use of timber from the colonies to spare
native woodlands. One thing to be addressed in this chapter is how
Shakespeare's writing about natural resources, so conspicuous in *The
Tempest*, meshes with what Dryden says about him as a natural
poet and poet of Nature,[7] a compliment which goes back through
Milton and Leonard Digges[8] to Heminge and Condell in the Folio.[9]
I plan to measure the distance between the springing root described
in the prologue to *The Enchanted Island* and what the poet Edward
Young wrote around and about Shakespeare in his *Conjectures on
Original Composition* (1759): 'An *Original* may be said to be of a *vegetable*
nature; it rises spontaneously from the vital root of genius; it *grows*, it
is not *made*.'[10]

That will bring me back to the starting-point of this book, with
Charlotte Lennox challenging the claims for Shakespeare's originality
that crescendo in the 1750s.[11] Before I get to the mid-eighteenth
century, however, I want to be Lennox-like myself, and return to the
sources of *The Tempest*. These have been, since the days of Malone,
considerably filled out by scholarship. In any reputable edition, you
will now find discussion of pamphlets about the Virginia colony, while
Jonson's *Hymenaei* (1606) is cited as inspiration (if only by reaction) for
the betrothal masque of Ferdinand and Miranda which constitutes a
climax both in plot terms and in the play's use of spectacle. Like
others, I shall reflect on Shakespeare's reading in Montaigne's essay
'Of the Caniballes', but I want to dig deeper into William Strachey's

narrative about the *Sea Venture*, Bermuda, and Virginia, in 'A True Reportory' (*c.*1610),[12] in relation to the betrothal masque. Doing so throws into relief an argument that *The Tempest* shares with the colonial pamphlets: the merits of labour as against idyllic idleness. I shall consequently turn to Virgil, going beyond the *Aeneid*[13]—so often discussed in relation to this play—to his great agricultural poem the *Georgics*.

* * *

Let me begin with a counter-view. It has been argued that New World, postcolonial accounts of *The Tempest* are misplaced because its geography is Mediterranean (Milan, Naples, Algiers) and because it is 'not at all interested in the things that colonization is primarily interested in: gold, spices, tobacco'.[14] The contention asks to be qualified and the play's fusion of Old and New worlds reassessed. Gold and tobacco are associated with Sir Walter Ralegh's adventures in Guiana (1595), where he searched for El Dorado. Spices were a magnet to empire in the East Indies. But the Bermuda and Virginia pamphlets reckon up more mundane resources: corn, peas, wood, fish, water fowl, berries.[15] The colony was a testing ground for the agricultural revolution, for that '*Improuement of the Ground*' which, in Bacon's words, is 'the most Naturall Obtaining of *Riches*'.[16] It should be thought about in relation to the teaching of the *Georgics* in grammar schools[17] and the spread of agrarian poetry, from the best-selling Tusser through Du Bartas to Chapman's Hesiod, dedicated to Bacon.[18] *The Sea Voyage* makes explicit what *The Tempest* draws from the pamphlets, that gold is not what empire is or should be about, least of all gold pillaged from rival colonists in the style of the privateering Ralegh. In Fletcher, the shipwrecked crew fight and injure one another as they quarrel over treasure, lose a boat to earlier castaways, and are left so hungry that they agree to cannibalize the play's equivalent of Miranda.

Any of the pamphlets could be quoted at this point, but take Robert Johnson's *Nova Britannia* (1609). He tells us of 'hills and mountaines making a sensible proffer of hidden treasure', but this is a natural resource which needs to be worked with and for, not stolen from the Spanish: 'the land is full of mineralles, plentie of woods'.[19] Fertility is a given, yet it requires laborious husbandry. The Indians 'shalbe most friendly welcome to conioyne their labours with ours', but if they 'obstinatly refuse' they will be 'dealt with as enemies' (C2r). For the planting of a colony is also the cultivation of men. The pamphlets are keen to propose, like Bacon in his essay 'Of Plantations', that crafts-men should go to Virginia, but they also say (with Johnson) that jokers like Trinculo 'shall haue there imployment enough, ... for no man must liue idle' (D3r). Compare the *True Declaration*, published by the Council of Virginia in 1610, which admits that the colony failed, for a time, due to a 'tempest of dissention: euery man ouervaluing his own worth, would be a Commander: euery man vnderprising an others value, denied to be commanded.'[20] The same diagnosis is given in *The Tempest*, where disaffected noblemen and low characters sink into sniping, usurpation, and rebellion. What there should be is productive labour. 'Now, I demand', the Council writes, 'whether *Sicilia*, or *Sardinia*, (sometimes the barnes of *Rome*) could hope for increase with-out manuring? A Colony is therefore denominated, because they should be *Coloni*, the tillers of the earth, and stewards of fertilitie' (35–6).

Shakespeare is realistic about the unattractiveness of work to those who can avoid it (his own occupation was playing).[21] Strachey says that, during the storm, the governor of Virginia and other gentlemen laboured with the mariners to keep the *Sea Venture* afloat.[22] In *The Tempest*, the courtiers on the ship are captious, uncooperative, and (as the sailors complain) in the way: 'You mar our labour' (1.1.12). Onshore, Ferdinand may resemble the well-born who, in Strachey, do physical work (1750) when he takes over from Caliban the task of carrying logs for Prospero; but he does this under duress, and he turns his 'wooden slavery' into a trial of his devotion to Miranda (3.1.62). He is so far from being a 'patient log man' (67) that he goes on and on about labour. But then, he has a point; for reasons to be given later, he is not exaggerating when he says that he 'must remove | Some thousands of these logs and pile them up' (3.1.9–10)—surely too much wood to keep Prospero's home fires burning.

If labour is unwelcome in *The Tempest* to those at the top of a hierarchy that commends it to others (as in plantation treatises), idleness is not idealized. True, Gonzalo speaks in its favour in a celebrated speech in Act 2. 'Had I plantation of this isle, my lord', he says to Alonso,

                                    no kind of traffic
                    Would I admit, no name of magistrate;
                    Letters should not be known; riches, poverty,
                    And use of service, none; contract, succession,
                    Bourn, bound of land, tilth, vineyard, none;
                    No use of metal, corn, or wine, or oil;
                    No occupation, all men idle, all;
                    And women too—but innocent and pure; . . .
                    All things in common nature should produce
                    Without sweat or endeavour . . . .   (2.1.154–66)

That this recycles a passage in Florio's translation of Montaigne's 'Of the Caniballes'[23] is consistent with that essay itself recycling the myth of the Golden Age from Lucretius, the *Georgics*, and Ovid. The received contours of the idyll, the intimations of *so it is said* that go back (source-study can show) to immediate but also originary indebtedness, make the material the more assignable—in an act of reinvention—to a character with a patrician, Panglossian outlook and a liking for commonplaces. This opens a critical angle for audiences, one that is sharpened by deft rewriting,[24] by the reweighting of words in the transposition of prose to verse,[25] and by a shift from description (of the Indians) in Montaigne to wishfulness, so that the speech is left the more exposed to jibes from Sebastian and Antonio.

Shakespeare's divergences from Montaigne here have been almost as little noticed as the originality of his re-characterizing the material by giving it to Gonzalo.[26] As a result, two points have been neglected, though they have consequences and resonance in an audience's response to the situation and to the play as a whole: first, Shakespeare adds the lines, 'nature should bring forth | Of its own kind all foison, all abundance, | To feed my innocent people' (68–70), which throws into sharp relief the question of what people eat, and how they can get it from the ground, in unfamiliar, American locations;[27] second, Montaigne moves seamlessly from the Indians into *Georgics* II: '*Hos natura modos primùm dedit.* | Nature at first vprise, | These manners did devise.'[28] In Virgil this describes the wild sprouting of trees, but only by way of introduction to an account that was widely read in the early modern period of the planting and management of woodlands. It is as though even natural fecundity and the life of man within it cannot be thought about for Montaigne

without a georgic dimension. Much the same—we shall now see—
could be said of *The Tempest*.

If Gonzalo gives us one version of the New World, the betrothal
masque gives us another: a planter's project, enacted by spirits, of
what labour can achieve. The contrast is deliberately pointed. I agree
with Margaret Tudeau-Clayton—though her tack is quite different
from mine—that the Masque of Ceres owes much to the opening of
the *Georgics*,[29] which calls upon 'alma Ceres' (the goddess who taught
men agriculture and civility, after the Golden Age) and then ushers
in 'you...Fauns...(come trip it [*pedem*, foot it], Fauns, and Dryad
maids...!)';[30] that is, 'you...Nymphs', according to a gloss in Fleming's
translation for schoolboys (see Fig. 9),[31] 'set hither-ward your foot'.[32] The
masque starts with Iris calling up 'Ceres, most bounteous lady'[33] and
it climaxes in the revels that Prospero will curtail, in which figures even
more georgic than the fauns in the *Georgics* ('You sunburned sicklemen,
of August weary') are called out to dance with 'temperate *nymphs*...In
country *footing*' (4.1.132, 134–8).

This much is obvious enough, and it would have informed the
response of audiences in 1610–11 even if they had got no further
than the first page of the *Georgics* at school. What Shakespeare *does* with
the source is more interesting, for he contaminates (in both senses)[34]
Virgil. Prospero's masque depicts a landscape improved by the sort
of agricultural science that was advocated by such contemporaries
as Sir Hugh Plat in his *Arte of Setting of Corne*—the title page of which
is reproduced as Fig. 10[35]—and variously by Francis Bacon.[36] The
Bermuda and Virginia pamphlets are low on incident and high on
improvement discourse. The masque was Shakespeare's way of turn-
ing this discourse into action,[37] and he does it partly by mixing
specific, unnoticed source material into the *Georgics*. The material is
drawn from Strachey's 'True Reportory', just before his account of
how 'men of ranke and quality' labour in the colony:

> no Countrey yeeldeth goodlier Corne, nor more manifold increase:
> large Fields wee haue, as prospects of the same, and not farre from our
> Pallisado. Besides, wee haue thousands of goodly Vines in euery
> hedge, and Boske running along the ground, which yeelde a plentifull
> Grape in their kinde. Let mee appeale then to knowledge, if these
> naturall Vines were planted, dressed, and ordered by skilfull Vinear-
> oones,[38] whether wee might not make a perfect Grape, and fruitefull

The first Booke of Virgill his Georgiks,

or otherwise called his Rurals or Husbandrie,
Made for the climat of Italie
specially, &c.

The argument of *Modestinus* a lawyer
upon the first Booke.

THe poet Virgill [in this first booke of his Georgiks here] [*Iustine,*
Hath plainly taught what thing wil make the corne fields ranke and
[Or corne delightsome, whose increase makes th' owners merry mart]
What fier: [what season,] [& husbandman should duly marke and keepe,
How he should cut up easie would with plough, and how his seeds
Are to be throwne into the ground. [and lie hath plainly taught]
The tilling and good husbanding of places [his therefore,]
And harvest is to be made [reford] with great increase and gaine.

The first Booke of the Georgiks, written to
Mecænas, a noble man.

LEarned, and in great favour with *Augustus Cæsar:*
Unto this *Mecænas* was *Virgil* and *Horace* much
Beholden, not only for the familiaritie which he vouch-
Safed them, but also for the manifold good courtesies
And benefites wherewith he releeved them, &c.

O My *Mecænas,* sle begin hereafter to ᵃ declare, (and ranke
ᵇ What thing may make corne-grounds to be [in yeelding] ᶜ fat
And under what starrs [influence] it were convenient [meete]
ᵈ To turne [with plow] the land, and ᵉ some the vines to trees of elme,
And what regard were to be had of oxen, and what care
ᶠ Of cattell, and how to great a profit in [thistlice] ᵍ sparing bees,
Upon the deerest things [that be] of all the world [so round,]

Bacchus

Bacchus and Ceres nourishing, which leade about the part
Falling from heaven, [which is the cause of seasons in their course,]
Sith that the earth by your [good] gifts hath changed ʰ Chaon akorns
[o] bread-corne ranke and ripe [to repe,] and mingled hath [also]
ⁱ Achelo pots with grapes, found out [water I meane] with wine,]
And O you Fawnes [o c Woods the Gods and Cattell-keepers too,]
Dou present Gods of Woodland-nets, you Fawns, and Dryads, put
[The Nymphs of Trees, a thicke place,] set hither unto your foote,
Your gifts [bestow] I sing aboard: And thou O Neptune God,
Of whome the earth smitten with greet thre-fold mace brought forth
The first fierce snorting horse that was: And o ᵏ [Ariftey,] thou
The saving friend of wods, to whom three hundred snow-white heifers
Do crop the bushie places ranke [with leaves] of Ceula.
O Pan o *Tege* [Citte,] [doung] thy natiuell mountaines be
A care to thee, thou leaving quite the wood where thou wast borne,
And keeper of the Sherpe upon *Lycæan* loftie hills,
Assist me: am *Minerua* th' inuentor of th' Oliue tree,
And O thou youth [Triptolemus] of crooked plow bruiser:
And o *Syluanus* setting of the tender Cypres tree,
[Springing] out of the roote [assift am present to wish me.]
O all you Gods and Goodesses, in whome there is a care
To keepe and saue the fallow feelds, and nourish with some feere
[O natures secret force] the corne nens [sowne] and which send downe
[O heaven] large large showrs of rain vpõ for lano to seco-corne sownt.
And thou O *Cæsar,* whome it is uncertaine what assemblies
Of Gods shall haue thee them among, or that thou wouldst vochsafe
To visite cities, and likewise of countries take the charge,
Am [so] most [part of all the] world should take and knowledge thee
ᵐ First the author, and of stormes [the ruler] [strong to be:
O compassing about thy brad with] ᵐ mothers * mystie leaves,
Shouldst come [to be] of seas most huge the God, am sea-men [so]
Now worship all alone thy maieftie most excellent.
The utmost ilam *Thule* should thee serue, am ᵐ Thetis hop
Thee for to be her sonne in law with [gulf of] waters all,
But maps't thou not much rather ioyne thy selfe a new bright star,
Betweene [the signes,] *Erigone,* am *Chelies* following next:
Now fcortching *Scorpius* himselfe in his armes [o crooked clawes]
Am leaueth roome enough in heaven [o] the, sken, and come to spare,
(Whatsoeuer [Cæsar] thou wilt be for fer-tro [bel-hounds] hope
For thee to be a King to them; ne let so curst a wish
O' reigning happen vnto thee: though Greece [enuiling life]

Doth

Fig. 9. The opening of Virgil's *Georgics* in Abraham Fleming's widely used translation (1589). Reproduced by

The nevv and admi-
rable Arte of setting of
Corne:

With all the necessarie Tooles and other
Circumstances belonging to the same : the
particular titles whereof, are set
downe in Page the
following.

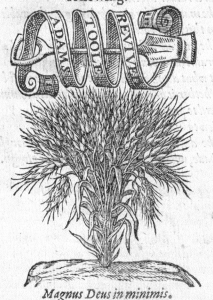

Magnus Deus in minimis.

Imprinted at London by *Peter Short*, dwelling at the
signe of the Starre on Bredstreet hill.
1600.

vintage in short time? And we haue made triall of our owne *English* seedes, kitchen Hearbs and Rootes, and finde them to prosper as speedily as in *England*. (1750)

Enter Iris, invoking Ceres, with her 'rich leas | Of wheat, rye, barley, vetches, oats and pease; . . . Thy banks with pionèd and twillèd brims'.[39] This is in line with Strachey, on English seeds and roots growing in the colonies.[40] It also marks out the bounds rejected in Gonzalo's idyll of the idle: 'pionèd' and 'twillèd' refer to military-style trenches and hedges tangled with roots or plaited with wood. Science comes to the aid of Ceres, but so does Adamic spadework, as on the title page of Plat's *Arte of Setting of Corne* (see Fig. 10 again). Trenches are the more salient because, in the *Georgics*, agriculture is frequently represented as a kind of warfare. This is how colonizing farmers, often enough veterans of the legions, master and manage nature. 'Thy pole-clipped vineyard,' Iris continues, 'And thy sea-marge, sterile and rocky-hard, . . . ' (68–9). 'Clipped' can mean 'embraced', but the thought is raised to be rejected; the poles are stiffly excluding— 'hedged in by tall stakes' like a palisade.[41] For Prospero, on the Stracheyan and Virgilian theme of cultivating vines on rods, stakes, and forks,[42] growth depends on cutting back and enclosure. Even the coastline is sterile and hard. Into these 'bosky acres' (81), Iris summons Ceres to celebrate a 'contract' between Ferdinand and Miranda that could not more sharply contrast with the idle sexual relations that obtain in Gonzalo's idyll.[43]

Echoes of Strachey accumulate: the defensive 'Pallisado', the 'Boske' through which the 'naturall Vines' run that should be 'planted, dressed, and ordered' (i.e. grown on poles). The masque is about 'increase' (Strachey's word), and the phrase added by Shakespeare to Montaigne, 'all foison, all abundance':

> Earth's increase, and foison plenty,
> Barns and garners never empty,
> Vines with clust'ring bunches growing,
> Plants with goodly burden bowing;
> Spring come to you at the farthest,
> In the very end of harvest.
> Scarcity and want shall shun you,
> Ceres' blessing so is on you. (110–17)

Shakespeare so often introduces a sceptical, countervailing note. The masque is devoted to plenty, but it is tainted with the downsides of improvement. Those who do the labouring are erased, yet the farm is a fortress of work. Even the plants are burdened, like Caliban and Ferdinand bearing logs, by the produce that they carry: 'with goodly burden bowing'. The harvest is contained—not distributed—in barns and garners. The threat against which this stands is the recurrent early modern one which the lyric calls 'Scarcity and want', as in the mid-1590s and again during the Midlands Rising (and so *Coriolanus*) of 1607. There is hunger on the island—not as extreme as in Fletcher's play, but the unfed courtiers are tantalized with a banquet that Ariel whisks away (3.3.52). You could say that the plenty represented by the masque, staged by spirits and soon to melt into air, equally tantalizes the audience with a vision of fruition.

Is this Prospero Shakespeare? In some ways and to an extent, including unattractive ways. We know that he hoarded grain illegally in barns and garners in Stratford[44] to sell at inflated prices. In 1605, 'he paid a large sum ... for a half interest in a lease of "tithes of corn, grain, blade, and hay".' He stocked up on malt and sold it on, prosecuting one neighbour, the apothecary Philip Rogers, for non-payment.[45] That he was willing to accept the enclosures at Welcombe as long as his interests were protected seems incontrovertible on the documentary evidence.[46] It should be said on his behalf, first that he had no pension scheme, and second that, in going with the flow of reform, in the matter of enclosure at least, which increased production in the regions that most adopted it, he was playing his part in the growth of general prosperity through improvement. He participated in developments in the artful control of Nature that, at their scientific leading edge, included Plat, Bacon, the Hartlib circle of the 1650s, and the 'Georgical Committee'[47] of the Royal Society.

We could still be negative about the lyric. When Ceres says to the lovers, 'Spring come to you at the farthest, | In the very end of harvest!', she is wishing for them no winter. This was said of the American colonies, with their supposedly equable climate. It is also the sort of thing that Ceres would regard as desirable, because, in a myth alluded to in the masque (87–101), she loses her daughter to Dis in the winter. If there were no winter, she would never be without Proserpina, whose importance to the play, as she is important in

The Winter's Tale,[48] is shown by her anagrammatic presence in 'Prospero'. But Prospero's name also glances at prosperity—another Strachey word ('to prosper as speedily')[49]—much as Caliban is about being called a cannibal. His vision of prosperity puts the seasons out of joint for the sake of increased production. Without winter the land can't rest. Without winter we have global warming.

* * *

That we have entered a new period in the history of the planet—one in which human activity does not just respond to climatic conditions but marks the record through the changes it effects in weather patterns, sediment discharge, pollen distribution, and so on—is agreed. But when did this period begin? In a recent, well-substantiated article, published in the journal *Nature*, Simon L. Lewis and Mark A. Maslin ask whether the Anthropocene started in 1964, when radioactivity from nuclear tests peaked in stratigraphic deposits, or with the 'Orbis spike' of 1610.[50] They opt for the Orbis spike, when 'The arrival of Europeans in the Caribbean . . . and subsequent annexing of the Americas, led to the largest human population replacement in the past 13,000 years, the first global trade networks . . . , and the resultant mixing of previously separate biotas.' This spike saw, among other things, 'the globalization of human foodstuffs. . . . Old World crops such as sugarcane and wheat were planted in the New World' (174). To conclude, with Lewis and Maslin, that 1610 initiated the Anthropocene, is to highlight the importance of power relationships within empire, economic growth, globalization, and the use of fossil fuels.[51]

This is a very big picture, but the invitation to home in on 1610, the year in which Shakespeare was writing *The Tempest*, encourages more precise contextualization which associates the play with this great shift in earth history. The late sixteenth and early seventeenth centuries were a time of experimentation with land, fertility, crops, manuring, and with curing the idle from sickness by putting them to work. These 'experiments' are often reported as such in the Virginia pamphlets.[52] The pressure felt by scientists such as Plat to increase yields or find substitutes for wheat in bread-making came from the population growth, shortfall in agricultural production, and escalation of food prices that characterized the period. The search for improvement came at a time when the biosphere was under strain, not just from disruption to the rural economy brought about by improvement itself, but from weather events which precipitated famine.

In Shakespeare, this goes back to *A Midsummer Night's Dream*, which, for all its entanglement in the wild wood, is not in flight from georgic. The play comically and mythically traces the troublingly bad weather that reduced the productiveness of agriculture in the mid-1590s to a quarrel between Oberon and Titania. The fairy queen describes a scene of fog and flood, the opposite of the bountiful cornfields and cared-for sheep in the Masque of Ceres:

> the green corn
> Hath rotted ere his youth attained a beard.
> The fold stands empty in the drownèd field,
> And crows are fatted with the murrain flock. (2.1.94–7)

The seasons are radically disrupted. According to both Quarto and Folio, 'The humane mortals want their winter heere.'[53] Global warming already. Even if we adopt Theobald's dubious emendation 'cheer', what comes next muddles winter into the other seasons:

> The spring, the summer,
> The childing autumn, angry winter change
> Their wonted liveries, and the mazèd world
> By their increase now knows not which is which; ... (111–14)

Titania and Oberon are spirits of Nature, disordered at its origin—at the origin we might say of this play without a narrative source—further confused by magic. 'This same progeny of evils', Titania tells her spouse, 'comes | From our debate, from our dissension. | We are their parents and *original*' (115–17).

The play's appeal to the supernatural in explaining the weather is not as unscientific as it seems, because early modern science was not what it became. Experimentalists like Plat and Bacon drew on the 'natural magic' of Cornelius Agrippa, who said that magicians could do miraculous-seeming things by manipulating and bringing forward ordinary phenomena, as when making roses flower and grapes ripen in March 'and greater thinges then these, as Cloudes, Raine, Thunder'.[54] Garrick is right when he says, in the 'Argument' to his version of *The Tempest*, that Prospero pursues 'the study and exercise of natural magic'.[55] This is shown, give or take—since his powers are also demonological—in his monologue 'Ye elves of hills . . . ' where he declares that he has darkened the sun at noon (as Nature does, by night), created 'rattling thunder' and earthquakes (5.1.33–50). In the *Magnalia Naturae*, Bacon listed some of the things he wanted to achieve: 'Acceleration *of* germination. Making Rich Composts *for the* Earth. Impressions *of the* Aire, *and* Raising *of* Tempests.'[56] This goes from Plat-style agricultural science to the sort of weather with which *The Tempest* opens—as reported by Miranda:

> The sky, it seems, would pour down stinking pitch,
> But that the sea, mounting to th' welkin's cheek,
> Dashes the fire out.   (1.2.3–5)

Acid rain, El Niño, apocalypse? By now, well into the Anthropocene, we can manipulate the elements and cannot but affect them. Baconian science[57] and *The Tempest* are in this respect prophetic.

Yet not unexpectedly so. That human activity is degrading the environment—especially woodland—is a fear that goes back to antiquity. So does the idea that this impacts on weather patterns (see the writings of Theophrastus).[58] Such anxieties were heightened during the early modern period by the spread of empire, which brought out the capacity of mankind to create large-scale changes in land use, from draining fens to logging forests. The prominence of scientific thinking within imperialist agendas, from Bacon (who was on the Council of the Virginia Company) to Boyle, eliding their desire for an empire of knowledge with involvement in colonial schemes,[59] further enhanced awareness of the negative impact of improvement. As Richard H. Grove notes in *Green Imperialism*, 'the seeds of modern conservationism developed as an integral part of the European encounter with the tropics and with local classifications and interpretations of the natural world and its symbolism.'[60] This is one way in which Caliban, with his hunter-gatherer catalogue of things to eat and barren places, is the flip side of Prospero as magus/scientist. Grove dates to the mid-seventeenth century a realization that development was threatening the degradation of oceanic island colonies (5–6) but Shakespeare already intuited this beyond the horizon of 1610.

One can see how Prospero has inherited the medieval and early modern mantle of Virgil as a magus and—in the *Georgics*—natural philosopher, with knowledge of the stars and the weather.[61] Where is the evidence, though, for his implication in damaging development? Let us return to Prospero's woodpile.[62] When Caliban resists his master's command to bring in firing he says 'There's wood enough within' (1.2.316). This would simply be recalcitrance did he not also say to Stephano, when promising to introduce him to the riches of the isle—crab apples, marmosets, scamels—'I'll ... get thee wood enough' (2.2.160). Perhaps he is fed up with being anyone's log man, but the repeated 'enough' is consistent with the modest demands on the environment made by a hunter-gatherer. Contrast Prospero requiring Ferdinand to pile up 'thousands' of logs. We have noted, along with Lewis and Maslin, the increasing use of fossil fuels—that is, sea coal carried from Newcastle—as timber stocks ran down in England, used for shipbuilding, metal and glass manufacture, and firewood. Shakespeare's audience would have recognized that Prospero is doing what was often recommended in colonial projects: stockpiling logs to process ore. 'From thence we may haue Iron and Copper', writes Johnson, of Virginia,

> in great quantitie, about which the expence and waste of woode ... will be no hurt, but great seruice to that countrey: the great superfluity whereof, the continuall cutting downe, in manie hundred yeares, will not be able to ouercome, whereby will likewise grow a greater benefite to this land, in preseruing our woodes and tymber at home, ...   (C3v)

Within decades, not many hundreds of years, the deforestation of the West Indies had created massive soil erosion. It matters, in other words, that, when Ariel complains of his labour, Prospero says that he must resent 'To do me business in the veins o'th' earth' (1.2.256). Iron and copper come out of those veins.[63] Remember Johnson: 'the land is full of mineralles' (B4v); Strachey says much the same, as does Richard Rich, who writes of 'Iron promist, for tis true | their Mynes are very good.'[64] Ariel is a miner, one of the 'straunge shapes and spirites' that, in early modern lore, 'digge after the veine, to carrie togither oare';[65] Caliban brings fuel to the furnace. In Montaigne's 'Of the Caniballes', as in Gonzalo's utopian speech, we are told that, in the state of nature, man has 'no apparell but naturall, no manuring of lands, no vse of wine, corne, or mettle' (102). Critics have long recognized the importance of apparel and wine in *The Tempest*, and they are catching up with the tillage that is so prominent in the

Masque of Ceres.[66] To which we can now add the making of metal,
and its environmental impact.

* * *

Dryden's image of Shakespeare as a tree stump, regrowing from its
root, can be read as a tangential outcome of the concern about
deforestation that we have found in *The Tempest*. In 1667, it would
also have recalled the stock emblem of the Stuart monarchy as a royal
oak, cut down at the execution of Charles I but reviving with the
restoration of his son. '*Shakespear*'s pow'r', Dryden tells us in his
prologue, 'is sacred as a King's.' The restaging of *The Tempest* figures
from this point of view a larger cultural recovery, across the fields of
science and the arts, centred on the patrilineal authority that is
represented by Prospero. Certainly, Davenant and Dryden look
back to the interregnum. They recast Stephano, Trinculo, and
Caliban as an absurd, self-defeating group of republican and Crom-
wellian rebels. They also add in a plot about duelling, with Ferdinand
mortally wounding Hippolito and being condemned to death by
Prospero, until Ariel, using herbs and the 'sympathetic magic'
endorsed by Bacon, brings the wounded man back to life.[67] This
reflects (it seems to me) on royal and legislative steps taken in the
mid-1660s to curb a rash of duels exacerbated by the settling of scores
between triumphant cavaliers and their enemies.[68] Yet the new plot
does not simply endorse the Carolean authority that was insisting, at
this date, on capital punishment for those who killed other men in
duels, because Ferdinand's execution would be a disaster. It resolves
Prospero's difficulties by drawing out and inflecting the Baconian
elements in *The Tempest* and dramatizing the magic of science.

A movement away from the topic of Nature and planting in
Shakespeare can be seen in Davenant and Dryden's excision of the
Masque of Ceres and the expanded sequence in which a feast is
promised to the courtiers by Ariel with a line from Prospero's masque
('*Ceres* blessing so is on you'). 'O for a heavenly Vision of Boyl'd, |
Bak'd, and Roasted!' is Gonzalo's response—very much that of Restoration London. The vision becomes concrete after a dance of '*eight
fat Spirits, with Cornu-Copia in their hands*' leads the hungry to an offstage
'Table ... set out and furnisht | With all varieties of Meats and
fruits' (37). The focus has shifted from production (in Shakespeare)

to consumption, from agriculture to urban life. The masque would be changed again, into a celebration of Britain's oceanic power in Shadwell's more operatic version of Davenant and Dryden's play,[69] and then, at the end of Garrick's *Tempest*, into a sung, hymeneal dialogue between Ferdinand and Miranda which concludes in a chorus that includes only a trace of fruition: '*nobly fruitful be their bed*'.[70]

Yet if the ecological is not foregrounded in the post-Restoration *Tempest*, it is structurally active. From Shadwell to Garrick, the island is divided into a more civil section associated with Prospero and a '*A wild Island*' or '*wilder part . . . compos'd of divers sorts of Trees, and barren places*'.[71] The encroachments of the city generate by reaction a sphere in which Nature is irregular but sensuous—as in Sycorax's 'cool Plashes' and 'soft Fens, | . . . Flags and Bull-rushes' in Davenant-Dryden, and the haunting lines given to Hippolito: 'I have within me all, all the various Musick of | The Woods'.[72] Eventually, he is socialized; we are shown not a colony but a natural man being cultivated.[73] The post-Restoration comprehension of Nature—as in the Royal Society-like curing of Hippolito—shapes the profile of *The Enchanted Island*, rendering the accomplishment of the play overall as much as its action evidence of those advances that were stretching the semantics of 'cultivation' beyond its agricultural base.[74]

At least as symptomatic, and tied up with the alteration of plays, is the enlarged scope of 'improvement'. Take the uses of the word in Gerard Langbaine's *Account of the English Dramatick Poets* (1691), mentioned in the Introduction and Chapter 1. Quick to allege plagiarism, especially when it comes to Dryden, Langbaine is willing to soften the charge when adaptation has enhanced a play. Aphra Behn's *Abdelazar*, for example, has 'much improv'd' *Lust's Dominion*.[75] *Troilus and Cressida* was 'first written by *Shakespear*, and revis'd by Mr. *Dryden*', who 'cultivated and improv'd what he borrow'd from the Original' (173). In his historical survey *The Invention of Improvement*, Paul Slack shows how the ethos of improvement, centred on agricultural development, was extended to many fields in the seventeenth century—science, the arts, manners.[76] Langbaine's phrase 'cultivated and improv'd' is symptomatic, not incidental.

Post-Restoration alterations of Shakespeare often employ the language of improvement. John Crowne said that, in adapting *2 and 3 Henry VI*, he had 'undertaken to cultivate one of the most barren

Places' (Caliban's phrase) in the output.[77] 'The Tragedy we represent
to Day', wrote John Dennis in the prologue to his version of *Coriolanus*,

> Is but a Grafting upon *Shakespear*'s Play,
> In whose Original we may descry,
> Where Master-strokes in wild Confusion lye...[78]

Yet even as he edged *Coriolanus* towards correctness, Dennis expressed
concern lest 'Nature should be lost in Quest of Art'. The model was
becoming not a 'pole-clipped vineyard' but the 'natural' gardens of
William Kent and the landscapes of Capability Brown with their
wildernesses and open country. 'The light of Nature was his guide',
wrote Arthur Murphy of Shakespeare in 1753 (a year to conjure with).
Who could prefer regular vistas to his freely branching trees and 'wild
variety' of prospect?[79]

As attitudes to what Murphy called 'tedious culture' changed, the
notion of Shakespeare as a poet of Nature assumed more awesome
proportions. Pope declared, 'If ever any Author deserved the name of
an *Original*, it was *Shakespear*....he is not so much an Imitator, as an
Instrument, of Nature; and 'tis not so just to say that he speaks from
her, as that she speaks thro' him.'[80] *The Tempest* was an obvious text for
securing this thesis because of its inclusion of so much natural lore,
reaching into the supernatural. The play would underpin bardol-
atrous commentary when Shakespeare became 'the universal master
of Nature',[81] '*as another nature*',[82] or, in Coleridge out of Schelling,
natura naturans, great creating nature.[83] Yet Pope also noted that
Shakespeare 'had a taste of natural Philosophy, Mechanicks' (I, ix),
and this helped shape interpretation. Like Bacon, Boyle, and Newton,
as characterized by Thomson, Akenside, and others, Shakespeare was
said to offer analytically penetrating accounts of nature.[84] 'He was a
most diligent Spie upon Nature, trac'd her through her darkest
Recesses', wrote Nahum Tate;[85] the poet Smart describes him 'Pier-
cing all Nature with a single glance'.[86]

In late Shakespeare, 'Nature' is crossed with Art[87] and constrained
by georgic improvement. In *The Enchanted Island*, the same word
registers the innocent or Hobbesian condition of man in a state
of nature. Only incipient at this date—yet emerging in accounts of
The Tempest—was the Romantic reconception of Nature as wild, set
over against culture.[88] Does the word mean anything settled? Charles

Gildon objected in 1710 that '*Nature* is an equivocal Word, whose Sense is too various and Extensive ever to be able to appeal to';[89] but this is why it was useful, in allowing for innovation without appearing to change the terms of argument. Pope's extravagant view of Shakespeare was thus upped by William Guthrie: 'It is not Shakespeare who speaks the language of nature, but nature rather speaks the language of Shakespeare.... Nature is a stranger to objects which Shakespeare has rendered natural.'[90] What this means, in plain English, is that Shakespeare can go beyond the natural but still produce scenes and characters as Nature would have made them—a claim which *The Tempest* supported because of the plausibility of Caliban and Ariel.[91] That Shakespeare went beyond Nature by extrapolating its nature now became an orthodoxy. In the *Dream* and *The Tempest*, according to Warburton, he 'soars above the Bounds of Nature... or, more properly, carries Nature along with him beyond her established Limits.'[92]

Predictably there was some blurring back into the older idea of Shakespeare as (in Milton's words) 'fancy's child, | Warbl[ing] his native Wood-notes wild'.[93] *The Tempest* shows us his roots in local scenery and folklore: 'The Banks of the *Avon* were then *haunted* on every Side', writes Seward in 1750, '*there Sorcery bedimn'd* | *The Noon-tide Sun* ...' (adapting Prospero), 'So that *Shakespear* can scarcely be said to create a new World in his *Magic*; he went but back to his native Country'.[94] An Ossianic version of this thesis stirs after the publication of Macpherson's *Fragments* (1760)[95] and breaks out in William Duff's *Essay on Original Genius* (1767), which argues that 'original Poetic Genius' of the Homeric and Shakespearean variety is 'most remarkably displayed in an early and uncultivated period of society'. There genius 'shoots up' tree-like 'to the noblest height; it spreads forth all its luxuriance in the peaceful vale of rural tranquillity'.[96]

As the passage in Seward shows, Shakespeare easily morphed from child of nature to Prospero-like magician,[97] less in continuity with science than against what it was becoming when assertively mechanistic. Resisting the notion that Shakespeare was a poetic Newton, Morgann wrote: 'Nature,... has drawn through human life a regular chain of visible causes and effects: But... True Poesy is *magic*, not *nature*; an effect from causes hidden or unknown.'[98] That Morgann adds in a footnote, 'the magic of the *Tempest* is lasting and universal' is, by this date (1777), unsurprising. Long since anticipated by Dryden, the new formation came into view with Charles Churchill's *The Rosciad* (1761), in which Shakespeare is given a wand and globe. Knowing that he could be seen as a scientist, Churchill wants to claim more for the magus, who

> look'd through Nature at a single view:
> A loose he gave to his unbounded soul,
> And taught new lands to rise, new seas to rowl;
> Call'd into being scenes unknown before,
> And, passing Nature's bound, was something more.[99]

This image of a Bard who (in Warburton's words) carries Nature beyond her established limits evidently has *The Tempest* in mind, not just in the wand and globe but the new lands and seas.[100]

* * *

There was a tipping point mid-century. Let me date it to 1753 and, in a tribute to Lewis and Maslin, call it the 'Originality spike'. This was a moment of climax and contested transition.[101] On the one hand, it saw the publication of the first volume of Lennox's *Shakespear Illustrated*, which assailed Shakespeare's claims to originality and critiqued his use of his originals on grounds of coherence and probability that looked back to neoclassicism. On the other, this was the year in which Joseph Warton published his celebrated essay on *The Tempest* in *The Adventurer*.[102] Warton carried with him such conservative readers as Elizabeth Montagu[103] because he upheld the Aristotelian case. Shakespeare is great in *The Tempest* because 'the unities of action, of place, and of time are ... exactly observed' (68) and because he achieves that continuity of characterization (as in Caliban) that Horace, in the *Art of Poetry*, insisted upon: '"Whoever ventures", says Horace,' according to Warton, '"to form a character totally original, let him endeavour to preserve it with uniformity and consistency: but the formation of an original character is a work of great difficulty and hazard"' (64). Horace did not write anything as bracing as 'totally original',[104] but, at the height of the Originality spike, such an enhancement could be expected.

Secured by neoclassicism, Warton can say that in *The Tempest* Shakespeare 'has carried the romantic, the wonderful, and the wild to the most pleasing extravagance' (61). Though his appreciation of *The Tempest* starts on the same Aristotelian ground as that of Charles

Gildon, half a century earlier,[105] it moves towards Romanticism. When he concludes that the author of the play 'is a more powerful magician than his own Prospero' (64), he is within striking distance of Coleridge: 'Prospero, the mighty wizard, . . . seems a portrait of the bard himself.'[106] This was a view of *The Tempest* that left husbandry far behind. The play shared its moment of inception with the sprouting wheat and spade on the front of Plat's *Arte of Setting of Corne* (as seen in Fig. 10), but it was moving, by the 1750s, towards its visionary trans-formation in such works as Joseph Wright of Derby's depiction of the Masque of Ceres (Fig. 11), where Prospero points with his wand towards exalted and elusive spirits, where no trace is registered of 'wheat, rye, barley, vetches, oats and pease' and we are shown wild Nature raging with flashes of lightning outside the magus's cave.

1753 also coincides with a growing hostility to adaptation.[107] Gildon, decades earlier, had mounted a principled attack on the inferiorities of *The Enchanted Island*. Starting in 1750, Arthur Murphy wrote a series of well-argued pieces about the inadequacies of altered Shakespeare.[108] That Shakespeare was known—in detail after Lennox—to have adapted his sources no longer justified adapting him in turn. This rebuke from 1752 is typical of the moment: 'Mr *Dryden* and Sir *William D'Avenant* judiciously made Choice of *The Tempest*, the most regular and correct of all our Poet's Works, and the Result was natural: they formed a very bad Play out of a very good one.'[109] Garrick's 1756 reduction of *The Tempest*, written just after the Originality spike, did not stand a chance. Its imposing stage effects, dulcet airs, and comic songs did not make up for (in Garrick's own words) 'the omission of many passages of the first Merit'.[110] Smollett denounced it as 'cruelly mangled' while Theophilus Cibber called it '*The Tempest* castrated into an Opera'.[111] Within a year, Garrick was back with a Folio-based *Tempest*.[112] His *King Lear* (perf. 1756), like that of George Colman (1768), substantially reversed Tate's revisions. Bolder alterations, such as Richard Cumberland's *Timon*, were now offered with apologies.[113]

So the idea of Shakespeare as a natural poet and poet of Nature intersected in the middle of the century with a theatrical return to original texts—and with an editorial return to the same.[114] That the latter developments went together is demonstrable from scholarly practice[115] and echoed in the interchangeability of such terms as

Fig. 11. Prospero pointing with his wand at a spiritous Masque of Ceres, by Joseph Wright of Derby, engraved by Robert

'altering' and 'editing'.[116] There was a reaction against neoclassicizing emendation, no less ingenious and interventionist, often enough, than had been the civilizing efforts of Pope,[117] a reversion to original readings that was not helped when it came to, for example, the Masque of Ceres by a growing separation between urban cultivation and agricultural practice.[118] The claim was that, when your author is an original, it is right to see and read his original texts, however reconstructed. These developments meshed, during the 1750s, with a grander cult of originality for which (as we have noted) Shakespeare became the exemplar.

How, though, did this prevail in the face of Lennox's evidence that Shakespeare was a derivative artist? One persuasive response was to argue, as Johnson does in the dedication to *Shakespear Illustrated*—as cited in Chapter 1—that the greatness of the plays does not lie in 'the naked Plot' but in 'the Representation of life'. This turns out, once unpacked, to mean that he was attracted to 'such Tales as ... exhibited many Characters ... These Characters', Johnson goes on, 'are so copiously diversified, and some of them so justly pursued, that his Works may be considered as a Map of Life'.[119] Several factors were involved in the late eighteenth-century growth of 'character criticism'—from the analyses of Falstaff, Polonius, and Bertram in Johnson's edition (1765) through William Richardson on Hamlet (1784)[120] to Hazlitt's *Characters of Shakespear's Plays* (1817); but it was partly driven by the urge to rebuild the case for Shakespeare's originality on ground that Lennox's arguments about the derivativeness and improbability of his plotting could not reach.

Concentration on character was not the only defensive manoeuvre available. Some rearmed the notion of Shakespeare as a natural poet. Thomas Warton, for example, said that he showed his powers by refining 'without labour or deliberation' the base matter found in the library.[121] Others denied indebtednesss with a forcefulness which indicates that *Shakespear Illustrated* provoked a reaction despite its relatively low citation rate in the period. Robert Lloyd declared in a poem to Garrick, in flat contradiction of Lennox's evidence, that Shakespeare

> scorn'd the modes of imitation,
> Of altering, pilfering, and translation, ...
> The bright original he took,
> And tore the leaf from nature's book.[122]

Because Shakespeare had a copyright on Nature, he was both new, close to origins, and (more interestingly) himself inimitable. Paradoxes of this kind became the stuff of exalted criticism, as in Martin Sherlock's observation, in 1786, that 'the darling child, of Nature' was 'like [his] mother . . . inexhaustible. Always original, always new'.[123]

Every age has its cant, which can be more instructive, because representative, than the efforts of active intelligence. But plenty of the latter was lavished on squaring the circle produced by the Originality spike. For Richard Hurd, following 'originals' reduced the risk of a writer straying into 'affectation and bombast' and helped keep the plots of Shakespeare free of 'unnatural incidents'.[124] What makes the Bard '*original*' is his accenting of the '*particular*' in natural descriptions.[125] Yet the evidence was beginning to accumulate that Shakespeare's particularities sometimes followed his sources so closely as to be more or less pasted into place. In such cases, even character criticism could not rescue originality. Arthur Murphy, his notable defender, took up this point in 1757 in relation to *Henry VIII*:

> Holinshed, it appears, was our Author's historical Guide, the Characters being copied from him; and in general many of the Sentiments and not seldom whole Speeches are the original Property of the Historian. In treating Facts so well ascertained, . . . Shakespeare's Invention was fettered, and he could not make any considerable Departure from authenticated Tradition. However, he seems upon most Occasions . . . to create the Thoughts of others: Every Thing comes from him with an Air of Originality.[126]

Murphy does not explain how this 'Air of Originality' was contrived. But then, he did not need to, because he had an ace to play against the Lennox view, that just because Shakespeare's work was fettered by this or that, here and there, his powers of invention were original.

Hence the incorrigible Duff:

> Were we to establish the Genius of Shakespeare by the number of incidents which he has really invented, we should not be apt to rank him among the most complete originals; . . . But we ought not to form our opinion of his abilities in this way, by what he hath actually performed . . . but on what we have reason to think, from a view of the extent of his Genius, displayed in a higher species of *invention*, he could have performed, had he chosen to employ the powers of his mind in the manner above mentioned.[127]

From this we can see clearly, and almost finally, how, in the mid-eighteenth century, the work of Charlotte Lennox if anything drew greater ingenuity into the enterprise of arguing for Shakespeare's originality and encouraged the elevation of a play that—as I have indicated, and this is crucial—was not known (until 1808) to have any significant sources. *The Tempest* came to stand, in its originality, for more than itself: for the characteristics of Shakespearean drama and therefore of Shakespeare himself, as the poet of Nature and human nature—corn, crab apples, berries, courtly and savage people. Supreme in characterization, the play was stocked with preternatural figures that indexed the dramatist's ability to be natural beyond nature, and thus to create poetic magic, a poetry of effects untied from causes.

Despite the waves of critical scholarship that have broken over *The Tempest* in the course of the last century—symbolist, Christian, feminist, poststructuralist, postcolonial—and the many reconceptions of its material in film, theatre, opera, and fiction, the play itself still stands in the afterglow of its eighteenth-century status. To my chagrin I see that, in my youthful edition of *Love's Labour's Lost*, I declare that *The Tempest* is one of three Shakespeare plays (along with *Love's Labour's* and the *Dream*) that can 'best claim to be sourceless'.[128] 'Best claim' probably shows that I knew better than what I wanted to say. Yet even the editors of the Arden *Tempest*, massively well-informed, conclude, in their revised edition of 2011, at the end of a new, ten-page essay on 'Sources Revisited', that '*The Tempest*'s precise origins remain elusive' (149). We still have a need, it seems, to believe in original genius, and find an emblem for it in Prospero's play. I hope that this book has shown, not exactly how misguided this impulse is, but how much light and shade and depth and nuance are needed to comprehend Shakespeare's use of sources, and how his recognizably early modern versions of originality are worth thinking about not because of the questions they answer but because of those they raise.

Notes

Introduction

1. See e.g. Jakob Böhme, *A Description of the Three Principles of the Divine Essence* (1648), 'God the Father in his originality, out of which this world hath its beginning' (26), 'the originality of the essence and creatures of this world' (58), and 'the minde generateth againe a will . . . and the Originality of this will ariseth out of . . . the anguished minde' (146). Politically the word is used in R. W., *The Originall of the Dominion of Princes* (1660, dated by *OED* 1648), e.g. '*The Sacrilege of arrogating the Originality of the least Particle of Power*' (21r). Cf. 'originalness' in Thomas Brewer, *Gospel Publique Worship* (1656), anticipating by several decades the earliest *OED* citation: 'the fundamental and fontal originalness of the word it self, as the proper truth of *God*' (198).

2. *OED*, originality, *n.*, 2, 'original thought or action; independent exercise of one's creative faculties; the power of originating new or fresh ideas' (1742).

3. *OED*, original, *adj.* and *n.*

4. *OED*, originality, *n.*, 2, see n. 2 above, adding 3 a, 'The quality of being independent of and different from anything that has gone before; novelty or freshness of style or character, esp. in a work of art or literature' (1782), 3 b, 'An original trait, action, idea, etc.' (1808).

5. Quoted in *Twelfth Night*, ed. Keir Elam, Arden Shakespeare (London: Bloomsbury, 2008), 3.

6. Forman's notebook is quoted from *The Norton Shakespeare*, gen. ed. Stephen Greenblatt (New York: Norton, 1997), 3336–8.

7. *The Lives and Characters of the English Dramatick Poets: Also an Exact Account of all the Plays that were ever yet Printed in the English Tongue, . . . First Begun by Mr Langbain, Improv'd and Continued down to this Time* (1699).

8. *Of Dramatick Poesie: An Essay* (1668), 47.

9. Edward Capell, *Notes and Various Readings to Shakespeare*, 3 vols ([1774], 1779–83), esp. the third, posthumous volume, entitled *The School of Shakespeare*; *Six Old Plays*, ed. John Nichols, 2 vols (1769); *The Plays of William Shakspeare*, ed. Samuel Johnson and George Steevens, 10 vols (1778); *The Plays and Poems of William Shakspeare*, ed. Edmond Malone, 10 vols (1790).

10. *School of Shakespeare*, 3.

11. E.g. Collier, *Shakespeare's Library*, quoted by Mary Ann McGrail, 'From Plagiarism to Sources', *Poetica: An International Journal of Linguistic-Literary Studies*, 48 (1997), 169–85, p. 180: 'He employed the materials supplied by

some of his predecessors and contemporaries merely as a great painter uses what is called a lay figure: he borrowed the position, but invested it himself with drapery, colour, character, and sentiment.'

12. John Dennis, 'The Grounds of Criticism in Poetry' (1704), in *John Milton: The Critical Heritage*, Vol. I, *1628–1731*, ed. John T. Shawcross (London: Routledge, 1970), 128–36, pp. 128–9.

13. John Douglas, *Milton Vindicated from the Charge of Plagiarism, Brought Against him by Mr Lauder* (1750), 8.

14. See e.g. Thomas M. Greene, *The Light in Troy: Imitation and Discovery in Renaissance Poetry* (New Haven: Yale University Press, 1982), chs 2–3.

15. See the closing pages of David Quint, *Origin and Originality in Renaissance Literature* (New Haven: Yale University Press, 1983), but also Gordon Teskey, *The Poetry of John Milton* (Cambridge, Mass.: Harvard University Press, 2015), ch. 10.

16. *OED*, 1 d, 3 b. On 'invention and disposition' in classical and Renaissance treatises leading up to Shakespeare see Quentin Skinner, *Forensic Shakespeare* (Oxford: Oxford University Press, 2014), ch. 1.

17. Roland Greene, 'Invention' in *Five Words: Critical Semantics in the Age of Shakespeare and Cervantes* (Chicago: University of Chicago Press, 2013), 15–40.

18. *Reflections on Originality in Authors* (1766), 9–10.

19. See e.g. Richard S. Peterson, *Imitation and Praise in the Poems of Ben Jonson*, 2nd edn (Farnham: Ashgate, 2011).

20. Edward Young, *Conjectures on Original Composition*, 2nd edn (1759), 78, 80.

21. *Sejanus* (perf. 1603; pub. 1605).

22. See e.g. Thomas Hanmer, in his edition of 1745, cited by McGrail, 'From Plagiarism to Sources', 176.

23. *Reflections on Originality*, 64.

24. Cf. Robert Macfarlane, *Original Copy: Plagiarism and Originality in Nineteenth-Century Literature* (Oxford: Oxford University Press, 2007), 21–3, 34–6.

25. *Original Copy*, 36–7, 41–3.

26. 'Quotation and Originality', in *The Collected Works of Ralph Waldo Emerson*, Vol. VIII, *Letters and Social Aims*, ed. Joel Myerson (Cambridge, Mass.: Harvard University Press, 2010), 93–107, p. 94.

27. 'Shakspeare, or the Poet', in *The Collected Works of Ralph Waldo Emerson*, Vol. IV, *Representative Men: Seven Lectures*, ed. Douglas Emory Wilson (Cambridge, Mass.: Harvard University Press, 1987), 109–25, p. 110.

28. See Glenn W. Most, 'The Rise and Fall of *Quellenforschung*', in Ann Blair and Anja-Silvia Goeing, eds, *For the Sake of Learning: Essays in Honor of Anthony Grafton*, 2 vols (Leiden: Brill, 2016), II, 933–54.

29. J. O. Halliwell, *The Remarks of M. Karl Simrock on the Plots of Shakespeare's Plays. With Notes and Additions* (London: Shakespeare Society, 1850).

30. See e.g. the many volumes of the New Variorum Shakespeare, ed. Horace Howard Furness Sr and Jr, 1871–1928, and continued until 1955.

31. Geoffrey Bullough, *Narrative and Dramatic Sources of Shakespeare*, 8 vols (London: Routledge & Kegan Paul, 1957–75), VIII, 342–3.

32. Quoted by Macfarlane, *Original Copy*, 206, 190.

33. Macfarlane, *Original Copy*, alluding, in 'prating about originality', to Walter Jackson Bate, *The Burden of the Past and the English Poet* (London: Chatto & Windus, 1971), 105.

34. See Marjorie Perloff, *Unoriginal Genius: Poetry by Other Means in the New Century* (Chicago: University of Chicago Press, 2010).

35. *OED*, source, *n.*, 3 a, 4 a.

36. *OED*, source, *n.*, 2 a.

37. For stirrings see Ferdinand Fyldinge's sonnet, in Pierre de Ronsard, *A Discours of the Present Troobles in Fraunce*, tr. Thomas Ieney (1568), D4v: 'As Homers streaminge source, of springinge head doth flow | In Grekishe cloustred camps'.

38. See Quint, *Origin and Originality*, esp. chs 2 and 5.

39. E.g. Quint, *Origin and Originality*, ch. 7.

40. Elisabeth M. Magnus, 'Originality and Plagiarism in *Areopagitica* and *Eikonoklastes*', *English Literary Renaissance*, 21:1 (1991), 87–101.

41. G. W. Pigman III, 'Versions of Imitation in the Renaissance', *Renaissance Quarterly*, 33 (1980), 1–32.

42. Preface to William Lauder's *An Essay on Milton's Use and Imitation of the Moderns in his Paradise Lost* (1750), a3r–4v, at a4r.

43. *An Essay on the Learning of Shakespeare* (1767), 14–15.

44. *Plays of William Shakespeare*, ed. Johnson and Steevens, I, 103–4.

45. *Notes and Various Readings to Shakespeare*, I, 172.

46. *An Essay on Original Genius* (1767), 140.

47. Usage and methodology are shifting here from the search for 'analogous' material that we noted in the work of Capell. See W. C. Hazlitt's explanation, when introducing the term 'analogue', possibly for the first time in Shakespeare studies, in *Shakespeare's Library: A Collection of the Plays, Romances, Novels, Poems, and Histories Employed by Shakespeare in the Composition of his Works*, ed. John Payne Collier, rev. and enlarged by William Carew Hazlitt, 6 vols (London: Reeves & Turner, 1875), I, ix–x: 'Another group of productions there is, which are apt to secure a certain share of our attention by reason of being analogues, or of being derivatives from a common source, rather than as originals, to which the bard of Stratford was immediately under obligations.' For scientific, evolutionary uses see *OED*, analogue, *n.* and *adj.*, from 1808 and more saliently 1835 and 1870.

48. Cf. Colin Burrow, 'Montaignian Moments: Shakespeare and the *Essays*', in Neil Kenny, Richard Scholar, and Wes Williams, eds, *Montaigne in Transit: Essays in Honour of Ian Maclean* (Cambridge: Legenda, 2016), 239–52.

49. Kenneth Muir, *Shakespeare's Sources*, Vol. I, *Comedies and Tragedies* (London: Methuen, 1957), *The Sources of Shakespeare's Plays* (London: Routledge, 1977), Preface.

50. Roland Barthes, *S/Z*, tr. Richard Howard (New York: Hill and Wang, 1974), 21.

51. Julia Kristeva, 'Word, Dialogue, and Novel', in her *Desire in Language: A Semiotic Approach to Literature and Art*, ed. Leon S. Roudiez, tr. Thomas Gora, Alice Jardine, and Leon S. Roudiez (Oxford: Blackwell, 1981), 64–91, p. 66.

52. See e.g. Stephen J. Lynch, *Shakespearean Intertextuality: Studies in Selected Sources and Plays* (Westport, Conn.: Greenwood Press, 1998), Murray J. Levith, *Shakespeare's Cues and Prompts: Intertextuality and Sources* (London: Continuum, 2007).

53. On quotation and *sententiae*, see Julie Maxwell, 'How the Renaissance (Mis)Used Sources', in Laurie Maguire, ed., *How to Do Things with Shakespeare: New Approaches, New Essays* (Oxford: Blackwell, 2007), 54–76; on translation, see Peter Burke, 'The Renaissance Translator as Go-Between', in Andreas Höfele and Werner von Koppenfels, eds, *Renaissance Go-Betweens: Cultural Exchange in Early Modern Europe* (Berlin: Walter de Gruyter, 2005), 17–31, esp. pp. 24–31; the fluidity of texts in transcription is familiar to anyone who has spent time with early modern literary manuscripts.

54. The most potent historicist critique of source study remains that of Stephen Greenblatt, 'Shakespeare and the Exorcists', in his *Shakespearean Negotiations: The Circulation of Social Energy in Renaissance England* (Oxford: Clarendon Press, 1988), 94–128.

55. See e.g. *King Henry VIII*, ed. Gordon McMullan, Arden Shakespeare (London: Arden Shakespeare, 2000) and *Much Ado About Nothing*, ed. Claire McEachern, Arden Shakespeare, rev. edn (London: Bloomsbury, 2016).

56. Emrys Jones, *The Origins of Shakespeare* (Oxford: Clarendon Press, 1977); cf. Leah Scragg, *Shakespeare's Mouldy Tales: Recurrent Plot-Motifs in Shakespearian Drama* (London: Longman, 1992), *Shakespeare's Alternative Tales* (London: Longman, 1996).

57. *Narrative and Dramatic Sources*, VIII, 346.

58. Raphael Lyne, *Memory and Intertextuality in Renaissance Literature* (Cambridge: Cambridge University Press, 2016).

59. Linda Woodbridge, 'Patchwork: Piecing the Early Modern in England's First Century of Print Culture', *English Literary Renaissance*, 23:1 (1993), 5–45, pp. 6–12; Charlotte Artese, *Shakespeare's Folktale Sources* (Newark: University of Delaware Press, 2015).

60. *Shakespeare Survey*, 68 (2015).

61. See esp. Gary Taylor and Rory Loughnane, 'The Canon and Chronology of Shakespeare's Works', in Taylor and Gabriel Egan, eds, *The New Oxford Shakespeare: Authorship Companion* (Oxford: Oxford University Press, 2017), 417–602, and note the forthcoming collection, Dennis Austin Britton and Melissa Walter, eds, *Rethinking Shakespeare Source Study: Audiences, Authors, and Digital Technologies* (Basingstoke: Palgrave, 2017).

62. For a list and discussion see Laurie Maguire and Emma Smith, 'What is a Source? Or, How Shakespeare Read His Marlowe', *Shakespeare Survey*, 68 (2015), 15–31, pp. 16–17.

63. See e.g. Adam Fox, *Oral and Literate Culture in England 1500–1700* (Oxford: Clarendon Press, 2000).

64. William H. Sherman, *Used Books: Marking Readers in Renaissance England* (Philadelphia: University of Pennsylvania Press, 2008), 3.

65. Evelyn B. Tribble, *Margins and Marginality: The Printed Page in Early Modern England* (Charlottesville: University of Virginia Press, 1993); William W. E. Slights, *Managing Readers: Printed Marginalia in English Renaissance Books* (Ann Arbor: University of Michigan Press, 2001).

66. Peter Mack, 'Rhetoric, Ethics and Reading in the Renaissance', *Renaissance Studies*, 19 (2005), 1–21, pp. 2–6.

67. Gabriel Harvey's annotation to Ramus' *Oikonomia*, quoted in Eugene R. Kintgen, *Reading in Tudor England* (Pittsburgh: Pittsburgh University Press, 1996), 69.

68. For access to the evidence see Sasha Roberts, *Reading Shakespeare's Poems in Early Modern England* (Basingstoke: Palgrave Macmillan, 2003) and Sonia Massai, 'Early Readers' in Arthur F. Kinney, ed., *The Oxford Handbook of Shakespeare* (Oxford: Oxford University Press, 2011), 143–64.

69. Jeffrey Todd Knight, *Bound to Read: Compilations, Collections, and the Making of Renaissance Literature* (Philadelphia: University of Pennsylvania Press, 2013), 5.

70. Knight, *Bound to Read*, 8–9.

71. Mary Thomas Crane, *Framing Authority: Sayings, Self, and Society in Sixteenth-Century England* (Princeton: Princeton University Press, 1993), 92.

72. Terence Cave, *The Cornucopian Text: Problems of Writing in the French Renaissance* (Oxford: Clarendon Press, 1979), 35.

73. Knight, *Bound to Read*, 16.

74. Heidi Brayman Hackel, *Reading Material in Early Modern England: Print, Gender, and Literacy* (Cambridge: Cambridge University Press, 2005), 157–8.

75. 'In the margin next to Sidney's description of the slaying of Amphialus' young squire Ismenus, this annotator has written "Imitation of Virgil at the very end of his Aeneids about Turnus death...."...He notes the similarity again to Turnus' death when Lycurgus is slain', Brayman Hackel, *Reading Material*, 167.

76. Folger Shakespeare Library Manuscript V.b 83 'opens with three pages taken from Greene's *Arcadia or Menaphon*...Carefully written on the rest of the nearly sixty folio sheets are selections from Sidney's *Arcadia*, Lodge's *Rosalynde*...and *Euphues Shadow*, John Dickenson's *Arisbas Euphues*, and one unidentified text'; Brayman Hackel, *Reading Material*, 187–8.

77. Brayman Hackel, *Reading Material*, 189–91.

78. Stephen Orgel, *The Reader in the Book: A Study of Spaces and Traces* (Oxford: Oxford University Press, 2015), 17, citing Gavin Alexander, 'Sir Philip

Sidney's *Arcadia*', in Andrew Hadfield, ed., *The Oxford Handbook of English Prose 1500–1640* (Oxford: Oxford University Press, 2013), 233.

79. Women's reading was for the most part less interventionist, adversarial, and directed to action; Sherman, *Used Books*, ch. 3; Brayman Hackel, *Reading Material*, ch. 5; Helen Smith, *'Grossly Material Things': Women and Book Production in Early Modern England* (Oxford: Oxford University Press, 2012), ch. 5.

80. See the classic article by Lisa Jardine and Anthony Grafton, ' "Studied for Action": How Gabriel Harvey Read his Livy', *Past and Present*, 129 (1990), 30–78.

81. For ways into the field see William B. Long, ' "Precious Few": English Manuscript Playbooks', in David Scott Kastan, ed., *A Companion to Shakespeare* (Oxford: Blackwell, 1999), 414–33, Paul Werstine, *Early Modern Playhouse Manuscripts and the Editing of Shakespeare* (Cambridge: Cambridge University Press, 2013).

82. E.g. Richard Dutton, *Mastering the Revels: The Regulation and Censorship of English Renaissance Drama* (Basingstoke: Macmillan, 1991), Janet Clare, *Art Made Tongue-tied by Authority: Elizabethan and Jacobean Dramatic Censorship*, 2nd edn (Manchester: Manchester University Press, 1999).

83. See Grace Ioppolo, *Dramatists and their Manuscripts in the Age of Shakespeare, Jonson, Middleton and Heywood: Authorship, Authority and the Playhouse* (London: Routledge, 2006).

84. See most recently James Purkis, *Shakespeare and Manuscript Drama: Canon, Collaboration and Text* (Cambridge: Cambridge University Press, 2016), chs 4–6.

85. See e.g. John Kerrigan, 'Shakespeare as Reviser (1987)', in my *On Shakespeare and Early Modern Literature: Essays* (Oxford: Oxford University Press, 2001), 3–22, pp. 6–8.

86. 'Shakespeare as Reviser', 17–22.

87. John Kerrigan, 'Stages and Plots', *Times Literary Supplement*, 7 October 2015, 3–5, p. 5.

88. *Christopher Marlowe: The Plays and their Sources*, ed. Vivien Thomas and William Tydeman (London: Routledge, 1994).

89. See R. W. Dent, *Webster's Borrowing* (Berkeley: University of California Press, 1960).

1 Upstarts and *Much Ado*

1. Miguel de Cervantes, *The History of the Valorous and Wittie Knight-errant, Don-Quixote of the Mancha . . . The First Parte*, tr. Thomas Shelton (1612), 38–40.

2. Cid Hamete Benengeli; see e.g. Cervantes *Don-Quixote*, tr. Shelton, 66.

3. *Mr William Shakespeare his Comedies, Histories and Tragedies*, ed. Edward Capell, 10 vols (1768), I, 65.

4. Matteo Bandello, *La prima parte de le novelle* (1554), translated in Geoffrey Bullough, *Narrative and Dramatic Sources of Shakespeare*, 8 vols (London:

Routledge & Kegan Paul, 1957–75), II, 112–34. There was a French version by François de Belleforest, in *Le troisième tome des Histoires tragiques* (Paris, 1570).

5. Her critical chemistry thus resembles, at her most polemical, that of Thomas Rymer, whose notorious attack on the plausibility of *Othello* can be found in his *Short View of Tragedy: Its Original, Excellency, and Corruption* (1693).

6. [Samuel Johnson], 'To the Right Honourable John, Earl of Orrery', in Charlotte Lennox, *Shakespear Illustrated: Or, The Novels and Histories, On which the Plays of Shakespeare are Founded*, 3 vols (1753–4), I, iii–xii.

7. See e.g. Elizabeth L. Mann in 'The Problem of Originality in English Literary Criticism, 1750–1800', *Philological Quarterly*, 18 (1939), 97–118; Walter Jackson Bate, *The Burden of the Past and the English Poet* (London: Chatto & Windus, 1971), 104–7; George J. Buelow, 'Originality, Genius, Plagiarism in English Criticism of the Eighteenth Century', *International Review of the Aesthetics and Sociology of Music*, 21 (1990), 117–28.

8. '[On Genius and Common Sense:] The Same Subject Continued', in *Table Talk: Or, Original Essays* (London: John Warren, 1821), 93–111, pp. 94–6. Cf. *Characters of Shakespear's Plays* (London: R. Hunter, C. and J. Ollier, 1817), 16.

9. E.g. 'Same Subject Continued', 93–4.

10. Brean S. Hammond, 'Plagiarism: Hammond versus Ricks on Plagiarism', in Paulina Kewes, ed., *Plagiarism in Early Modern England* (Basingstoke: Palgrave Macmillan, 2003), 41–55, pp. 48–9.

11. Paulina Kewes, *Authorship and Appropriation: Writing for the Stage in England, 1660–1710* (Oxford: Clarendon Press, 1998), 2.

12. *OED* cites Joseph Hall, *Virgidemiarum: The Three Last Bookes* (1598).

13. *OED* cites Richard Montague, *Diatribae vpon the First Part of the Late History of Tithes* (1621).

14. Roland Greene, 'Invention' in *Five Words: Critical Semantics in the Age of Shakespeare and Cervantes* (Chicago: University of Chicago Press, 2013), 15–40.

15. *OED*, discover, *v.*, 6 b (from 1553), 2 a (from 1375).

16. *Dictionary of Medieval Latin from British Sources Online* (Brepolis, accessed 29 May 2017); *OED*, original, *adj.* and *n.*; B. *n.* 1 a (till late 19C).

17. *Greenes Groatsworth of Witte* (1592), F1v.

18. See now Gary Taylor and Rory Loughane, 'The Canon and Chronology of Shakespeare's Works', in Taylor and Gabriel Egan, eds, *The New Oxford Shakespeare: Authorship Companion* (Oxford: Oxford University Press, 2017), 417–602, pp. 424–5, 493–9, 513–17.

19. Gary Taylor, 'Collaboration', in Dympna Callaghan and Suzanne Gossett, eds, *Shakespeare in our Time* (New York: Bloomsbury, 2016), 141–9, p. 146.

20. That the accusation stuck (and was linked to collaboration) is suggested by Leonard Digges' insistence that Shakespeare did not 'Plagiari-like from

others gleane, | Nor begges he from each witty friend a Scene | To peece
his Acts with', in *Poems: Written by Wil. Shake-speare* (1640), *3r.

21. *The Myrrour of Modestie* (1584), dedication; *Francescos Fortunes: Or, The Second
    Part of Greenes Neuer too Late* (1590), C1r.
22. Gabriel Harvey, *Foure Letters* (1592), 23.
23. Thomas Nashe, 'To the Gentlemen Students of both Uniuersities', in
    Robert Greene, *Menaphon* (1589), **1r-A3r, A2v.
24. See the examples from John Hooper, Thomas Cranmer, L. Blundeston,
    Sidney, the author of *Vlysses vpon Aiax* (1596), Nicholas Breton, and
    Richard Brathwait, in Harold Ogden White, *Plagiarism and Imitation During
    the English Renaissance* (Cambridge, Mass.: Harvard University Press,
    1935); further instances can be found in such contributions to the debate
    as John Dover Wilson, 'Malone and the Upstart Crow', *Shakespeare Survey*,
    4 (1951), 56–68 and Peter Berek, 'The "Upstart Crow", Aesop's Crow,
    and Shakespeare as a Reviser', *Shakespeare Quarterly*, 35 (1984), 205–7.
25. As does Brian Vickers, most recently, in his ' "Upstart Crow"? The Myth
    of Shakespeare's Plagiarism', *Review of English Studies*, 68 (2017), 244–67.
26. See e.g. R. B., *Greenes Funeralls* (1594), Sonnet 9, apparently responding to
    the passage: 'the men, that so Eclipst his fame: | Purloynde his Plumes,
    can they deny the same?' (C1r).
27. It adds more to Shakespeare's biography if we assume—as we probably
    should not—that Chettle went on to apologize to him for the *Groatsworth*
    in *Kind-Harts Dreame* (1592): 'I am as sory, as if the originall fault'—the
    fault in mistaking his originality—'had beene my fault, because my selfe
    haue seene his demeanor no lesse ciuill than he exelent in the qualitie he
    professes: Besides, diuers of worship haue reported, his vprightnes of
    dealing, which argues his honesty, and his facetious grace in writting,
    that aprooues his Art' (A3v–4r). Against a Chettle/Shakespeare reading
    of this passage see Lukas Erne, 'Biography and Mythography: Rereading
    Chettle's Alleged Apology to Shakespeare', *English Studies*, 79:5 (1998),
    430–40; the case for Chettle having a leading role is revived by Katherine
    Duncan-Jones in *Shakespeare: Upstart Crow to Sweet Swan 1592–1623*
    (London: Methuen Drama, 2011), 37–54.
28. Cf. the perceptive discussion in Janet Clare, *Shakespeare's Stage Traffic:
    Imitation, Borrowing and Competition in Renaissance Theatre* (Cambridge:
    Cambridge University Press, 2014), 5–11.
29. Robert Greene, *The Defence of Conny Catching* (1592), C3r–v; *The Historie of
    Orlando Furioso, One of the Twelue Peeres of France* (1591?, pub. 1594).
30. See e.g. Martha Hale Shackford, 'Shakespeare and Greene's *Orlando
    Furioso*', *Modern Language Notes*, 39 (1924), 54–6, Jason Lawrence, ' "The
    Story is Extant, and Writ in Very Choice Italian": Shakespeare's Drama-
    tization of Cinthio', in Michele Marrapodi, ed., *Shakespeare, Italy, and
    Intertextuality* (Manchester: Manchester University Press, 2004), 91–106,
    p. 96. On Shakespeare's sustained engagement with Greene, see e.g.
    Steven R. Mentz, 'Wearing Greene: Autolycus, Robert Greene, and the

Structure of Romance in *The Winter's Tale*', *Renaissance Drama*, 30 (1999), 73–92 and Jonathan Baldo, 'The Greening of Will Shakespeare', *Borrowers and Lenders: The Journal of Shakespeare and Appropriation*, 3:2 (Spring/summer 2008), 1–30.

31. 'To the Gentlemen Students', in Greene, *Menaphon*, A2v.
32. 'Would not this, sir, and a forest of feathers,... with two Provençal roses on my razed shoes, get me a fellowship in a cry of players, sir?' (3.2.263–6).
33. See Catherine Howey, 'The Vain, Exotic, and Erotic Feather: Dress, Gender, and Power in Sixteenth- and Seventeenth-Century England', in Alexandra Cuffel and Brian Britt, eds, *Religion, Gender, and Culture in the Pre-modern World* (Basingstoke: Palgrave Macmillan, 2007), 211–40.
34. *Groatsworth*, F2r.
35. See Frances Elizabeth Baldwin, *Sumptuary Legislation and Personal Regulation in England* (Baltimore: Johns Hopkins Press, 1926).
36. James Pilkington, attrib., 'An Homyly against Excesse of Apparell', in John Jewel, *The Seconde Tome of Homelyes* (1563), fols 112v–121r.
37. *A Quip for an Vpstart Courtier: Or, A Quaint Dispute Between Veluet Breeches and Cloth-Breeches* (1592), A3v.
38. Stephen Gosson, *The School of Abuse* (1579), 22.
39. 'The Player', in *Micro-cosmographie* (1628), E3r–v.
40. The window is erotic—figuring sexual access—but *Much Ado* like Bandello is also concerned about a gentlewoman putting the security of the house at risk (e.g. of theft) by night. Hence the constables in the streets. George Sandys writes of Messina, the scene of the play, in *A Relation of a Iourney begun An. Dom. 1610* (1615): 'they dare not venture to keepe [money] in their houses, so ordinarily broken open by theeues ... for all their crosse-bard windowes, iron doores, locks, bolts, and barres on the inside' (245).
41. Lennox, *Shakespear Illustrated*, III, 262.
42. 5.1.95, 1.3.61—the only such appearance of 'start-up' in the canon, though 'upstart' appears twice, as a noun, *1 Henry VI*, 4.7.87 (Joan la Pucelle) and an adjective, *Richard II*, 2.3.121 (Bolingbroke).
43. *Orlando Furioso*, tr. Sir John Harington (1591), Bk V, st 25.
44. See e.g. *Orlando Furioso*, tr. Harington, Bk V, st 49, where Dalinda says of her mistress, in a near-identical rhyme: 'When in her robes I had my selfe arayd, | Me thought before I was not much unlike her, | But certaine now I seemed very like her' (D1r).
45. Peter Beverley, *The Historie of Ariodanto and Ieneura* (1575), G8r.
46. 'Afar off', according to Borachio—a distance that would point to a failure of judgement and leadership—but close enough, Pedro assures Claudio, to 'see her, hear her ... Talk with a ruffian at her chamber window' (4.1.91–2), which points to a failure of understanding.
47. Greene, *Quip for an Vpstart Courtier*, 'or will you bee Frenchefied with a loue locke downe to your shoulders,...?' (C3v); Nashe, *Pierce Penilesse his*

Supplication to the Diuell (1592), 'his nittie loue lock' (B2r) and *Nashes Lenten Stuffe* (1599), 'his hairie tuft or loue-locke' (41).

48. *The Vnlouelinesse of Loue-lockes* (1628), 34.

49. Philip Stubbes, *The Anatomie of Abuses* [Part I] (1583), B7v.

50. On divergence from what is meet, see e.g. Susan Vincent, *Dressing the Elite: Clothes in Early Modern England* (Oxford: Berg, 2003), 129. To situate the critique of fashion in *Much Ado* in a fuller, more complex context, note that arguments against 'singularitie' could favour keeping up 'measurablie' with 'the fashion of the time' in hair, beards, and dress and using clothes to deflect attention away from actual, physical 'deformitie' (Giovanni della Casa, *Galateo*, tr. Robert Peterson [1576], 18–19, 108, 109).

51. *Anatomie of Abuses*, D7v [inc. marginal note]. On sumptuary excess, see Amanda Bailey, '"Monstrous Manner": Style and the Early Modern Theater', *Criticism*, 43 (2001), 249–84, largely reprinted in her *Flaunting: Style and the Subversive Male Body in Renaissance England* (Toronto: University of Toronto Press, 2007), ch. 2.

52. Michael Drayton, *Idea: The Shepheards Garland* (1593), 58; John Taylor, *The Nipping and Snipping of Abuses* (1614), D3v.

53. Cf. Portia on her English suitor, 'I think he bought his doublet in Italy, his round hose in France, his bonnet in Germany, and his behaviour everywhere' (*The Merchant of Venice*, 1.2.71–3). For contexts see Roze Hentschell, *The Culture of Cloth in Early Modern England: Textual Constructions of a National Identity* (Aldershot: Ashgate, 2008), esp. ch. 4.

54. 'An Homyly against Excesse of Apparell', 118v.

55. Such is the value placed on clothing that not even the constables strictly speaking avoid excess: Dogberry asserts his status as 'one that hath two gowns, and everything handsome about him' (4.2.82–3), yet the 'Homyly against Excesse of Apparell' cites Matthew 10: 'Our Sauiour Chryst bad his Disciples they should not haue two coates' (fol. 115r).

56. For the prohibition against cutting sidelocks see Leviticus 19:27. The Talmud reasserts this (Makkoth 20b). Cf. Philip Ferdinand, the converted Polish Jew who lived in London and Cambridge in the 1590s and published a Latin commentary on the Hebrew Bible, including, at Leviticus 19:27, 'Ne circumcidito pilos ad latus capitis' (*Haec sunt verba Dei* [1597], B4r). For a Venetian Jew's account, see the treatise that Leon Modena wrote *c.*1616 for Sir Henry Wotton, *The History of the Rites, Customes, and Manner of Life, of the Present Jews*, 1650 edn (13). Visual depictions of unshorn sidelocks and what Nashe calls hairy tufts (see n. 47) can be found from the adapted Michelangelo Jeremiah in the Mantua Passover Haggadah (1560) through the widely reproduced illustrations in the 1593 Venetian Book of Customs (*Sefer Minhagim*) to Rembrandt's portraits of Jews in Amsterdam. Old Gobbo's inadvertent parody of Abraham's blessing of Jacob based on a misapprehension of their sons' hairiness (2.2.87–99) confirms the interest of *The Merchant of Venice* in the place of hair in Jewish tradition.

57. Barnabe Riche, *My Ladies Looking Glasse* (1616), 20.

58. For contexts see Natasha Korda, *Labors Lost: Women's Work and the Early Modern English Stage* (Philadelphia: University of Pennsylvania Press, 2011), ch. 3, 'Froes and Rebatoes'.

59. Cf. the 'coloured periwig' in *The Two Gentlemen of Verona* (4.4.188). Stubbes, predictably, writes against those who are 'not simply contente with their owne haire, but buy other heyre, dying it of what color they list themselues', *Anatomy of Abuses* [Part I], F2v, but disapproval is also registered in Shakespeare's Sonnet 68.

60. Attempts to localize the Duchess of Milan's gown could be overdone, but see Janet Arnold, *Patterns of Fashion: The Cut and Construction of Clothes for Men and Women c.1560–1620* (London: Macmillan, 1985), on slashed, double-bodiced gowns, 'a style described as "the Italian fashion" in England', in a Milanese tailor's book *c.*1555–80 and Vecellio's depiction of clothes from Lombardy (7–9), and related discussion in her *Queen Elizabeth's Wardrobe Unlock'd* (1988; Leeds: Maney, 2014), including a picture from the mid-1570s which 'shows the slashes on a short-waisted bodice with long sleeves … This bodice is made with tabs at the waist, or "little skirts" as they are described in the warrants. This is probably the Italian fashion in England at this date' (129).

61. Richard Brathwait, *The English Gentlewoman* (1631), 23.

62. John Stephens, *Satyrical Essayes, Characters and Others* (1615), 248.

63. See e.g. the dressing of the boy in Thomas Tomkis, *Lingua: Or, The Combat of the Tongue, and the Fiue Senses for Superiority* (1607), 4.6: ' … Purles, Falles, Squares, Buskes, Bodies, Scarffes, Neck laces, Carcanets, Rebatoes, Borders, … '. On this description see e.g. Karen Newman, *Fashioning Femininity and English Renaissance Drama* (Chicago: University of Chicago Press, 1991), 123–4.

64. Mary Augusta Scott, '*The Book of the Courtyer*: A Possible Source of Benedick and Beatrice', *PMLA*, 16 (1901), 475–502. Cf. Philip D. Collington, '"Stuffed with all honourable virtues": *Much Ado About Nothing* and *The Book of the Courtier*', *Studies in Philology*, 103 (2006), 281–312.

65. Quoting from the summary, 'Of the chief conditions and qualityes in a waytyng gentylwoman', in *The Courtyer of Count Baldessar Castilio*, tr. Thomas Hoby (1561), Z3r–4v.

66. Miguel de Cervantes, *The Second Part of the History of the Valorous and Witty Knight-errant, Don Quixote of the Mançha*, tr. Thomas Shelton (1620), 'and that over and besides, shee have twenty Ducats delivered unto her, to buy her some good clothes withall' (500).

67. 'Item I gyve and bequeath vnto my saied sister Jone xx.li. and all my wearing Apparrell to be paied and deliuered within one yeare after my deceas.' From the transcription in E. K. Chambers, *William Shakespeare: A Study of Facts and Problems*, 2 vols (Oxford: Clarendon Press, 1930), II, 170–4.

68. Thomas Nashe, *Strange Newes* (1592), E4v–F1r.

69. Arnold, *Queen Elizabeth's Wardrobe Unlock'd*, 99–103.

70. Catherine Richardson, *Shakespeare and Material Culture* (Oxford: Oxford University Press, 2011), 70–1, citing the Revels accounts.

71. For contexts see Ann Rosalind Jones and Peter Stallybrass, *Renaissance Clothing and the Materials of Memory* (Cambridge: Cambridge University Press, 2000), 1–2.

72. On players' parts see Simon Palfrey and Tiffany Stern, *Shakespeare in Parts* (Oxford: Oxford University Press, 2007); on their physical make-up, Grace Ioppolo, 'Early Modern Handwriting', in Michael Hattaway, ed., *A New Companion to English Renaissance Literature and Culture*, 2 vols (Oxford: Blackwell, 2010), I, 177–89, p. 187.

73. Ben Jonson, *Timber: Or, Discoveries*, in *The Workes of Benjamin Jonson* (1641), 85–132, p. 96.

74. 'To the Comicke, Play-readers, Venery, and Laughter', in *The Roaring Girle: Or, Moll Cut-Purse* (1611), A3r.

75. 2.1.344–6, 2.2.38–42; cf. the Friar at 4.1.236–8.

76. For an iconographical and Platonic approach, with little purchase on the play, see David Ormerod, 'Faith and Fashion in "Much Ado About Nothing"', *Shakespeare Survey*, 25 (1972), 93–105; Thomas Moisan, 'Deforming Sources: Literary Antecedents and their Traces in *Much Ado About Nothing*', *Studies in English Literature*, 31 (2003), 165–83, is altogether more astute, though it owes more to Derrida on discourse than the materiality of fashion.

77. Cf. *Much Ado About Nothing*, ed. Claire McEachern, Arden Shakespeare, rev. edn (London: Bloomsbury, 2016), 4.

78. Anthony Munday, *Fedele and Fortunio: The Deceites in Loue* (1585).

79. Some of them, the more obscurely, leaving only traces in the record and what can be divined from their titles—e.g. *Panecia* (for *Fenicia*?) played by Leicester's Men in 1574/5 and *Ariodant and Jenevora* performed to the court (probably at Richmond Palace) by the boys of Merchant Taylor's school in 1583.

80. D. J. Gordon, '*Much Ado About Nothing*: A Possible Source for the Hero-Claudio Plot', *Studies in Philology*, 39 (1942), 279–90.

2 Shakespeare Afoot

1. William Hazlitt, *Characters of Shakespear's Plays* (London: R. Hunter, C. and J. Ollier, 1817), 231. For the effect in performance, see Peter Holland, 'Opening', in Stuart Hampton-Reeves and Bridget Escolme, eds, *Shakespeare and the Making of Theatre* (Basingstoke: Palgrave Macmillan, 2012), 14–31, pp. 18–21.

2. Anon., *The True Tragedie of Richard the Third* (pub. 1594), A3v.

3. *The History of King Richard III/Historia Richardi Tertii*—best consulted in Vols II and XV of the Yale *Complete Works of St Thomas More*, ed. Richard S. Sylvester et al., 15 vols (New Haven: Yale University Press,

1963–97)—was read by Shakespeare in Edward Hall's *Vnion of the Two Noble and Illustre Famelies of Lancastre [and] Yorke* (1548) and the 2nd edn of Holinshed's *Chronicles* (1587).

4. Cf. *King Richard III*, ed. James R. Siemon, Arden Shakespeare (London: Methuen, 2009), 3. For lame and wooden-legged veterans, see Nick de Somogyi, *Shakespeare's Theatre of War* (Aldershot: Ashgate, 1998), ch. 1.

5. Antony Sher, *The Year of the King: An Actor's Diary* (London: Chatto & Windus, 1985), 144.

6. The phrase, which is widely diffused, goes back inter alia to interpretations of Genesis 3:21.

7. *The Essaies of Sir Francis Bacon*, enlarged edn (1612), 142–3.

8. See Sigmund Freud, 'Some Character-Types Met with in Psycho-analytic Work' (1916), in *The Standard Edition of the Complete Psychological Works of Sigmund Freud*, tr. James Strachey et al. (London: Hogarth Press, 1953–74), 24 vols, XIV, 309–33.

9. Georges Bataille, 'Le gros orteil', with photographs by Jacques-André Boiffard, in *Documents*, 6 (November, 1929), 297–302. Reprinted in *Œuvres complètes*, Vol I, ed. Denis Hollier (Paris: Gallimard, 1970), 200–4; 'The Big Toe', tr. Allan Stoekl, in Bataille, *Visions of Excess: Selected Writings, 1927–1939*, ed. Stoekl (Manchester: University of Manchester Press, 1985), 20–3.

10. 1.1.153–4; cf. 'The Life of Caius Martius Coriolanus', in Plutarch, *The Lives of the Noble Grecians and Romanes*, tr. Thomas North (1579), 237–59, p. 240.

11. E.g. René Weis, *Shakespeare Revealed: A Biography* (London: John Murray, 2007), 165–7.

12. *The Wound and the Bow: Seven Studies in Literature* (Cambridge, Mass.: Riverside Press, 1941).

13. Several Elizabethan measures are relevant, beginning with a proclamation of 3 January 1572 and statute 14 Elizabeth, c. 5, in the same year. See e.g. Peter Roberts, 'Elizabethan Players and Minstrels and the Legislation of 1572 against Retainers and Vagabonds', in Anthony Fletcher and Peter Roberts, eds, *Religion, Culture and Society in Early Modern Britain: Essays in Honour of Patrick Collinson* (Cambridge: Cambridge University Press, 1994), 29–55.

14. Robert Greene, *Greenes Groatsworth of Witte* (1592), D4v: 'What though the world once went hard with me, when I was faine to carry my playing Fardle a footebacke; *Tempora mutantur*'. The same jibe can be found earlier, in Nashe's 'To the Gentlemen Students of both Uniuersities', in Robert Greene, *Menaphon* (1589), **1r–A3r, A2v, and later, in *The Second Part of the Return from Parnassus*, 5.1 (lines 1918–28), in *The Three Parnassus Plays (1598–1601)*, ed. J. B. Leishman (London: Ivor Nicholson & Watson, 1949).

15. See Andrew Gurr, *The Shakespearian Playing Companies* (Oxford: Clarendon Press, 1996), ch. 3.

16. Thomas Dekker, *Satiro-Mastix: Or, The Vntrussing of the Humorous Poet* (1602), G3v; Jonson, *Poetaster*, 3.4 (Folio version, *Workes of Beniamin Ionson* [1616], 267). Cf. the players in John Marston, *Histrio-Mastix* (1610), C3v, 'we that trauell, with pumps full of grauel, | Made all of such running leather', and Thomas Dekker, in *The Belman of London* (1608), on actors who during the time of plague 'trauell vpon the hard hoofe, from village to village' (C1r).

17. William Kemp, *Kemps Nine Daies Wonder, Performed in a Daunce from London to Norwich* (1600).

18. Andrew Gurr, 'Who Strutted and Bellowed?', *Shakespeare Survey*, 16 (1963), 95–102. Cf. Tiffany Stern, 'Tragedy and Performance', in Michael Neill and David Schalkwyk, eds, *The Oxford Handbook of Shakespearean Tragedy* (Oxford: Oxford University Press, 2016), 489–504, pp. 493–4.

19. Ben Jonson, *Timber: Or, Discoveries*, in *The Workes of Benjamin Jonson* (1641), 85–132, p. 100.

20. This is registered the more strongly by his misogynistic use of 'ambling', from a verb used almost exclusively of horses at this date. For a possibly significant exception see Plutarch, on Cleopatra, in 'The Life of Marcus Antonius', in *Lives*, tr. North, 970–1010, p. 983; cf. Hamlet's 'You jig, you amble, and you lisp', 3.1.147.

21. 'Oft have I seen him leape into a grave | Suiting the person (which hee vs'd to haue) | Of a mad lover', from 'On the Death of the Famous Actor R. Burbadge', printed from a *c.*1630–40 manuscript in the *Gentleman's Magazine*, 95 (1825), 497–9 and reproduced in G. P. Jones, 'A Burbage Ballad and John Payne Collier', *Review of English Studies*, 40 (1989), 393–7. On the elegy and its texts see Bart van Es, *Shakespeare in Company* (Oxford: Oxford University Press, 2013), 232–4.

22. Cf. 'An Excellent Actor', often attributed to the dramatist Webster, and said to be about Burbage, in *Sir Thomas Ouerburie his Wife...: Whereunto are Annexed, New Newes and Characters* (1616), M2r–3r, at M2r–v, 'He doth not striue to make nature monstrous, she is often seene in the same Scæne with him; but neither on Stilts nor Crutches'.

23. Samuel Rowlands, 'To the Gentlemen Readers' in *Humors Ordinarie* (1605), '*Gallants*, like *Richard* the Vsurper swagger. | That had his hand continuall on his dagger' (A2r).

24. Robert Speaight, quoted in Anthony Holden, *Olivier* (London: Weidenfeld & Nicolson, 1988), 192.

25. Sher, *Year of the King*, 39, 42.

26. Tarquin Olivier, *My Father Laurence Olivier* (London: Headline, 1992), 151, Thomas Kiernan, *Olivier: The Life of Laurence Olivier* (London: Sidgwick & Jackson, 1981), 265.

27. See e.g. Richard Flecknoe, 'A Short Discourse of the English Stage', appended to his *Love's Kingdom: A Pastoral Trage-comedy* (1664), G4r–8r at G6v.

28. Thomas Heywood, *An Apology for Actors* (1612), B3v.

29. Stephen Gosson, *Playes Confuted in Fiue Actions* (1582), B7r.
30. Michel de Montaigne, 'An Apologie of Raymond Sebond', 'Of Experi-
    ence', in *The Essayes*, tr. John Florio (1603), 252–351, p. 328; 633–64,
    p. 652.
31. Cf. Natasha Korda, 'How to Do Things with Shoes', in Patricia Lennox
    and Bella Mirabella, eds, *Shakespeare and Costume* (London: Bloomsbury,
    2015), 85–104, p. 88.
32. Tiffany Stern, '"You That Walk i'th Galleries": Standing and Walking in
    the Galleries of the Globe Theatre', *Shakespeare Quarterly*, 51 (2000),
    211–16.
33. Thomas Dekker, *The Guls Horne-booke* (1609), 26.
34. *OED* spurn, *v.*[1], 1–5.
35. Montaigne, 'Of the Lame or Cripple', in *Essayes*, 612–17, p. 616.
36. Ignoto, 'I loue thee not for sacred chastitie', in John Davies and Christo-
    pher Marlowe, *Epigrammes and Elegies by I. D. and C. M.* (1599), D4r–v, at
    D4v. On the sex appeal of the role there is also John Manningham's diary
    (1602): 'Vpon a tyme when Burbidge played Rich. 3. there was a citizen
    greue so farr in liking wth him, that before shee went from the play shee
    appointed him to come that night vnto hir by the name of Ri: the 3 . . . . ';
    quoted in *Richard III*, ed. Siemon, 83.
37. Performed in 1580, and extant in nine manuscripts according to
    E. K. Chambers, *The Elizabethan Stage*, 4 vols (Oxford: Clarendon Press,
    1923), III, 408, the play was not printed until 1884.
38. Geoffrey Bullough, *Narrative and Dramatic Sources of Shakespeare*, 8 vols
    (London: Routledge & Kegan Paul, 1957–75), III, 239.
39. Quintilian, *Institutio oratoria*, ed. and tr. Donald A. Russell, Loeb Classical
    Library, 5 vols (Cambridge, Mass.: Harvard University Press, 2001),
    11.3.85–135.
40. *Institutio oratoria*, ed. and tr. Russell, 11.3.112.
41. Aristotle, *Nicomachean Ethics*, 1125a.
42. *The Seuenth Tragedie of Seneca, entituled Medea*, tr. John Studley (1566), 17. On
    Latin material in general, see Timothy M. O'Sullivan, *Walking in Roman
    Culture* (Cambridge: Cambridge University Press, 2011).
43. Thomas Hill, *The Contemplation of Mankinde Contayning a Singuler Discourse
    after the Art of Phisiognomie* (1571), fol. 202v.
44. For the transmission of this from Aristotle see e.g. Thomas Wright, *The
    Passions of the Minde in Generall* (1604), 134.
45. James Cleland, *Hero-paideia: Or, The Institution of a Young Noble Man* (1607),
    170.
46. *2 Henry IV*, 2.4.66–106, 159–66.
47. *The English Gentleman* (1630), 6.
48. *English Gentleman*, 362.
49. Richard Brathwait, *The English Gentlewoman* (1631), 82.
50. *English Gentlewoman*, 83.
51. *My Ladies Looking Glasse* (1616), 43.

52. See e.g. Fani Loula et al., 'Recognizing People from their Movement', *Journal of Experimental Psychology: Human Perception and Performance*, 31 (2005), 210–20, p. 210, Galit Yovel and Alice J. O'Toole, 'Recognizing People in Motion', *Trends in Cognitive Sciences*, 20 (2016), 383–9, pp. 388–9.

53. *English Gentlewoman*, 81.

54. This is not to deny that 'entrances and exits were moves which had a certain duration, rather than single actions which were completed immediately' (Mariko Ichikawa, *Shakespearean Entrances* [Basingstoke: Palgrave Macmillan, 2002], 3).

55. The Rose stage was initially as short as 15 feet 6 inches deep; the Fortune contract specifies that the 'Stadge shall conteine in length Fortie and Three foote of lawfull assize and in breadth to extende to the middle of the yarde [i.e. 27 feet 6 inches]'. See Andrew Gurr, *The Shakespearean Stage 1574–1642*, 4th edn (Cambridge: Cambridge University Press, 2009), 158, 168–70.

56. *Second Part of the Return from Parnassus*, 4.3 (lines 1757–61).

57. Rebecca Solnit, *Wanderlust: A History of Walking* (London: Verso, 2001), 9.

58. Philip Sidney, *An Apology for Poetry*, ed. Geoffrey Shepherd, 3rd edn rev. by R. W. Maslen (Manchester: Manchester University Press, 2002), 110–11.

59. Henry King, 'The Labyrinth', in his *Poems, Elegies, Paradoxes, and Sonets* (1664), 134–5, p. 134.

60. Alan C. Dessen and Leslie Thomson, eds, *A Dictionary of Stage Directions in English Drama 1580–1642* (Cambridge: Cambridge University Press, 1999), 245.

61. Thomas Lodge, *Rosalynde: Euphues Golden Legacie* (1592), D3v.

62. Noted by William Oldys, supposedly from a conversation with one of Shakespeare's brothers; quoting David Bevington, *Shakespeare and Biography* (Oxford: Oxford University Press, 2010), 29.

63. 1.2.200–09; cf. Celia at 3.2.207–8, 'young Orlando, that tripped up the wrestler's heels and your heart both in an instant'.

64. 'Thus for two or three dayes he walked vp and downe with his brother, to shew him all the commodities that belonged to his walke' (K4r).

65. 3.2.9, 5.1.61, 5.4.196.

66. Cf. Laura Levine, *Men in Women's Clothing: Anti-Theatricality and Effeminization, 1579–1642* (Cambridge: Cambridge University Press, 1994), 21, discussing Gosson, *Playes Confuted*.

67. *As You Like It*, ed. Cynthia Marshall, Shakespeare in Production (Cambridge: Cambridge University Press, 2004), 15, 3.

68. John Earle, *Micro-cosmographie* (1628), I11v.

69. *Second Part of the Return from Parnassus*, 4.3 (line 1772).

70. Cf. his account of the stages of a quarrel, 5.4.76–101.

71. Michel de Certeau, *The Practice of Everyday Life*, tr. Steven Rendall (Berkeley, Calif.: University of California Press, 1984), esp. ch. 7.

72. Joseph Amato, *On Foot: A History of Walking* (New York: New York University Press, 2004), 4.

73. Tim Ingold and Jo Lee Vergunst, 'Introduction' to Ingold and Vergunst, eds, *Ways of Walking: Ethnography and Practice on Foot* (Aldershot: Ashgate, 2008), 1–19, p. 1. Cf. Ingold's 'Culture on the Ground: The World Perceived Through the Feet', *Journal of Material Culture*, 9 (2004), 315–40.

74. When Clifford, in *2 Henry VI*, calls him a 'foul indigested lump' (5.1.155), as when Henry denounces him as 'an indigested...lump (*3 Henry VI*, 5.6.51) and Richard compares himself to 'a chaos, or an unlicked bear whelp' (*3 Henry VI*, 3.2.161), they echo Ovid's account of the creation: 'quem dixere chaos rudis indigestaque moles', *Metamorphoses*, I.7 ('which state have men called chaos: a rough, unordered mass of things')— quoting *Metamorphoses*, tr. Frank Justus Miller, rev. G. P. Goold, 2 vols, Loeb Classical Library (Cambridge, Mass.: Harvard University Press, 2014). Cf. '*Chaos*...A heauie lump', in *The XV Bookes of P. Ouidius Naso, entytuled Metamorphosis*, tr. Arthur Golding (1567), B1r. It is a passage that Shakespeare associated (as in the Sonnets) with invention and, of course, with the shape-shifting, Protean qualities that Richard wants to achieve through acting. 'My mind is bent to tell of bodies changed into new forms', Ovid's work begins.

75. *Richard III*, 1.1.20, *3 Henry VI*, 5.6.71–2. Cf. Hall, quoting More, in testimony that goes back to Richard's contemporary, John Rous (who adds that Richard was two years in the womb): 'his mother the duches had muche a dooe in her travaill...he came into the worlde the fete forwarde,...and as the fame ranne, not untothed' (Bullough, *Narrative and Dramatic Sources*, III, 253).

76. 3.2.110. On 'poetic feet' that run, stop, skip, limp, or stumble', see Paula Blank, *Shakespeare and the Mismeasure of Renaissance Man* (Ithaca, NY: Cornell University Press, 2006), 67.

77. *The Plays of William Shakespeare*, ed. Samuel Johnson, 8 vols (1765), II, 54.

78. See Bruce R. Smith on Puttenham, in his 'Finding Your Footing in Shakespeare's Verse', in Jonathan F. S. Post, ed., *The Oxford Handbook of Shakespeare's Poetry* (Oxford: Oxford University Press, 2013), 323–39, pp. 326–7.

79. *The Etymologies of Isidore of Seville*, tr. Stephen A. Barney et al. (Cambridge: Cambridge University Press, 2006), I.xvii.21.

80. Cited by Robert Stagg, 'Shakespeare's Feet: Puns, Metre, Meaning', *Literature Compass*, 12/3 (2015), 83–92, p. 85.

81. Cf. the voices of commentary on the cruel, warped Richard's complaint in William Baldwin, *A Myrrour for Magistrates* (1563): 'Seyng than that kyng Rychard never kept measure in any of his doings,...it were agaynst the *decorum* of his personage, to vse eyther good Meter or order.... It is not meete that so disorderly and vnnatural a man as kyng Rychard was, shuld observe any metrical order in his talke' (fo. 154v–155r).

82. Reginald Scot, *The Discouerie of Witchcraft* (1584), 7, 110.

83. Cuthbert Bede, '*Macbeth* on the Stage', *Notes and Queries*, 7th series, 8 (13 July 1889), 21–2, p. 21; cf. *Macbeth*, ed. John Wilders, Shakespeare in Production (Cambridge: Cambridge University Press, 2004), 85.

84. David Garrick, *An Essay on Acting… To which Will be Added, A Short Criticism on his Acting Macbeth* (1744), 17–18. After the murder, he advised, an actor should 'wear *Cork Heels* to his Shoes, as in this Scene he should seem to *tread on Air*' (9).

85. F. W. Hawkins, *The Life of Edmund Kean*, 2 vols (London: Tinsley Brothers, 1869), I, 272.

86. Quoted by David Roberts, 'Ravishing Strides: Signs of the Peripatetic in Early Modern Performance', *New Theatre Quarterly*, 17 (2001), 18–30, n. 1.

87. Hilary Spurling, 'Convulsion', in *The Spectator*, 217, no. 7218 (28 October 1966), 550–1, p. 551.

88. *Macbeth*, ed. Wilders, 116, quoting Richard David, 'The Tragic Curve: Two Productions of *Macbeth*', *Shakespeare Survey*, 9 (1956), 122–31, pp. 128–9.

89. See Marvin Rosenberg, *The Masks of Macbeth* (Berkeley, Calif.: University of California Press, 1978), 313.

90. John Coleman, 'Facts and Fancies about *Macbeth*', *The Gentleman's Magazine*, 266 (March 1889), 218–32, p. 223.

91. Arthur Colby Sprague, *Shakespeare and the Actors* (Cambridge, Mass.: Harvard University Press, 1944), 240–1.

92. E. R. Russell, 'Mr Irving's Interpretation of Shakspeare', *Fortnightly Review*, 1 October 1883, quoted in Sprague, *Shakespeare and the Actors*, 241.

93. Henry Higden, *A Modern Essay on the Thirteenth Satyr of Juvenal* (1686), 45; noted by Sprague, *Shakespeare and the Actors*, 254.

94. Thomas Tomkis, *Lingua: Or, The Combat of the Tongue, and the Fiue Senses for Superiority* (1607), 5.18; Ludwig Lavater, *Of Ghostes and Spirites Walking by Nyght*, tr. R. H. (1572), 48–9.

95. Hazlitt, *Characters of Shakespear's Plays*, 22.

96. Harriet Walter, *Macbeth* (London: Faber, 2002), 56, though the implicit exchange with Macbeth ('No more o' that, my lord,' and so on [34–65]) arguably makes the monologue, in some sense, the final scene between king and queen that the audience is denied because they are estranged by murder.

97. E.g. Sarah Bernhardt, Judith Anderson, Kate Fleetwood.

98. Hamish Fulton, *Wild Life: Walks in the Cairngorms* (Edinburgh: Pocketbooks, 2000), 202.

99. Reported by John Forster, in Forster and George Henry Lewes, *Dramatic Essays* (London: W. Scott, 1896), 36.

100. For discussion see e.g. Robert S. Miola, *Shakespeare and Classical Tragedy: The Influence of Seneca* (Oxford: Clarendon Press, 1992), 97–8.

101. Quoted in *Macbeth*, ed. A. R. Braunmuller, New Cambridge Shakespeare (Cambridge: Cambridge University Press, 1997), 57–8, p. 58.

102. Peter Brook, *The Empty Space* (1968; Harmondsworth: Penguin, 1972), 11.

103. Declan Donnellan, *The Actor and the Target*, rev. edn (London: Nick Hern Books, 2005), 131.

3 *King Lear* and its Origins

1. *The Tragedy of King Lear: The Folio Text*, 4.5.1–4. Except where otherwise indicated, all quotations from the play come from this Folio-based edition.
2. For discussion see the admirable essays by Richard Knowles, 'How Shakespeare Knew *King Leir*', *Shakespeare Survey*, 55 (2002), 12–35, Meredith Skura, 'Dragon Fathers and Unnatural Children: Warring Generations in *King Lear* and its Source', *Comparative Drama*, 42 (2008), 121–48 and her 'What Shakespeare Did with the Queen's Men's *King Leir* and When', *Shakespeare Survey*, 63 (2010), 316–25.
3. *Shakespear Illustrated: Or, The Novels and Histories, On which the Plays of Shakespeare are Founded*, 3 vols (1753–4), III, 273–308, p. 291.
4. Philip Sidney, *The Countesse of Pembrokes Arcadia* (1590), 142–3.
5. Note the reference to 'th' Egyptian thief' (Thyamis) in Heliodorus, at *Twelfth Night*, 5.1.116. *An Æthiopian Historie written in Greeke by Heliodorus*, tr. Thomas Underdown, was published in 1569 (enlarged 1577, 1587, and 1605).
6. Philip Sidney, *An Apology for Poetry*, ed. Geoffrey Shepherd, 3rd edn rev. by R. W. Maslen (Manchester: Manchester University Press, 2002), 91.
7. *Thebais*, tr. Thomas Newton, in *Seneca his Tenne Tragedies, translated into Englysh*, ed. Newton (1581), 40–54, p. 41.
8. *Phoenissae*, line 63, in Seneca, *Tragedies*, ed. and tr. John J. Fitch, 2 vols, Loeb Classical Library (Harvard, Mass: Harvard University Press, 2002), *Thebais*, tr. Newton, 42.
9. 'An Apologie of Raymond Sebond', in *The Essayes*, tr. John Florio (1603), 252–351, p. 346: 'Nay some there are, that can scarcely thinke or heare of such heights. . . . I haue sometimes made triall of it vpon our mountaines on this side of *Italie*, yet am I one of those that wil not easily be afrighted with such things, and I could not without horror to my minde, and trembling of legges and thighes endure to looke on those infinit precipices and steepe downefalles, though . . . vnlesse I had willingly gone to the perill, I could not possibly have falne. . . . we cannot without some dread and giddines in the head, so much as abide to looke vpon one of those even and down-right precipices: . . . Which is an evident deception of the sight. Therfore was it, that a worthy Philosopher pulled out his eies, that so he might discharge his soule of the debauching and diverting he received by them, and the better and more freely apply himselfe vnto philosophie. But by this accompt, he should also have stopped his eares, which . . . are the most dangerous instruments we have to receive violent and sodaine impressions to trouble and alter vs.' Cf. W. B. Drayton Henderson, 'Montaigne's *Apologie of Raymond Sebond*, and *King Lear*', *The Shakespeare Association Bulletin*, 14 (1939), 209–25 and 15 (1940), 40–54, pp. 41–3.
10. John W. Cunliffe, *The Influence of Seneca on Elizabethan Tragedy* (London: Macmillan, 1893), 23–4, 136, 137, 139, 144–5, 146, 147, 152.

11. The last wave of the older scholarship breaks in Hardin Craig, 'The Shackling of Accidents: A Study of Elizabethan Tragedy', *Philological Quarterly*, 19 (1940), 1–19, p. 10 (on Seneca's *Oedipus*, *Phoenissae*, and *King Lear*).

12. Gordon Braden, *Renaissance Tragedy and the Senecan Tradition: Anger's Privilege* (New Haven: Yale University Press, 1985), Robert S. Miola, *Shakespeare and Classical Tragedy: The Influence of Seneca* (Oxford: Clarendon Press, 1992), Colin Burrow, *Shakespeare and Classical Antiquity* (Oxford: Oxford University Press, 2013).

13. Kenneth Muir, *The Sources of Shakespeare's Plays* (London: Methuen, 1977) 202, *King Lear*, ed. Muir, Arden Shakespeare (London: Methuen, 1972), xxxviii, n. 4; M. L. Stapleton, *Fated Sky: The* Femina Furens *in Shakespeare* (Newark: University of Delaware Press, 2000), 18–20.

14. George Puttenham, *The Arte of English Poesie* (1589), 27, 30–1; cf. Thomas Heywood, *An Apology for Actors* (1612), B1v–2v, D1v–2r, F1v.

15. Tanya Pollard, 'What's Hecuba to Shakespeare?', *Renaissance Quarterly*, 65 (2012), 1060–93, p. 1064. Cf. Pollard's 'Greek Playbooks and Dramatic Forms', in Allison K. Deutermann and András Kiséry, eds, *Formal Matters: Reading the Materials of English Renaissance Literature* (Manchester: Manchester University Press, 2013), 99–123, pp. 110–11.

16. Roger Ascham, *The Scholemaster* (1570), 53.

17. Ben Jonson, 'To the Memory of my Beloued, the Author Mr William Shakespeare: and What He Hath Left Vs', in *Mr William Shakespeares Comedies, Histories, and Tragedies* (1623), A4r–v, at A4r.

18. Louise Schleiner, 'Latinized Greek Drama in Shakespeare's Writing of *Hamlet*', *Shakespeare Quarterly*, 41 (1990), 29–48. Anticipated by Emrys Jones' account of Euripides' *Hecuba* as a template for *Titus Andronicus*, and his *Iphigenia at Aulis* as one source of *Julius Caesar*, in *The Origins of Shakespeare* (Oxford: Clarendon Press, 1977), chs 3–4, see Laurie Maguire, *Shakespeare's Names* (Oxford: Oxford University Press, 2007), 97–103, Sarah Dewar-Watson, 'The *Alcestis* and the Statue Scene in *The Winter's Tale*', *Shakespeare Quarterly*, 60 (2009), 73–80, Pollard, 'What's Hecuba to Shakespeare' and 'Greek Playbooks and Dramatic Forms', Myron Stagman's eccentric *Shakespeare's Greek Drama Secret* (Newcastle: Cambridge Scholars Publishing, 2010), Robert S. Miola, 'Early Modern Antigones: Receptions, Refractions, Replays', *Classical Receptions Journal*, 6 (2014), 221–44. For contexts, see J. W. Binns, 'Latin Translations from Greek in The English Renaissance', *Humanistica Lovaniensia*, 27 (1978), 128–59.

19. In George Gascoigne, *A Hundreth Sundrie Flowres* (1573), 71–164. See Robert S. Miola, 'Euripides at Gray's Inn: Gascoigne and Kinwelmersh's *Jocasta*', in Naomi Conn Liebler, ed., *The Female Tragic Hero in English Renaissance Drama* (New York: Palgrave Macmillan, 2002), 33–50; Sarah Dewar-Watson, '*Jocasta*: "A Tragedie Written in Greek"', *International Journal of the Classical Tradition*, 17 (2010), 22–32. The standard edition is in George Gascoigne, *A Hundreth Sundrie Flowres*, ed. G. W. Pigman III (Oxford: Clarendon Press, 2000).

20. John Harvey, 'A Note on Shakespeare and Sophocles', *Essays in Criticism*, 27 (1977), 259–70. Some Victorian scholars did look for echoes of Greek tragedy. J. Churton Collins in his *Studies in Shakespeare* (Westminster: Archibald Constable and Co., 1904) compares 'Lear and Gloucester with Edgar and Cordelia' to 'Oedipus and Antigone of the end of the *Phoenissae*' (75), judges Eteocles a lot less plausibly to be 'the archetype of Hotspur' and alludes to unspecified 'parallels' between *Oedipus at Colonus* and Cordelia with Lear (80–1). Others were more abstemious, as in Samuel Lee Wolff on Oedipus, Sidney, and Heliodorus, *The Greek Romances in Elizabethan Prose Fiction* (New York: Columbia University Press, 1912), 366. Recent commentary, wary of implying influence, has been glancing or suggestive in proportion to being merely comparative; see esp. Peter Stallybrass, 'The Mystery of Walking', *Journal of Medieval and Early Modern Studies*, 32 (2002), 571–80.

21. Desiderius Erasmus, *Apophthegmes*, tr. Nicholas Udall (1542), 91–2, Thomas Cooper, *Thesaurus Linguae Romanae et Britannicae* (1578), under Antigone and Oedipus. Cf. Thomas Heywood, on 'the *Theban* History, notorious in *Oedipus* and *Iocasta*, with the deathes of the two Brothers *Eteocles*, and *Polynices*' (*Troia Britanica: Or, Great Britaines Troy* [1609], '*Proemium*').

22. *A Declaration of Egregious Popish Impostures* (1603), 16.

23. For signs of ignorance about Oedipus' final days, see e.g. Niels Hemmingsen, *A Postill, or, Exposition of the Gospels*, tr. Arthur Golding (1569), which says that 'fleeing his Realm, hee liued blinde and a beggar, vntil hee perrished beeing swalowed vppe in despaire' (G5v) and Giovanni della Casa, *Galateo*, tr. Robert Peterson (1576): 'being banished and driuen out of his countrie (vppon what occasion I know not) he fled to King *Theseus* at *Athens,* the better to saue him selfe and his life, from his enemies, that mainely pursued him' (53). Both references remind us that the Oedipus story linked English readers with a European-wide body of lore.

24. For lists see Rudolf Hirsch, 'The Printing Tradition of Aeschylus, Euripides, Sophocles and Aristophanes', *Gutenberg-Jahrbuch*, 39 (1964), 138–46.

25. *Paradise Regain'd . . . to which is added Samson Agonistes* (1671), I5r.

26. *De finibus*, V.1.3.

27. Raphael Holinshed, *The First and Second Volumes of Chronicles*, 2nd edn (1587), 10.

28. *Oedipus at Colonus*, line 192, in *Antigone, Women of Trachis, Philoctetes, Oedipus at Colonus*, ed. and tr. Hugh Lloyd-Jones, Loeb Classical Library (Cambridge, Mass.: Harvard University Press, 1994).

29. Quoting *Sophoclis Tragoediæ VII., ex aduerso respondet Latina interpretatio*, tr. Vitus Winsemius (Heidelberg, 1597). In the Loeb edn this is line 212. On the case for Melanchthon as translator, see Stefan Rhein, 'Melanchthon and Greek Literature', in Timothy J. Wengert and M. Patrick Graham, eds, *Philip Melanchthon (1497–1560) and the Commentary* (Sheffield: Sheffield Academic Press, 1997), 149–70, pp. 153–4.

30. See the fine essay by Hester Lees-Jeffries, 'No Country for Old Men? Ciceronian Friendship and Old Age in Shakespeare's Second Tetralogy and Beyond', *Review of English Studies*, 62 (2011), 716–37, p. 737.

31. *De senectute* VII (22–3), in *De senectute, De amicitia, De divinatione*, ed. and tr. William Armistead Falconer, Loeb Classical Library (Cambridge, Mass.: Harvard University Press, 1923).

32. By Edgar's report, discussed below, Gloucester died of a broken heart when he revealed his identity to him (5.3.188–91).

33. Quoting Geoffrey Bullough, *Narrative and Dramatic Sources of Shakespeare*, 8 vols (London: Routledge & Kegan Paul, 1957–75), VII, 288.

34. 'Argument of the Tragedie', in Thomas Norton and Thomas Sackville, *The Tragedie of Gorboduc* (1565).

35. *Thebais*, 43.

36. *The Holie Bible* [Bishops' Bible, rev. edn] (1572), Genesis 1:1–7. In Ovid's account of the creation, Shakespeare would also have read of God: 'The earth from heauen, the sea from earth, he parted orderly' (*The XV Bookes of P. Ouidius Naso, entytuled Metamorphosis*, tr. Arthur Golding [1567], b2v).

37. Lancelot Andrewes, *Apospasmatia Sacra: Or, A Collection of Posthumous and Orphan Lectures* (1657), esp. 25, 27–34, 41–2, 48–9, 75, 103–4.

38. *First and Second Volumes of Chronicles*, 1.

39. *First and Second Volumes of Chronicles*, 13. Aganippus, who takes Cordeilla in marriage, 'was one of the twelue kings that ruled Gallia in those daies, as in the British historie it is recorded'.

40. See e.g. M. A. Screech, *Montaigne's Annotated Copy of Lucretius* (Geneva: Droz, 1998), Peter Mack, *Reading and Rhetoric in Montaigne and Shakespeare* (London: Bloomsbury, 2010), 26–7.

41. Dr Johnson wrote, 'The enumeration of the choughs and crows, the samphire-man and the fishers,... stops the mind in the rapidity of its descent' (*The Plays of William Shakespeare*, ed. Samuel Johnson, 8 vols [1765], VI, 123), and added, according to James Boswell, 'The crows impede your fall.... The impression is divided; you pass on by computation' (*The Life of Samuel Johnson*, 2 vols [1791], I, 317). Cf. division in the passage of Montaigne in note 9: 'if but a tree, a shrub, or any out-butting cragge of a Rocke presented it selfe vnto our eyes,... somewhat to vphold the sight, and divide the same, it doth somewhat ease and assure vs from feare, as if it were a thing, which in our fall might either helpe or vpholde vs.'

42. Richard P. Olenick et al., *The Mechanical Universe: Introduction to Mechanics and Heat* (Cambridge: Cambridge University Press, 2008), ch. 2.

43. Kenelm Digby, *Two Treatises* (Paris, 1644), 82. Cf. Mary Thomas Crane, *Losing Touch with Nature: Literature and the New Science in Sixteenth-Century England* (Baltimore: Johns Hopkins University Press, 2014), 132–8, 140–1.

44. Sir Roger L'Estrange, *Lestrange's Narrative of the Plot* (1680), 13; cf. John Yalden, *Huperēphanias Musērion: Or, Machiavil Redivivus* (1681), 14.

45. 'The Life of Marcus Antonius', in Plutarch, *The Lives of the Noble Grecians and Romans*, tr. Thomas North (1579), 970–1010, p. 980. For contexts see Gordon Braden, 'Tragedy', in Patrick Cheney and Philip Hardie, eds, *The Oxford History of Classical Reception in English Literature*, Vol. II, *1588–1660* (Oxford: Oxford University Press, 2015), 373–94, p. 377.

46. *Poetics*, 1449a 9–10, 1450a 49, in *Aristotle, 'Poetics', Longinus, 'On the Sublime', Demetrius, 'On Style'*, ed. and tr. Stephen Halliwell et al., Loeb Classical Library (Cambridge, Mass.: Harvard University Press, 1995).

47. *Oedipus Tyrannus*, lines 1–5, in *Ajax, Electra, Oedipus Tyrannus*, ed. and tr. Hugh Lloyd-Jones, Loeb Classical Library (Cambridge, Mass.: Harvard University Press, 1994).

48. Thomas G. Rosenmeyer, *Senecan Drama and Stoic Cosmology* (Berkeley: University of California Press, 1989), ch. 3, quoting p. 64.

49. *Oedipus*, line 709, in Seneca, *Tragedies*, ed. and tr. Fitch.

50. Lines 837–8. At the end of Seneca's play, Jocasta, with lethal logic, stabs herself in the womb (lines 1038–9).

51. *The Common Places*, tr. Anthonie Marten (1583), Pt III, 38–9, in a chapter 'Of Predestination'.

52. Daniel Javitch, 'The Emergence of Poetic Genre Theory in the Sixteenth Century', *Modern Language Quarterly*, 59 (1998), 139–69, p. 160.

53. Emrys Jones, *Scenic Form in Shakespeare* (Oxford: Clarendon Press, 1971), 64–5, quoted with approval in a related argument by Lorna Hutson, *The Invention of Suspicion: Law and Mimesis in Shakespeare and Renaissance Drama* (Oxford: Oxford University Press, 2007), 118–19.

54. Abraham Fraunce, *The Lawiers Logike* (1588), E4v.

55. 'For Quintilian and the ancient rhetoricians,' Barbara J. Shapiro reminds us, 'arguments might . . . be drawn from the causes of things done or that may be done' (*'Beyond Reasonable Doubt' and 'Probable Cause': Historical Perspectives on the Anglo-American Law of Evidence* [Berkeley: University of California Press, 1991], 117).

56. Quoting William Cornwallis, *Discourses vpon Seneca the Tragedian* (1601), B2r.

57. Oedipus' 'terrible birth/origin' is traumatic from *Oedipus Tyrannus* lines 1252–7, 1369–1415, 1496–9 to the closing chorus of *Oedipus at Colonus*. Seneca extracts lurid paradoxes from the womb as *ortus*: see *Oedipus*, lines 237–8, 637–9; his Jocasta, as noted, stabs herself in her womb. Cf. Statius, *Thebaid*, I.233–5.

58. 1.4.253–62, 4.5.121–6, 1.5.35–8.

59. *De rerum natura*, VI.96–107, with further discussion to line 521.

60. On this 'desire to recuperate origins', see Alvin Snider, *Origin and Authority in Seventeenth-Century England: Bacon, Milton, Butler* (Toronto: University of Toronto Press, 1994), 3.

61. Simon Palfrey, *Poor Tom: Living 'King Lear'* (Chicago: Chicago University Press, 2014), 104.

62. 'A Note to Young Writers', in Edward Bond, *Plays 4* (London: Methuen, 2002), 106–9, p. 109.

63. 4.6.68; cf. the immediate source, in *King Leir*, where the king and Cordelia kneel to one another, and the latter says, with less depth, 'you were the cause that I | Am what I am, who else had neuer bin' (H4r).

64. 'Of Coaches', in *Essayes*, tr. Florio, 538–49, p. 538.

65. 'Apologie of Raymond Sebond', in *Essayes*, tr. Florio, 307, 295.

66. 'Mothes' is a variant of 'motes'; 'Apologie of Raymond Sebond', in *Essayes*, tr. Florio, 315–16.

67. 'That a Man Ought Soberly to Meddle with Iudging of Divine Lawes', *Essayes*, tr. Florio, 107–8, p. 107.

68. 'Of Prognostications', *Essayes*, tr. Florio, 19–21, p. 21.

69. 'Of the Lame or Cripple', *Essayes*, tr. Florio, 612–17, pp. 612–13.

70. *The History of King Lear: The Quarto Text*, sc 2, 139–44.

71. 'The Life of Pyrrus', in Plutarch, *Lives*, tr. North, 426–50, p. 431.

72. Euripides, *Phoenician Women*, line 68, in *Helen, Phoenician Women, Orestes*, ed. and tr. David Kovacs, Loeb Classical Library (Cambridge, Mass.: Harvard University Press, 2002).

73. See the Latin parallel text by Rudolfus Collinus in *Euripidis ... Tragoediae XVIII* (Basel, 1541), i2v; on this translation and Dolce see *Hundreth Sundrie Flowres*, ed. Pigman, 510, citing John W. Cunliffe. The widely used Stiblinus Greek-Latin edition, *Euripides poeta tragicorum princeps* (Basel, 1562), has 'Acuto ferro ut hanc dilacerent domum' (*dilacerare*, 'to tear apart').

74. Minimally in Seneca's *Thebais*, as extravagantly in Statius (*Thebaid*, XI), there is a single combat between Eteocles and Polynices. Sidney turns this tangentially into a fatal duel between the mutually disguised brothers Tydeus and Telenor, alluding to Tydeus the friend of Polynices in Statius.

75. Euripides, *Phoenician Women*, lines 327–36. Arguably the paternal cursing is transferred from the Gloucester-as-Oedipus story to that of Lear (whose daughters are not cursed in *King Leir* or Spenser or Holinshed); see 1.1.203, 1.4.279–81, 2.2.318, 335–45.

76. *Countesse of Pembrokes Arcadia*, 146.

77. *The Works of Mr William Shakespear*, ed. Nicholas Rowe, 6 vols (1709), [V,] 2549.

78. *History of King Lear: Quarto*, sc 24, 213–14.

79. 'only the crossing counts', in C. D. Wright, *Cooling Time: An American Poetry Vigil* (Port Townsend, Washington: Copper Canyon Press, 2005).

80. A. C. Bradley, *Shakespearean Tragedy* (1904; London: Macmillan, 1957), 241.

4 *The Tempest* to 1756

1. Sir William Davenant and John Dryden, *The Tempest: Or, The Enchanted Island* (perf. 1667; 1670), A2v. Like some other commentators, to avoid confusion with Shakespeare, I refer to this play by its subtitle.

2. Alteration was legitimate, he insisted, if it improved upon originals and drew on creative labour; imitation—in the classical sense—was accepted practice; plots could be reused (as Scaliger had argued) so long as dialogue and scenic structure were reworked. See further Pauline Kewes, *Authorship and Appropriation: Writing for the Stage in England, 1660–1710* (Oxford: Clarendon Press, 1998), esp. 54–63, 124–8, 170–6.

3. 'Preface' and 'The Grounds of Criticism in Tragedy', in his *Troilus and Cressida: Or, Truth Found too Late* (1679), A4v–b3v, at A4v.

4. Edmond Malone, *An Account of the Incidents, from which the Title and Part of the Story of Shakespeare's 'Tempest' were Derived* (London: C. and R. Baldwin, 1808). Malone focused on Silvester Jourdain's *A Discovery of the Barmudas, Otherwise Called the Ile of Diuels* (1610); it was not until 1901 that Morton Luce identified William Strachey's 'True Reportory', which must have circulated in manuscript before its publication in Samuel Purchas' compilation, *Purchas His Pilgrimes* (1625), as the more immediate, written source of the play.

5. John Locke, *Two Treatises of Government* (1694), Bk II, ch. 5.

6. Sir Robert Filmer, *Patriarcha: Or, The Natural Power of Kings* (1680).

7. E.g. John Dryden, *Of Dramatick Poesie: An Essay* (1668), 47.

8. John Milton, 'L'Allegro', in *Poems* (1645), 30–6, p. 36, 'If *Jonsons* learned Sock be on, | Or sweetest *Shakespear* fancies childe, | Warble his native Wood-notes wilde'; Leonard Digges, 'Vpon Master William Shakespeare', in *Poems: Written by Wil. Shake-speare* (1640), *3r–4r, *3r, 'Next Nature onely helpt him'. Cf. Jonathan Bate, *The Genius of Shakespeare* (London: Picador, 1997), 160–1.

9. John Heminge and Henry Condell, 'To the Great Variety of Readers', 'Who, as he was a happie imitator of Nature, was a most gentle expresser of it', in *Mr William Shakespeares Comedies, Histories, and Tragedies* (1623), A3r.

10. *Conjectures on Original Composition*, 2nd edn (1759), 12.

11. Charlotte Lennox, *Shakespear Illustrated: Or, The Novels and Histories, On which the Plays of Shakespeare are Founded*, 3 vols (1753–4).

12. William Strachey, 'A true reportory of the wracke, and redemption of Sir *Thomas Gates* Knight; vpon, and from the Ilands of the *Bermudas*: his comming to *Virginia*, and the estate of that Colonie then, and after, vnder the gouernment of the Lord *La Warre*, Iuly 15. 1610', in Samuel Purchas, *Purchas His Pilgrimes*, 4 vols (1625), IV, 1734–58.

13. See e.g. John Pitcher, 'A Theatre of the Future: *The Aeneid* and *The Tempest*', *Essays in Criticism*, 34 (1984), 193–215, Donna B. Hamilton, *Virgil and 'The Tempest': The Politics of Imitation* (Columbus: Ohio University Press, 1990), Laurie Maguire and Emma Smith, 'What is a Source? Or, How Shakespeare Read His Marlowe', *Shakespeare Survey*, 68 (2015), 15–31.

14. Jonathan Bate, *Shakespeare and Ovid* (Oxford: Clarendon Press, 1993), 243.

15. E.g. for the Bermudas, Strachey, 'A True Reportory', 1739–41, Jourdain, *Discovery of the Barmudas*, 12–17, Lewes Hughes, *A Letter, Sent into England from the Summer Ilands* (1615), B1v–2r; for Virginia, Thomas Harriot,

    A Briefe and True Report of the New Found Land of Virginia, rev. edn (1590), 7–24, Council for Virginia, *A True Declaration of the Estate of the Colonie in Virginia* (1610), 28–31, 54–9, Richard Rich, *Newes from Virginia* (1610), B2v. Cf. John Gillies, 'Shakespeare's Virginian Masque', *ELH*, 53 (1986), 673–707, esp. pp. 681–3.

16. 'Of Riches', in *The Essayes or Counsels, Ciuill and Morall*, rev. edn (1625), 205–11, p. 207.

17. 'The *Bucolics* and *Georgics* were likely to be among the first poems read' (in the upper grammar school), 'Pretty clearly Shakspere had the *Bucolics* and *Georgics* in grammar school as was customary in his day'; T. W. Baldwin, *William Shakspere's Small Latine & Lesse Greeke*, 2 vols (Urbana: University of Illinois Press, 1944), II, 456, 479.

18. Thomas Tusser, *A Hundreth Good Pointes of Husbandrie* (1557), which became *Fiue Hundreth Points of Good Husbandry* (1573, etc.), shows no obvious knowledge of the *Georgics*, but Barnabe Googe added translated extracts to his scarcely less popular version of Conrad Heresbach's *Foure Bookes of Husbandry* (1577, etc.). Sylvester's translation of *Bartas: His Deuine Weekes and Workes* (1605) appeared in stages from the late 1590s and was often reprinted. *The Georgicks of Hesiod*, tr. Chapman, was published in 1618. For contexts see Andrew McCrae, *God Speed the Plough: The Representation of Agrarian England, 1500–1660* (Cambridge: Cambridge University Press, 1996), esp. ch. 5.

19. Robert Johnson, *Nova Britannia* (1609), B4v.

20. Council for Virginia, *True Declaration*, 34.

21. William Crashaw, father of the poet, asked in a sermon of 1609, 'why are the *Players* enemies to this Plantation and doe abuse it?' (in such plays as *Eastward Hoe* [1605]). 'First, they see that wee send of all trades to *Virginea*, but will send no *Players*,...Secondly,...wee resolue to suffer no *Idle persons in Virginea*, which course if it were taken in *England*, they know they might turne to new occupations' (*A Sermon Preached in London before the Right Honorable the Lord Lawarre, Lord Gouernour and Captaine Generall of Virginea, and Others of his Maiesties Counsell for that Kingdome* [1610], H4r).

22. 'A True Reportory', 1736.

23. 'It is a nation...that hath no kinde of traffike, no knowledge of Letters, no intelligence of numbers, no name of magistrate, nor of politike superioritie; no vse of service, of riches, or of poverty; no contracts, no successions, no dividences, no occupation but idle; no respect of kinred, but common, no apparell but naturall, no manuring of lands, no vse of wine, corne, or mettle. The very words that import lying, falshood, treason, dissimulation, covetousnes, envie, detraction, and pardon, were never heard of amongst them.' Michel de Montaigne, 'Of the Caniballes', in *The Essayes*, tr. John Florio (1603), 100–7, p. 102.

24. E.g. 'no occupation but idle' becoming 'all men idle, all', which invites rebuttal, or the hastily added, hastily qualified, 'And women too; but innocent and pure'.

25. E.g. the wishful, commanding 'All' and 'should' in the verse line 'All things in common nature should produce', pieced out of 'but common, . . . naturall, no manuring of lands'.

26. For prompts to the former see Fred Parker, 'Shakespeare's Argument with Montaigne', *Cambridge Quarterly*, 28 (1999), 1–18, pp. 3–5; on the latter see Janet Clare, 'Tracings and Data in *The Tempest*: Author, World and Representation', *Shakespeare Survey*, 68 (2015), 109–17, p. 115.

27. Kenji Go, 'Montaigne's "Cannibals" and *The Tempest* Revisited', *Studies in Philology*, 109 (2012), 455–73, p. 462, compares 'they yet enjoy that naturall vbertie and fruitefulnesse, which without labouring-toyle, doth in such plenteous aboundance furnish them' on p. 104 of the *Essayes*.

28. *Essayes*, 102.

29. Margaret Tudeau-Clayton, *Jonson, Shakespeare and Early Modern Virgil* (Cambridge: Cambridge University Press, 1998), 219–20.

30. *Georgics*, I.1–7, in Virgil, *Eclogues, Georgics, Aeneid I–VI*, ed. and tr. H. R. Fairclough, rev. G. P. Goold, Loeb Classical Library (Cambridge, Mass.: Harvard University Press, 1999).

31. The underlying influence is Ramus' commentary, *Georgica P. Rami praelectionibus illustrata* (Paris, 1556).

32. *The Georgiks*, A3v, in *The Bucoliks of Publius Virgilius Maro, Together with his Georgiks or Ruralls, Otherwise Called his Husbandrie*, tr. Abraham Fleming (1589).

33. On this echo of Virgil, see David Lindley's note in his rev. edn of *The Tempest*, New Cambridge Shakespeare (Cambridge: Cambridge University Press, 2013).

34. See *OED*, contamination, *n.* 1 c, 'The blending of two or more stories, plots, or the like into one' (from Latin).

35. Sir Hugh Plat, *The New and Admirable Arte of Setting of Corne: With all the Necessarie Tooles and other Circumstances belonging to the Same* (1600) quotes Book I of the *Georgics* on germination (B3r) and goes on to show (like Prospero's masque) '*How by setting and planting of Corne or vines; a great and plentifull encrease may be had*' (B4v); cf. Plat's *Floraes Paradise Beautified and Adorned with Sundry Sorts of Delicate Fruites and Flowers* (1608), which notes that gentlemen farmers are 'well acquainted with *Virgils Georgicks*' (9). For contexts see Deborah E. Harkness, *The Jewel House: Elizabethan London and the Scientific Revolution* (New Haven: Yale University Press, 2007), esp. ch. 6.

36. E.g. his *New Atlantis* (1658), 28–9. Bacon famously represented his larger philosophical enterprise as georgic: 'And surely if the purpose be . . . really to instruct and suborne Action and actiue life, these Georgickes of the mind concerning the husbandry and tillage therof, are no lesse worthy then the heroical descriptions of *vertue, duty,* and *felicity*' (*Aduancement of Learning* [1605], Ss4r).

37. There is a wedding in Strachey's 'True Reportory' between a cook and a maid servant (1746); not much like Ferdinand and Miranda, the couple conceivably led Shakespeare towards his masque.

38. *OED*, vigneron, *n.*, 'One who cultivates grape-vines'.
39. 4.1.60–4. The Oxford Shakespeare emendation, 'peonied' (Folio 'pioned'), is quaint.
40. Cf. e.g. Harriot, *Briefe and True Report*, 'For English corne ... Of the grouth you need not to doubt: for barlie, oates and peaze, we haue seene proof of' (15). Bacon, 'Of Plantations', in the 1625 edn of *Essayes*, 198–204: 'Then consider, what Victuall or Esculent Things there are, which grow speedily, and within the yeere; As Parsnips, Carrets, Turnips, Onions, Radish, Artichokes of Hierusalem, Maiz, and the like. For Wheat, Barly, and Oats, they aske too much Labour: But with Pease, and Beanes, you may begin' (199–200).
41. *The Tempest*, ed. Virginia Mason Vaughan and Alden T. Vaughan, Arden Shakespeare, rev. edn (London: Bloomsbury, 2011), 269.
42. Cf. *Georgics*, II.357–60; cf. (esp. on clipping) lines 397–419.
43. On contracts compare 2.1.157 with 4.1.19, 84, 134. As Sebastian and Antonio quip, there is, in Gonzalo's utopia, 'No marrying ... all idle: whores and knaves' (2.1.171–2).
44. On the foot of fine that confirmed Shakespeare's acquisition of New Place ('two granaries, and two gardens with appurtenances') see B. Roland Lewis, *The Shakespeare Documents*, 2 vols (Stanford, Calif.: Stanford University Press, 1940–41), docs 111–12.
45. Jayne Elisabeth Archer, Richard Marggraf Turley, Howard Thomas, 'The Autumn King: Remembering the Land in *King Lear*', *Shakespeare Quarterly*, 63 (2012), 518–43, p. 537. For contexts see Bruce Boehrer, *Environmental Degradation in Jacobean Drama* (Cambridge: Cambridge University Press, 2013), 88–90.
46. Samuel Schoenbaum, *William Shakespeare: A Compact Documentary Life*, rev. edn (New York: Oxford University Press, 1987), 281–5, p. 283; Robert Bearman, *Shakespeare's Money: How Much Did He Make and What Does This Mean?* (Oxford: Oxford University Press, 2016), 138–45, esp. pp. 140, 145.
47. On this committee see Michael Hunter, *Science and Society in Restoration England* (Cambridge: Cambridge University Press, 1981), 92–3.
48. In Greene's *Pandosto* (1588), the King of Bohemia harries his wife to death for an imagined affair with his friend, the King of Sicily, and sends the child whose paternity he doubts into exile. Fawnia ends up in Sicily, where she is brought up by shepherds. She marries the son of the King of Sicily, and everything works out well enough when they visit Bohemia and her tyrannical father goes mad and dies. Scholars have wondered why Shakespeare reversed all the locations he found in Greene. At a mythical level, Perdita is a version of Proserpina taken from Sicily—as in the legend—to elsewhere, proposing for her suitor Florizel 'flowers ... From Dis's wagon' (4.4.117–18). The play can only come right, bring her father and still-living mother back to new life together, when she returns to Sicily bringing fertility through her marriage to the prince.

49. For other contexts, many of them speculative, see Richard Abrams, '"The Name of Prosper": A Philological Engagement', *Review of English Studies*, 66 (2015), 258–79.

50. 'Defining the Anthropocene', *Nature*, 519 (12 March 2015), 171–80.

51. 'Defining the Anthropocene', 177. For a challenge see Jan Zalasiewicz and others, 'Disputed Start Dates for Anthropocene', *Nature*, 520 (23 April 2015), 436.

52. Harriot, *Briefe and True Report*, 'The ground being thus set according to the rate by vs experimented' (15), 'all which I haue before spoken of, haue bin discouered and experimented not far from the sea coast where was our abode' (31); Council for Virginia, *True Declaration*, 'Our transported Cattell, as Horses, Kine, Hogs, and Goats, do thriue most happily: which is confirmed by a double experiment' (30), 'The like experiment was long since in the regiment of *Sir Raph Lane*, . . . To close vp this part with *Sir Thomas Gates* his experiment: he professeth, that in a fortnights space he recouered the health of most of them by moderat labour, whose sicknesse was bred in them by intemperate idlenes' (32–3).

53. Quoting Q1, *A Midsommer Nights Dreame* (1600), B4v.

54. Cornelius Agrippa, *Of the Vanitie and Vncertaintie of Artes and Sciences*, tr. James Sanford (1569), 55.

55. *The Tempest, An Opera: Taken from Shakespeare* (1756).

56. Sir Francis Bacon, *Sylua Syluarum* (1627), g3r–v, at g3v.

57. See e.g. the Father of Salomon's House in Bacon, *New Atlantis*, 27: '*We have also* Great *and spacious* Houses, *where we imitate and demonstrate* Meteors; *As* Snow, Hail, Rain, *some* Artificial Rains *of* Bodies, *and not of* Water, Thunders, Lightnings.'

58. J. Donald Hughes, 'Theophrastus as Ecologist', *Environmental Review*, 9 (1985), 296–307, pp. 302–3.

59. See e.g. Sarah Irving, *Natural Science and the Origins of the British Empire* (2008; London: Routledge, 2016).

60. Richard H. Grove, *Green Imperialism: Colonial Expansion, Tropical Island Edens, and the Origins of Environmentalism, 1600–1860* (Cambridge: Cambridge University Press, 1995), 3.

61. See e.g. John Wilson Spargo, *Virgil the Necromancer: Studies in Virgilian Legends* (Cambridge, Mass.: Harvard University Press, 1934); David Scott Wilson-Okamura, *Virgil in the Renaissance* (Cambridge: Cambridge University Press, 2010), ch. 3.

62. For Geraldo U. de Sousa, 'Alien Habitats in *The Tempest*', in Patrick M. Murphy, ed., *The Tempest: Critical Essays* (London: New York, 2001), 439–62, the woodpile is evidence of 'a *feitoria* . . . dedicated to logging and the export of timber' (448); Gabriel Egan, *Green Shakespeare: From Ecopolitics to Ecocriticism* (Abingdon: Routledge, 2006), sees the clearing of trees as a step towards plantation, as in Ireland (157); Randall Martin, *Shakespeare and Ecology* (Oxford: Oxford University Press, 2015), argues that Prospero is engaged in glass-making (41–3); Vin Nardizzi, ingeniously, suggests that

the logs are being 'stockpiled' for 'the building of a theatre' but that they also have their uses in 'Energy, Murder, and Trothplight' (*Wooden Os: Shakespeare's Theatres and England's Trees* [Toronto: University of Toronto Press, 2013], ch. 4).

63. See *OED*, vein, *n.*, 7, 'A deposit of metallic or earthy material having an extended or ramifying course underground; a seam or lode; *spec.* a continuous crack or fissure filled with matter (esp. metallic ore) different from the containing rock' (from late 14C).

64. On '*Iron oare*' along with '*abundance of Wood*', see Strachey, 'True Reportory', 1758; Rich, *Newes from Virginia* (B2v).

65. Ludwig Lavater, *Of Ghostes and Spirites Walking by Nyght*, tr. R. H. (1572), 73.

66. See esp. Charlotte Scott, *Shakespeare's Nature: From Cultivation to Culture* (Oxford: Oxford University Press, 2014), ch. 6.

67. The key source, by general agreement, is Kenelm Digby's atomistic disquisition, *A Late Discourse ... Touching the Cure of Wounds by the Powder of Sympathy* (1658), with its epigraph from *Georgics*, II.490, 'Foelix qui potuit *Rerum* cognoscere *causas*' ('Happy the Man, who, studying Nature's Laws, | Thro' known Effects can trace the secret Cause', in *The Works of Virgil*, tr. Dryden [1697], 92) and its invocation of Bacon on sympathetic magic (4–5) in *Sylva Sylvarum*, 264–5. Cf. Seth Lobis, *The Virtue of Sympathy: Magic, Philosophy, and Literature in Seventeenth-Century England* (New Haven: Yale University Press, 2015), ch. 1.

68. On these measures and their context see Markku Peltonen, *The Duel in Early Modern England: Civility, Politeness and Honour* (Cambridge: Cambridge University Press, 2002), 203–8.

69. Thomas Shadwell, *The Tempest: Or, The Enchanted Island* (1674), 77–81.

70. Garrick, *Tempest*, 47.

71. Shadwell, *Tempest*, 14, 26, 31, 37, 57; Garrick, *Tempest*, 12, 21, 28.

72. Davenant and Dryden, *Enchanted Island*, 39, 55.

73. *OED*, cultivate, *v.*, 3 (? 1631); cultivated, *adj.*, 3 a (1645), 3 b (1653).

74. *OED*, cultivation, *n.*, esp. 4 b (from 1662), 'The action of being cultivated; culture, refinement.'

75. *An Account of the English Dramatick Poets* (1691), 18.

76. *The Invention of Improvement: Information and Material Progress in Seventeenth-Century England* (Oxford: Oxford University Press, 2015).

77. *The Tempest*, 1.2.340; John Crowne, *Henry the Sixth* [also *The Misery of Civil War*] (1681), prologue (A2r) and dedication 'To Sir Charles Sidley' (A3r–4v, at A3v). Cf. the prologue to Thomas Otway, *The History and Fall of Caius Marius* (1680): 'And from the Crop of his luxuriant Pen | E're since succeeding Poets humbly glean' (A3r).

78. John Dennis, *The Invader of His Country: Or, The Fatal Resentment* (1720).

79. Arthur Murphy, 'Shakespeare vindicated, in a letter to Voltaire' (*Gray's-Inn Journal*, 1753), in *Shakespeare: The Critical Heritage*, ed. Brian Vickers, 6 vols (London: Routledge, 1974–81), IV, 90–4, p. 94.

80. *The Works of Shakespear*, ed. Alexander Pope, 6 vols (1725), I, ii.

81. Peter Whalley, *An Enquiry into the Learning of Shakespeare* (1748), excerpted in *Shakespeare: Critical Heritage*, ed. Vickers, III, 271–89, p. 281.

82. 'An Oration in Honour of Shakespeare', intended to be spoken by Garrick at the 1769 Jubilee, in *Shakespeare: Critical Heritage*, ed. Vickers, V, 355–60, p. 357.

83. *Lectures 1808–1819: On Literature*, ed. R. A. Foakes, 2 vols, in *The Collected Works of Samuel Taylor Coleridge*, ed. Kathleen Coburn, 5 (London: Routledge, 1987), II, 147–9; also, 'On Poesy or Art', in *The Literary Remains of Samuel Taylor Coleridge*, ed. Henry Nelson Coleridge, Vol. I (London: William Pickering, 1836), 216–30, p. 222.

84. See esp. Akenside's 'Hymn to Science'. In Thomson's *The Seasons* (1746), Shakespeare follows Boyle and Newton in a list of British and Irish worthies modelled on a passage in the *Georgics* praising those of Italy; Boyle's search for God 'Amid the dark Recesses of his Works' anticipates Shakespeare's 'Inspection keen | Thro the deep Windings of the human Heart' (115).

85. Nahum Tate, 'To Edward Tayler Esq', in *The Loyal General* (1680), A2r–5v, at A5r.

86. Christopher Smart, 'An Occasional Prologue and Epilogue to *Othello . . .* 1751', in his *Poems on Several Occasions* (1752), 216–19, p. 217.

87. 'The art itself is nature', says Polixenes in *The Winter's Tale*, 4.4.97, on grafting.

88. Hazlitt's Caliban, resembling 'the God Pan . . . in contact with the pure and original forms of nature . . . uncouth and wild' is one outcome of this trend; see his *Characters of Shakespear's Plays* (London: R. Hunter, C. and J. Ollier, 1817), 118.

89. Charles Gildon, 'An Essay on the Art, Rise and Progress of the Stage in Greece, Rome and England' (1710), excerpted in *Shakespeare: Critical Heritage*, ed. Vickers, II, 216–26, p. 220.

90. William Guthrie, *An Essay upon English Tragedy* (1747), excerpted in *Shakespeare: Critical Heritage*, ed. Vickers, III, 191–205, pp. 194–5.

91. The conceit starts with Dryden on Caliban, 'He seems there to have created a person which was not in Nature', 'Grounds of Criticism in Tragedy', in his *Troilus and Cressida*, b1r. Cf. e.g. Guthrie, *Essay upon English Tragedy*, excerpted in *Shakespeare: Critical Heritage*, ed. Vickers, III, 195: 'Nature never created a Caliban till Shakespeare introduced the monster, and we now take him to be nature's composition.'

92. *Works of Shakespear*, ed. Pope and Warburton, I, 3.

93. 'L'Allegro', here quoting *The Poetical Works of Mr John Milton*, 2 vols (1705), II, 192–9, p. 198. For *The Tempest* in relation to this see e.g. William Collins, *Verses Humbly Address'd to Sir Thomas Hanmer. On his Edition of Shakespeare's Works* (1743), in *Shakespeare: Critical Heritage*, ed. Vickers, III, 113–17, esp. 116 ('and Spring diffusive decks th' *enchanted Isle*'), and Joseph

Warton, *The Enthusiast: Or, The Lover of Nature* (1744), on '*Shakespear*'s
Warblings wild': 'Whom on the winding *Avon*'s willow'd Banks | Fair
Fancy found, . . . ' (12–13).

94. *The Tempest*, 5.1.41–2; Thomas Seward, 'Preface', in *The Works of
Mr Francis Beaumont and Mr John Fletcher*, ed. Lewis Theobald, Thomas
Seward, and Sidrach Sympson, 10 vols (1750), I, v–lxxvi, p. lii.

95. For a Shakespeare/Ossian comparison, presided over by Ariel, see John
Ogilvie, *Solitude: Or, The Elysium of the Poets, A Vision* (1765), 24–8.

96. *An Essay on Original Genius* (1767), 265 (Homer, Ossian, and Shakespeare),
294.

97. See e.g. the sweep of Garrick's 'An Ode upon Dedicating a Building,
and Erecting a Statue, to Shakespeare, at Stratford upon Avon', in
Testimonies to the Genius and Merits of Shakespeare (1769): '*When Nature, smiling,
hail'd his birth, | To him unbounded pow'r was given; | The whirlwind's wing to
sweep the sky*' (4).

98. Maurice Morgann, *An Essay on the Dramatic Character of Sir John Falstaff*
(1777), 70–1.

99. Charles Churchill, *The Rosciad* (1761), 7.

100. The motif becomes familiar, in depictions of 'our *Magician*'—according
to Garrick at the Stratford Jubilee—'inspir'd, | By charms, and spells'
('Ode upon Dedicating a Building', 7).

101. On changing legal attitudes, and their (at most, indirect) relationship to
this shift, see Simon Stern, 'Copyright, Originality, and the Public
Domain in Eighteenth-Century England', in Reginald McGinnis, ed.,
Originality and Intellectual Property in the French and English Enlightenment (New
York: Routledge, 2009), 69–101.

102. From *The Adventurer*, 93 and 97 (1753), in *Shakespeare: Critical Heritage*, ed.
Vickers, IV, 60–8.

103. Elizabeth Robinson Montagu, *An Essay on the Writings and Genius of
Shakespear* (1769), 169.

104. *Ars poetica*, lines 125–7, in Horace, *Satires, Epistles, Art of Poetry*, ed. and tr.
H. R. Fairclough, Loeb Classical Library (Cambridge MA: Harvard
University Press, 1926), 'si quid inexpertum scaenae committis et audes
| personam formare novam, servetur ad imum, | qualis ab incepto
processerit, et sibi constet' ('If it is an untried theme you entrust to the
stage, and if you boldly fashion a fresh character, have it kept to the end
even as it came forth at the first, and have it self-consistent'). Meanwhile,
'great difficulty and hazard' overstates the challenge of making it new
(lines 128–30): 'tuque | rectius Iliacum carmen deducis in actus, | quam
si proferres ignota indictaque primus', 'you are doing better in spinning
into acts a song of Troy than if, for the first time, you were giving the
world a theme unknown and unsung.'

105. Charles Gildon, 'Remarks on the Plays of Shakespear', excerpted in
Shakespeare: Critical Heritage, ed. Vickers, II, 226–36.

106. *Coleridge's Shakespeare Criticism*, ed. T. M. Raysor, 2 vols, 2nd edn (London: Dent, 1960), II, 253. Cf. I, 119, where Prospero is 'the very Shakspeare himself, as it were, of the tempest'.

107. On this oft-noted, mid-century turn see e.g. Jean I. Marsden, *The Re-Imagined Text: Shakespeare, Adaptation, and Eighteenth-Century Literary Theory* (Lexington: University Press of Kentucky, 1995), 4, 76–8.

108. 'Free Remarks on the Tragedy of *Romeo and Juliet*', from *The Student*, 2 (1750), reprinted in *Shakespeare: Critical Heritage*, ed. Vickers, III, 374–9, esp. pp. 375–6. Cf. his 1757 regret at the cutting of *1 Henry IV* (IV, 275), his disapproval of Otway's alteration of *Romeo and Juliet* (while approving of Garrick's substitution [276–7], as he does his revision of *The Winter's Tale* [289]), and his 1758 attack on *Coriolanus* at Covent Garden, with the first two acts by Shakespeare and the other three by Thomson (IV, 349–50).

109. Anon., *Miscellaneous Observations on the Tragedy of Hamlet* (1752), excerpted in *Shakespeare: Critical Heritage*, ed. Vickers, III, 452–61, pp 454–5.

110. Garrick, *Tempest*, prelims.

111. *Shakespeare: Critical Heritage*, ed. Vickers, IV, 245, 252 (cf. 256).

112. At the Theatre Royal, Drury Lane, 20 October 1757. *The Tempest* would reincorporate elements of *The Enchanted Island* under Kemble, also at Drury Lane, in 1789, and at Covent Garden, in 1806; but after Garrick's revival of 1757, and even more durably after Macready's production of 1838, the Folio text prevailed. For a socio-political contextualization of Kemble's 'relapse', see Michael Dobson, ' "Remember First to Possess his Books": The Appropriation of *The Tempest*, 1700–1800', *Shakespeare Survey*, 43 (1991), 99–107, p. 106.

113. 'Many original Passages of the first Merit are still retained, and in the Contemplation of them, my errors, I hope, will be overlooked or forgiven: In examining the Brilliancy of a Diamond, few People throw away any Remarks upon the Dullness of the foil' (author's 'Advertisement', in Richard Cumberland, *Timon of Athens, Altered from Shakespeare* [1771]).

114. The process starts as early as *The Works of Shakespeare*, ed. Lewis Theobald, 7 vols (1733), though advances are anticipated in Johnson's *Proposals* (1756) and realized in his edition of *The Plays of William Shakespeare*, 8 vols (1765). *The Tempest* had a role in this return to original texts because editors who reacted against e.g. Pope's rejection of dialogue which he thought '*interpolated, (perhaps by the* Players*) . . . impertinent . . . ill plac'd Drollery*' (*Works of Shakespear*, ed. Pope, I, 25–7) found themselves dealing with a Folio-only play remarkably free of textual problems.

115. Emendations made by adapters from Tate to Garrick were taken up by such editors as Johnson, Capell, and Steevens; contrariwise, Steevens, contending that 'Shakespeare was always adding, without the least consideration whether his additions were consistently made or not',

encouraged Garrick to alter *Hamlet* (*Shakespeare: Critical Heritage*, ed. Vickers, V, 456–9, quoting p. 458).

116. An editor was often called a 'reviser' and an emendation an 'alteration', much as adapters could be called 'editors'; for some detail, and context, see Paulina Kewes, '"[A] Play, Which I Presume to Call *Original*": Appropriation, Creative Genius, and Eighteenth-Century Playwriting', *Studies in the Literary Imagination*, 34 (2001), 17–47, pp. 20–1; on editing and alteration, see Thomas Edwards, *The Canons of Criticism* (1750), excerpted in *Shakespeare: Critical Heritage*, ed. Vickers, III, 390–419, p. 391.

117. For a sampler, highlighting *The Tempest*, and satirical about the 'sacred rage of correcting!', see George Steevens' review of Benjamin Heath, *A Revisal of Shakespeare's Text* (1765), in *Shakespeare: Critical Heritage*, ed. Vickers, IV, 565–73.

118. Thus, in Steevens' astute review of Heath (just noted), the Folio reading 'twilled' is defended against emendation to 'tulip'd' or 'lilied' on the polite, misplaced grounds that 'the operation of *twilling*' produces 'the beautiful borders... on the damask and fine linen' of tablecloths, while among alternative readings F's '"*pole-clipt* vineyard"' ought to stand as being the most poetical, and signifying the vineyard whose poles are embraced by vines'—another correct conclusion but one ignorant of fencing (569).

119. [Samuel Johnson], 'To the Right Honourable John, Earl of Orrery', in Lennox, *Shakespear Illustrated*, I, ix–xi.

120. William Richardson, *Essays on Shakespeare's Dramatic Characters of Richard the Third, King Lear, and Timon of Athens. To which are added, an Essay on the Faults of Shakespeare and Additional Observations on the Character of Hamlet* (1784).

121. Thomas Warton, *The History of English Poetry*, 4 vols (1774), III, 484; cf. Kewes, '"[A] Play"', 32.

122. Robert Lloyd, *Shakespeare: An Epistle to Mr Garrick* [1760]), *Shakespeare: Critical Heritage*, ed. Vickers, IV, 419–23, p. 423.

123. Martin Sherlock, *A Fragment on Shakespeare* (1786), excerpted in *Shakespeare: Critical Heritage*, ed. Vickers, VI, 435–9, p. 436.

124. *Q. Horatii Flacci. Ars Poetica. Epistola ad Pisones*, ed. Richard Hurd (1749), 68.

125. *Q. Horatii Flacci. Epistola ad Augustum*, ed. Richard Hurd (1751), 120–1.

126. 'Drury-Lane, Feb. 17. 1757', in *Shakespeare: Critical Heritage*, ed. Vickers, IV, 278–9, p. 278. Murphy's promptness to compare plays with (alleged or actual) source material in other notices he wrote over this period— *Romeo and Juliet*, 'founded upon an Italian Novel, by Bandello' (276), *Hamlet* 'formed upon the story of Amleth in... Saxo-Grammaticus' (277), *Henry VIII* (Holinshed), *Measure for Measure*, 'from an Italian Narrative in Cinthio's Novels' (284), *The Winter's Tale*, 'from the old Story of Dorastus and Fawnia' [Greene's *Pandosto*] (287)—confirms that Lennox's *Shakespear Illustrated* (to which he explicitly refers his reader [277]),

though not widely written about, was influencing the questions asked by
the thoughtful.

127. William Duff, *Critical Observations on the Writings of the Most Celebrated Original Geniuses in Poetry* (1770), 127.

128. *Love's Labour's Lost*, New Penguin Shakespeare (Harmondsworth: Penguin, 1982), 11.

Select Bibliography

Shakespeare and Drama

Anon., *The True Tragedie of Richard the Third* (1594).

Anon., *The True Chronicle History of King Leir, and His Three Daughters* (1605).

Anon., *The Three Parnassus Plays (1598–1601)*, ed. J. B. Leishman (London: Ivor Nicholson & Watson, 1949).

Beckett, Samuel, *Footfalls* (London: Faber, 1976).

Bond, Edward, *Lear* (London: Eyre Methuen, 1972).

Davenant, Sir William and John Dryden, *The Tempest: Or, The Enchanted Island* (1670).

Della Porta, Giambattista, *Gli duoi fratelli rivali* (Venice, 1601).

Euripides, *Tragoediae XVIII* (Basel, 1541).

Euripides, *Euripides poeta tragicorum princeps*, ed. and tr. Gasparus Stiblinus (Basel, 1562).

Euripides, *Helen, Phoenician Women, Orestes*, ed. and tr. David Kovacs, Loeb Classical Library (Cambridge, MA: Harvard University Press, 2002).

Fletcher, John, *The Sea Voyage*, in Francis Beaumont and John Fletcher, *Comedies and Tragedies* (1647).

Garrick, David, *The Tempest, An Opera: Taken from Shakespeare* (1756).

Gascoigne, George and Francis Kinwelmarsh, *Iocasta: A Tragedie Written in Greke by Euripides* (1573), in George Gascoigne, *A Hundreth Sundrie Flowres* (1573).

The Geneva Bible: A Facsimile of the 1560 Edition, introd. Lloyd E. Berry (Peabody, MA: Hendrickson, 2007).

Greene, Robert, *The Historie of Orlando Furioso, One of the Twelue Peeres of France* (1594).

Jonson, Ben, *Sejanus His Fall* (1605).

Jonson, Ben, *The Workes of Beniamin Ionson* (1616).

Jonson, Ben, *The Workes of Benjamin Jonson* (1641).

Kemp, William, *Kemps Nine Daies Wonder, Performed in a Daunce from London to Norwich* (1600).

Legge, Thomas, *Richardus Tertius* (1579), ed. Dana F. Sutton, <http://www.philological.bham.ac.uk/rich/>.

Marlowe, Christopher, *The Complete Works of Christopher Marlowe*, gen. ed. Roma Gill, 5 vols (Oxford: Oxford University Press, 1987–98).

Milton, John, *Samson Agonistes*, in *Paradise Regain'd . . . to which is added Samson Agonistes* (1671).

Munday, Anthony, *Fedele and Fortunio: The Deceites in Loue* (1585).

Norton, Thomas and Thomas Sackville, *The Tragedie of Gorboduc* (1565).

Pasqualigo, Luigi, *Il fedele* (Venice, 1576).

Seneca, Lucius Annaeus, *The Eyght Tragedie of Seneca, entituled Agamemnon*, tr. John Studley (1566).

Seneca, Lucius Annaeus, *The Seuenth Tragedie of Seneca, entituled Medea*, tr. John Studley (1566).

Seneca, Lucius Annaeus, *Thebais*, tr. Thomas Newton, in *Seneca his Tenne Tragedies, translated into Englysh*, ed. Newton (1581).

Seneca, Lucius Annaeus, *Tragedies*, ed. and tr. John G. Fitch, 2 vols, Loeb Classical Library (Cambridge, MA: Harvard University Press, 2002).

Shadwell, Thomas, *The Tempest: Or, The Enchanted Island* (1674).

Shakespeare, William, *A Midsommer Nights Dreame* (1600).

Shakespeare, William, *True Chronicle Historie of the Life and Death of King Lear and his Three Daughters* (1608).

Shakespeare, William, *Mr William Shakespeares Comedies, Histories, and Tragedies* (1623).

Shakespeare, William, *The Works of Mr William Shakespear*, ed. Nicholas Rowe, 6 vols (1709).

Shakespeare, William, *The Works of Shakespear*, ed. Alexander Pope, 6 vols (1725).

Shakespeare, William, *The Plays of William Shakespeare*, ed. Samuel Johnson, 8 vols (1765).

Shakespeare, William, *Love's Labour's Lost*, ed. John Kerrigan, New Penguin Shakespeare (Harmondsworth: Penguin, 1982).

Shakespeare, William, *The Norton Shakespeare*, gen. ed. Stephen Greenblatt (New York: Norton, 1997).

Shakespeare, William, *The Oxford Shakespeare, Complete Works*, 2nd edn, gen. eds Stanley Wells and Gary Taylor (Oxford: Oxford University Press, 2005), electronic edition.

Shakespeare, William, *King Richard III*, ed. James R. Siemon, Arden Shakespeare (London: Methuen, 2009).

Shakespeare, William, *The Tempest*, ed. Virginia Mason Vaughan and Alden T. Vaughan, Arden Shakespeare, rev. edn (London: Bloomsbury, 2011).

Shakespeare, William, *The Tempest*, ed. David Lindley, New Cambridge Shakespeare, rev. edn (Cambridge: Cambridge University Press, 2013).

Shakespeare, William, *Much Ado About Nothing*, ed. Claire McEachern, Arden Shakespeare, rev. edn (London: Bloomsbury, 2016).

Sophocles, *Sophoclis Tragoediæ VII., ex aduerso respondet Latina interpretatio*, tr. Vitus Winsemius (Heidelberg, 1597).

Sophocles, *Ajax, Electra, Oedipus Tyrannus*, ed. and tr. Hugh Lloyd-Jones, Loeb Classical Library (Cambridge, MA: Harvard University Press, 1994).

Sophocles, *Antigone, Women of Trachis, Philoctetes, Oedipus at Colonus*, ed. and tr. Hugh Lloyd-Jones, Loeb Classical Library (Cambridge, MA: Harvard University Press, 1994).

Tomkis, Thomas, *Lingua: Or, The Combat of the Tongue, and the Fiue Senses for Superiority* (1607).

Webster, John, *The Works of John Webster: An Old-Spelling Critical Edition*, ed. David Gunby et al., 3 vols (Cambridge: Cambridge University Press, 1995–2007).

Other Primary Sources

Agrippa, Cornelius, *Of the Vanitie and Vncertaintie of Artes and Sciences*, tr. James Sanford (1569).

Andrewes, Lancelot, *Apospasmatia Sacra: Or, A Collection of Posthumous and Orphan Lectures* (1657).

Ariosto, Ludovico, *Orlando Furioso*, tr. Sir John Harington (1591).

Aristotle, *Poetics*, in *Aristotle, 'Poetics', Longinus, 'On the Sublime', Demetrius, 'On Style'*, ed. and tr. Stephen Halliwell et al., Loeb Classical Library (Cambridge, MA: Harvard University Press, 1995).

B., R., *Greenes Funeralls* (1594).

Bacon, Sir Francis, *Aduancement of Learning* (1605).

Bacon, Sir Francis, *The Essaies of Sir Francis Bacon*, enlarged edn (1612).

Bacon, Sir Francis, *The Essayes or Counsels, Ciuill and Morall*, rev. edn (1625).

Bacon, Sir Francis, *Sylua Syluarum* (1627).

Bacon, Sir Francis, *New Atlantis* (1658).

Baldwin, William, *A Myrrour for Magistrates* (1563).

Beverley, Peter, *The Historie of Ariodanto and Ieneura* (1575).

Boydell, John and Josiah, *A Collection of Prints, from Pictures Painted for the Purpose of Illustrating the Dramatic Works of Shakespeare* (London: John and Josiah Boydell, Shakspeare Gallery, 1803).

Brathwait, Richard, *The English Gentleman* (1630).

Brathwait, Richard, *The English Gentlewoman* (1631).

Brumoy, Pierre, *The Greek Theatre of Father Brumoy*, tr. Charlotte Lennox, 3 vols (1759).

Bullough, Geoffrey, *Narrative and Dramatic Sources of Shakespeare*, 8 vols (London: Routledge & Kegan Paul, 1957–75).

Capell, Edward, *Reflections on Originality in Authors* (1766).

Capell, Edward, *Notes and Various Readings to Shakespeare*, 3 vols ([1774], 1779–83).

Castiglione, Baldassare, *The Courtyer of Count Baldessar Castilio*, tr. Thomas Hoby (1561).

Cervantes, Miguel de, *The History of the Valorous and Wittie Knight-errant, Don-Quixote of the Mancha ... The First Parte*, tr. Thomas Shelton (1612).

Cervantes, Miguel de, *The Second Part of the History of the Valorous and Witty Knight-errant, Don Quixote of the Mançha*, tr. Thomas Shelton (1620).

Chettle, Henry, *Kind-Harts Dreame* (1592).

Churchill, Charles, *The Rosciad* (1761).

Cicero, Marcus Tullius, *De senectute, De amicitia, De divinatione*, ed. and tr. William Armistead Falconer, Loeb Classical Library (Cambridge, MA: Harvard University Press, 1923).

Cleland, James, *Hero-paideia: Or, The Institution of a Young Noble Man* (1607).

Coleridge, Samuel Taylor, *Lectures 1808–1819: On Literature*, ed. R. A. Foakes, 2 vols, in *The Collected Works of Samuel Taylor Coleridge*, ed. Kathleen Coburn, 5 (London: Routledge, 1987).

Collier, John Payne, *Shakespeare's Library: A Collection of the Romances, Novels, Poems, and Histories, Used by Shakespeare as the Foundation of his Dramas*, 2 vols (London: Thomas Rodd, 1843).

Cornwallis, William, *Discourses vpon Seneca the Tragedian* (1601).

Council for Virginia, *A True Declaration of the Estate of the Colonie in Virginia* (1610).

Digby, Kenelm, *Two Treatises* (Paris, 1644).

Digby, Kenelm, *A Late Discourse . . . Touching the Cure of Wounds by the Powder of Sympathy* (1658).

Digges, Leonard, 'Vpon Master William Shakespeare', in *Poems: Written by Wil. Shake-speare* (1640), *3r–4r.

Douce, Francis, *Illustrations of Shakspeare, and of Ancient Manners* (London: Longman, Hurst, Rees, and Orme, 1807).

Douglas, John, *Milton Vindicated from the Charge of Plagiarism, Brought Against him by Mr Lauder* (1750).

Dryden, John, *Of Dramatick Poesie: An Essay* (1668).

Dryden, John, 'Preface' and 'The Grounds of Criticism in Tragedy', in his *Troilus and Cressida: Or, Truth Found too Late* (1679), A4v–b3v.

Duff, William, *An Essay on Original Genius* (1767).

Duff, William, *Critical Observations on the Writings of the Most Celebrated Original Geniuses in Poetry* (1770).

Earle, John, *Micro-cosmographie* (1628).

Emerson, Ralph Waldo, 'Shakspeare, or the Poet', in *The Collected Works of Ralph Waldo Emerson*, Vol. IV, *Representative Men: Seven Lectures*, ed. Douglas Emory Wilson (Cambridge, MA: Harvard University Press, 1987), 109–25.

Emerson, Ralph Waldo, 'Quotation and Originality', in *The Collected Works of Ralph Waldo Emerson*, Vol. VIII, *Letters and Social Aims*, ed. Joel Myerson (Cambridge, MA: Harvard University Press, 2010), 93–107.

Evelyn, John, *Sylva: Or, A Discourse of Forest-Trees* (1664).

Farmer, Richard, *An Essay on the Learning of Shakespeare* (1767).

Garrick, David, *An Essay on Acting . . . To which Will be Added, A Short Criticism on his Acting Macbeth* (1744).

Gosson, Stephen, *The School of Abuse* (1579).

Gosson, Stephen, *Playes Confuted in Fiue Actions* (1582).

Greene, Robert, *The Myrrour of Modestie* (1584).

Greene, Robert, *Pandosto: The Triumph of Time* (1588).

Greene, Robert, *Francescos Fortunes: Or, The Second Part of Greenes Neuer too Late* (1590).

Greene, Robert, *Greenes Groatsworth of Witte* (1592).

Greene, Robert, *A Quip for an Vpstart Courtier: Or, A Quaint Dispute Between Veluet Breeches and Cloth-Breeches* (1592).

Harriot, Thomas, *A Briefe and True Report of the New Found Land of Virginia*, rev. edn (1590).

Harsnett, Samuel, *A Declaration of Egregious Popish Impostures* (1603).

Hazlitt, William, '[On Genius and Common Sense:] The Same Subject Continued', in his *Table Talk: Or, Original Essays* (London: John Warren, 1821), 93–111.

Hazlitt, William Carew, *Shakespeare's Library: A Collection of the Plays, Romances, Novels, Poems, and Histories Employed by Shakespeare in the Composition of his Works*, 6 vols (London: Reeves and Turner, 1875).

Heliodorus of Emesa, *An Æthiopian Historie written in Greeke by Heliodorus*, tr. Thomas Underdown (1569).

Heminge, John and Henry Condell, 'To the Great Variety of Readers', in *Shakespeares Comedies, Histories, and Tragedies* (1623), A3r.

Heywood, Thomas, *An Apology for Actors* (1612).

Hill, Thomas, *The Contemplation of Mankinde Contayning a Singuler Discourse after the Art of Phisiognomie* (1571).

The Holie Bible [Bishops' Bible, rev. edn] (1572).

Holinshed, Raphael, *The First and Second Volumes of Chronicles*, 2nd edn (1587).

Horace, *Satires, Epistles, The Art of Poetry*, ed. and tr. H. Rushton Fairclough, Loeb Classical Library (Cambridge, MA: Harvard University Press, 1926).

Isidore of Seville, *The Etymologies of Isidore of Seville*, tr. Stephen A. Barney et al. (Cambridge: Cambridge University Press, 2006).

Johnson, Robert, *Nova Britannia* (1609).

[Johnson, Samuel], 'To the Right Honourable John, Earl of Orrery', in Lennox, *Shakespear Illustrated* (1753–4), I, iii–xii.

Jonson, Ben, 'To the Memory of my Beloued, the Author Mr William Shakespeare: and What He Hath Left Vs', in *Shakespeares Comedies, Histories, and Tragedies* (1623), A4r–v.

Jonson, Ben, *Timber: Or, Discoveries*, in *The Workes of Benjamin Jonson* (1641), 85–132.

Jourdain, Silvester, *A Discovery of the Barmudas, Otherwise Called the Ile of Diuels* (1610).

King, Henry, *Poems, Elegies, Paradoxes, and Sonets* (1664).

Langbaine, Gerard, *Momus Triumphans: Or, The Plagiaries of the English Stage Expos'd* (1687).

Langbaine, Gerard, *An Account of the English Dramatick Poets* (1691).

Lavater, Ludwig, *Of Ghostes and Spirites Walking by Nyght*, tr. R. H. (1572).

Lennox, Charlotte, *Shakespear Illustrated: Or, The Novels and Histories, On which the Plays of Shakespeare are Founded*, 3 vols (1753–4).

Lennox, Charlotte, *The Female Quixote: Or, The Adventures of Arabella*, ed. Margaret Dalziel, introd. Margaret Anne Doody (Oxford: Oxford University Press, 1989).

L'Estrange, Sir Roger, *Lestrange's Narrative of the Plot* (1680).

Lodge, Thomas, *Rosalynde: Euphues Golden Legacie* (1592).

Lodge, Thomas, *Lodge's 'Rosalynde', Being the Original of Shakespeare's 'As You Like It'*, ed. W. W. Greg (London: Chatto & Windus, 1907).

Lucretius Carus, Titus, *De rerum natura*, ed. and tr. W. H. D. Rouse, rev. Martin Ferguson, Loeb Classical Library (Cambridge, MA: Harvard University Press, 1992).

Montagu, Elizabeth Robinson, *An Essay on the Writings and Genius of Shakespear* (1769).

150 *Select Bibliography*

Montaigne, Michel de, *The Essayes*, tr. John Florio (1603).

More, Thomas, *The History of King Richard III/ Historia Richardi Tertii*, in *The Complete Works of St Thomas More*, ed. Richard S. Sylvester et al., 15 vols (New Haven: Yale University Press, 1963–97), Vols II and XV.

Morgann, Maurice, *An Essay on the Dramatic Character of Sir John Falstaff* (1777).

Nashe, Thomas, 'To the Gentlemen Students of both Uniuersities', in Robert Greene, *Menaphon* (1589), **1r-A3r.

Ovid, *The XV Bookes of P. Ouidius Naso, entytuled Metamorphosis*, tr. Arthur Golding (1567).

Ovid, *Metamorphoses*, tr. Frank Justus Miller, rev. G. P. Goold, 2 vols, Loeb Classical Library (Cambridge, MA: Harvard University Press, 2014).

Pilkington, James, attrib., 'An Homyly against Excesse of Apparell', in John Jewel, *The Seconde Tome of Homelyes* (1563), fols 112v–121r.

Plat, Sir Hugh, *The New and Admirable Arte of Setting of Corne: With all the Necessarie Tooles and other Circumstances belonging to the Same* (1600).

Plat, Sir Hugh, *Floraes Paradise Beautified and Adorned with Sundry Sorts of Delicate Fruites and Flowers* (1608).

Plutarch, *The Lives of the Noble Grecians and Romanes*, tr. Thomas North (1579).

Prynne, William, *The Vnlouelinesse of Loue-lockes* (1628).

Puttenham, George, *The Arte of English Poesie* (1589).

Quintilian, Marcus Fabius, *Institutio oratoria*, ed. and tr. Donald A. Russell, Loeb Classical Library, 5 vols (Cambridge, MA: Harvard University Press, 2001).

Rich, Richard, *Newes from Virginia* (1610).

Richardson, William, *Essays on Shakespeare's Dramatic Characters of Richard the Third, King Lear, and Timon of Athens. To which are added, an Essay on the Faults of Shakespeare and Additional Observations on the Character of Hamlet* (1784).

Riche, Barnabe, *My Ladies Looking Glasse* (1616).

Rowlands, Samuel, *Humors Ordinarie* (1605).

Scot, Reginald, *The Discouerie of Witchcraft* (1584).

Sidney, Philip, *An Apology for Poetry*, ed. Geoffrey Shepherd, 3rd edn rev. by R. W. Maslen (Manchester: Manchester University Press, 2002).

Sidney, Philip, *The Countesse of Pembrokes Arcadia* (1590).

Statius, *Thebaid, Books 1–7*, ed. and tr. D. R. Shackleton Bailey, Loeb Classical Library (Cambridge, MA: Harvard University Press, 2003).

Statius, *Thebaid, Books 8–12, Achilleid*, ed. and tr. D. R. Shackleton Bailey, Loeb Classical Library (Cambridge, MA: Harvard University Press, 2003).

Stephens, John, *Satyrical Essayes, Characters and Others* (1615).

Strachey, William, 'A true reportory of the wracke, and redemption of Sir *Thomas Gates* Knight; vpon, and from the Ilands of the *Bermudas*: his comming to *Virginia*, and the estate of that Colonie then, and after, vnder the gouernment of the Lord *La Warre*, Iuly 15. 1610', in Samuel Purchas, *Purchas His Pilgrimes*, 4 vols (1625), IV, 1734–58.

Stubbes, Philip, *The Anatomie of Abuses* (1583).

Taylor, John, *The Nipping and Snipping of Abuses* (1614).

Thomas, Vivien and William Tydeman, eds, *Christopher Marlowe: The Plays and their Sources* (London: Routledge, 1994).

Vecellio, Cesare, *De gli habiti antichi et moderni di diversi parti del mondo* (Venice, 1590).

Vermigli, Peter Martyr, *The Common Places*, tr. Anthonie Marten (1583).

Vickers, Brian, ed., *Shakespeare: The Critical Heritage*, 6 vols (London: Routledge, 1974–81).

Virgil, *The Bucoliks of Publius Virgilius Maro, Together with his Georgiks or Ruralls, Otherwise Called his Husbandrie*, tr. Abraham Fleming (1589).

Virgil, *Eclogues, Georgics, Aeneid I–VI*, ed. and tr. H. R. Fairclough, rev. G. P. Goold, Loeb Classical Library (Cambridge, MA: Harvard University Press, 1999).

Warton, Thomas, *The History of English Poetry*, 4 vols (1774).

Webster, John, attrib., 'An Excellent Actor', in *Sir Thomas Ouerburie his Wife...: Whereunto are Annexed, New Newes and Characters* (1616), M2r–3r.

Wright, C. D., *Cooling Time: An American Poetry Vigil* (Port Townsend, Washington: Copper Canyon Press, 2005).

Yalden, John, *Huperēphanias Musērion: Or, Machiavil Redivivus* (1681).

Young, Edward, *Conjectures on Original Composition*, 2nd edn (1759).

Secondary Sources

Amato, Joseph, *On Foot: A History of Walking* (New York: New York University Press, 2004).

Arnold, Janet, *Patterns of Fashion: The Cut and Construction of Clothes for Men and Women c.1560–1620* (London: Macmillan, 1985).

Artese, Charlotte, *Shakespeare's Folktale Sources* (Newark: University of Delaware Press, 2015).

Bailey, Amanda, '"Monstrous Manner": Style and the Early Modern Theater', *Criticism*, 43 (2001), 249–84.

Baldwin, T. W., *William Shakspere's Small Latine & Lesse Greeke*, 2 vols (Urbana: University of Illinois Press, 1944).

Barthes, Roland, *S/Z*, tr. Richard Howard (New York: Hill and Wang, 1974).

Bataille, Georges, 'Le gros orteil', *Documents*, 6 (November, 1929), 297–302.

Bate, Jonathan, *Shakespeare and Ovid* (Oxford: Clarendon Press, 1993).

Berek, Peter, 'The "Upstart Crow", Aesop's Crow, and Shakespeare as a Reviser', *Shakespeare Quarterly*, 35 (1984), 205–7.

Braden, Gordon, *Renaissance Tragedy and the Senecan Tradition: Anger's Privilege* (New Haven: Yale University Press, 1985).

Bradley, A. C., *Shakespearean Tragedy* (1904; London: Macmillan, 1957).

Brayman Hackel, Heidi, *Reading Material in Early Modern England: Print, Gender, and Literacy* (Cambridge: Cambridge University Press, 2005).

Brook, Peter, *The Empty Space* (1968; Harmondsworth: Penguin, 1972).

Burke, Peter, 'The Renaissance Translator as Go-Between', in Andreas Höfele and Werner von Koppenfels, eds, *Renaissance*

Go-Betweens: Cultural Exchange in Early Modern Europe (Berlin: Walter de Gruyter, 2005), 17–31.

Burrow, Colin, *Shakespeare and Classical Antiquity* (Oxford: Oxford University Press, 2013).

Burrow, Colin, 'Montaignian Moments: Shakespeare and the *Essays*', in Neil Kenny, Richard Scholar, and Wes Williams, eds, *Montaigne in Transit: Essays in Honour of Ian Maclean* (Cambridge: Legenda, 2016), 239–52.

Cave, Terence, *The Cornucopian Text: Problems of Writing in the French Renaissance* (Oxford: Clarendon Press, 1979).

Certeau, Michel de, *The Practice of Everyday Life*, tr. Steven Rendall (Berkeley, CA: University of California Press, 1984).

Clare, Janet, *Shakespeare's Stage Traffic: Imitation, Borrowing and Competition in Renaissance Theatre* (Cambridge: Cambridge University Press, 2014).

Collington, Philip D., '"Stuffed with all honourable virtues": *Much Ado About Nothing* and *The Book of the Courtier*', *Studies in Philology*, 103 (2006), 281–312.

Collins, J. Churton, *Studies in Shakespeare* (Westminster: Archibald Constable and co., 1904).

Crane, Mary Thomas, *Framing Authority: Sayings, Self, and Society in Sixteenth-Century England* (Princeton: Princeton University Press, 1993).

Cunliffe, John W., *The Influence of Seneca on Elizabethan Tragedy* (London: Macmillan, 1893).

Dent, R. W., *Webster's Borrowing* (Berkeley: University of California Press, 1960).

Dessen, Alan C. and Leslie Thomson, eds, *A Dictionary of Stage Directions in English Drama 1580–1642* (Cambridge: Cambridge University Press, 1999).

Dobson, Michael, '"Remember First to Possess his Books": The Appropriation of *The Tempest*, 1700–1800', *Shakespeare Survey*, 43 (1991), 99–107.

Donnellan, Declan, *The Actor and the Target*, rev. edn (London: Nick Hern Books, 2005).

Eliot, T. S., 'Tradition and the Individual Talent', in *The Sacred Wood: Essays on Poetry and Criticism* (1920; London: Methuen, 1950), 47–59.

Fox, Adam, *Oral and Literate Culture in England 1500–1700* (Oxford: Clarendon Press, 2000).

Freud, Sigmund, 'Some Character-Types Met with in Psycho-analytic Work' (1916), in *The Standard Edition of the Complete Psychological Works of Sigmund Freud*, tr. James Strachey et al. (London: Hogarth Press, 1953–74), 24 vols, XIV, 309–33.

Fulton, Hamish, *Wild Life: Walks in the Cairngorms* (Edinburgh: Pocketbooks, 2000).

Gillespie, Stuart, *Shakespeare's Books: A Dictionary of Shakespeare's Sources*, 2nd edn (London: Bloomsbury Arden Shakespeare, 2016).

Gordon, D. J., '*Much Ado About Nothing*: A Possible Source for the Hero-Claudio Plot', *Studies in Philology*, 39 (1942), 279–90.

Greenblatt, Stephen, 'Shakespeare and the Exorcists', in his *Shakespearean Negotiations: The Circulation of Social Energy in Renaissance England* (Oxford: Clarendon Press, 1988), 94–128.

Greene, Roland, 'Invention' in his *Five Words: Critical Semantics in the Age of Shakespeare and Cervantes* (Chicago: University of Chicago Press, 2013), 15–40.

Greene, Thomas M., *The Light in Troy: Imitation and Discovery in Renaissance Poetry* (New Haven: Yale University Press, 1982).

Grove, Richard H., *Green Imperialism: Colonial Expansion, Tropical Island Edens, and the Origins of Environmentalism, 1600–1860* (Cambridge: Cambridge University Press, 1995).

Gurr, Andrew, 'Who Strutted and Bellowed?', *Shakespeare Survey*, 16 (1963), 95–102.

Gurr, Andrew, *The Shakespearian Playing Companies* (Oxford: Clarendon Press, 1996).

Gurr, Andrew, *The Shakespearean Stage 1574–1642*, 4th edn (Cambridge: Cambridge University Press, 2009).

Hammond, Brean S., 'Plagiarism: Hammond versus Ricks on Plagiarism', in Paulina Kewes, ed., *Plagiarism in Early Modern England* (Basingstoke: Palgrave Macmillan, 2003), 41–55.

Harvey, John, 'A Note on Shakespeare and Sophocles', *Essays in Criticism*, 27 (1977), 259–70.

Hutson, Lorna, *The Invention of Suspicion: Law and Mimesis in Shakespeare and Renaissance Drama* (Oxford: Oxford University Press, 2007).

Ingold, Tim and Jo Lee Vergunst, 'Introduction' to Ingold and Vergunst, eds, *Ways of Walking: Ethnography and Practice on Foot* (Aldershot: Ashgate, 2008), 1–19.

Irving, Sarah, *Natural Science and the Origins of the British Empire* (2008; London: Routledge, 2016).

Jardine, Lisa and Anthony Grafton, ' "Studied for Action": How Gabriel Harvey Read his Livy', *Past and Present*, 129 (1990), 30–78.

Javitch, Daniel, 'The Emergence of Poetic Genre Theory in the Sixteenth Century', *Modern Language Quarterly*, 59 (1998), 139–69.

Jones, Emrys, *The Origins of Shakespeare* (Oxford: Clarendon Press, 1977).

Kewes, Paulina, *Authorship and Appropriation: Writing for the Stage in England, 1660–1710* (Oxford: Clarendon Press, 1998).

Kewes, Paulina, ' "[A] Play, Which I Presume to Call *Original*": Appropriation, Creative Genius, and Eighteenth-Century Playwriting', *Studies in the Literary Imagination*, 34 (2001), 17–47.

Knight, Jeffrey Todd, *Bound to Read: Compilations, Collections, and the Making of Renaissance Literature* (Philadelphia: University of Pennsylvania Press, 2013).

Kristeva, Julia, 'Word, Dialogue, and Novel', in her *Desire in Language: A Semiotic Approach to Literature and Art*, ed. Leon S. Roudiez, tr. Thomas Gora, Alice Jardine, and Leon S. Roudiez (Oxford: Blackwell, 1981), 64–91.

Lees-Jeffries, Hester, 'No Country for Old Men? Ciceronian Friendship and Old Age in Shakespeare's Second Tetralogy and Beyond', *Review of English Studies*, 62 (2011), 716–37.

Levith, Murray J., *Shakespeare's Cues and Prompts: Intertextuality and Sources* (London: Continuum, 2007).

Lewis, Simon L. and Mark A. Maslin, 'Defining the Anthropocene', *Nature*, 519 (12 March 2015), 171–80.

Lynch, Stephen J., *Shakespearean Intertextuality: Studies in Selected Sources and Plays* (Westport, CT: Greenwood Press, 1998).

Lyne, Raphael, *Memory and Intertextuality in Renaissance Literature* (Cambridge: Cambridge University Press, 2016).

Macfarlane, Robert, *Original Copy: Plagiarism and Originality in Nineteenth-Century Literature* (Oxford: Oxford University Press, 2007).

Maguire, Laurie and Emma Smith, 'What is a Source? Or, How Shakespeare Read His Marlowe', *Shakespeare Survey*, 68 (2015), 15–31.

Malone, Edmond, *An Account of the Incidents, from which the Title and Part of the Story of Shakespeare's 'Tempest' were Derived* (London: C. and R. Baldwin, 1808).

Mann, Elizabeth L., 'The Problem of Originality in English Literary Criticism, 1750–1800', *Philological Quarterly*, 18 (1939), 97–118.

Maxwell, Julie, 'How the Renaissance (Mis)Used Sources', in Laurie Maguire, ed., *How to Do Things with Shakespeare: New Approaches, New Essays* (Oxford: Blackwell, 2007), 54–76.

McGrail, Mary Ann, 'From Plagiarism to Sources', *Poetica: An International Journal of Linguistic-Literary Studies*, 48 (1997), 169–85.

Miola, Robert S., *Shakespeare and Classical Tragedy: The Influence of Seneca* (Oxford: Clarendon Press, 1992).

Most, Glenn W., 'The Rise and Fall of *Quellenforschung*', in Ann Blair and Anja-Silvia Goeing, eds, *For the Sake of Learning: Essays in Honor of Anthony Grafton*, 2 vols (Leiden: Brill, 2016), II, 933–54.

Muir, Kenneth, *The Sources of Shakespeare's Plays* (London: Methuen, 1977).

Orgel, Stephen, *The Reader in the Book: A Study of Spaces and Traces* (Oxford: Oxford University Press, 2015).

O'Sullivan, Timothy M., *Walking in Roman Culture* (Cambridge: Cambridge University Press, 2011).

Palfrey, Simon, *Poor Tom: Living 'King Lear'* (Chicago: Chicago University Press, 2014).

Peltonen, Markku, *The Duel in Early Modern England: Civility, Politeness and Honour* (Cambridge: Cambridge University Press, 2002).

Perloff, Marjorie, *Unoriginal Genius: Poetry by Other Means in the New Century* (Chicago: University of Chicago Press, 2010).

Pigman III, G.W., 'Versions of Imitation in the Renaissance', *Renaissance Quarterly*, 33 (1980), 1–32.

Pollard, Tanya, 'What's Hecuba to Shakespeare?', *Renaissance Quarterly*, 65 (2012), 1060–93.

Pollard, Tanya, 'Greek Playbooks and Dramatic Forms', in Allison K. Deutermann and András Kiséry, eds, *Formal Matters: Reading the Materials of English Renaissance Literature* (Manchester: Manchester University Press, 2013), 99–123.

Purkis, James, *Shakespeare and Manuscript Drama: Canon, Collaboration and Text* (Cambridge: Cambridge University Press, 2016).

Quint, David., *Origin and Originality in Renaissance Literature* (New Haven: Yale University Press, 1983).

Rhein, Stefan, 'Melanchthon and Greek Literature', in Timothy J. Wengert and M. Patrick Graham, eds, *Philip Melanchthon (1497–1560) and the Commentary* (Sheffield: Sheffield Academic Press, 1997), 149–70.

Roberts, David, 'Ravishing Strides: Signs of the Peripatetic in Early Modern Performance', *New Theatre Quarterly*, 17 (2001), 18–30.

Rosenmeyer, Thomas G., *Senecan Drama and Stoic Cosmology* (Berkeley: University of California Press, 1989).

Scott, Charlotte, *Shakespeare's Nature: From Cultivation to Culture* (Oxford: Oxford University Press, 2014).

Scott, Mary Augusta, '*The Book of the Courtyer*: A Possible Source of Benedick and Beatrice', *PMLA*, 16 (1901), 475–502.

Sher, Antony, *The Year of the King: An Actor's Diary* (London: Chatto & Windus, 1985).

Sherman, William H., *Used Books: Marking Readers in Renaissance England* (Philadelphia: University of Pennsylvania Press, 2008).

Simrock, Karl, *Die Quellen des Shakspeare in Novellen, Märchen und Sagen* (Berlin: In der Finckeschen Buchhandlung, 1831).

Skottowe, Augustine, *The Life of Shakespeare: Enquiries into the Originality of his Dramatic Plots and Characters* (London: Longman, Hurst, Rees, Orme, Brown, and Green, 1824).

Slack, Paul, *The Invention of Improvement: Information and Material Progress in Seventeenth-Century England* (Oxford: Oxford University Press, 2015).

Smith, Bruce R., 'Finding Your Footing in Shakespeare's Verse', in Jonathan F. S. Post, ed., *The Oxford Handbook of Shakespeare's Poetry* (Oxford: Oxford University Press, 2013), 323–39.

Snider, Alvin, *Origin and Authority in Seventeenth-Century England: Bacon, Milton, Butler* (Toronto: University of Toronto Press, 1994).

Solnit, Rebecca, *Wanderlust: A History of Walking* (London: Verso, 2001).

Stagg, Robert, 'Shakespeare's Feet: Puns, Metre, Meaning', *Literature Compass*, 12/3 (2015), 83–92.

Stapleton, M. L., *Fated Sky: The Femina Furens in Shakespeare* (Newark: University of Delaware Press, 2000).

Stern, Simon, 'Copyright, Originality, and the Public Domain in Eighteenth-Century England', in Reginald McGinnis, ed., *Originality and Intellectual Property in the French and English Enlightenment* (New York: Routledge, 2009), 69–101.

Stern, Tiffany, ' "You That Walk i'th Galleries": Standing and Walking in the Galleries of the Globe Theatre', *Shakespeare Quarterly*, 51 (2000), 211–16.

Taylor, Gary, 'Collaboration', in Dympna Callaghan and Suzanne Gossett, eds, *Shakespeare in our Time* (New York: Bloomsbury, 2016), 141–9.

Tudeau-Clayton, Margaret, *Jonson, Shakespeare and Early Modern Virgil* (Cambridge: Cambridge University Press, 1998).

Vickers, Brian, '"Upstart Crow"? The Myth of Shakespeare's Plagiarism',
    Review of English Studies, 68 (2017), 244–67.

Walter, Harriet, *Macbeth* (London: Faber, 2002).

White, Harold Ogden, *Plagiarism and Imitation During the English Renaissance*
    (Cambridge, MA: Harvard University Press, 1935).

Wilson, John Dover, 'Malone and the Upstart Crow', *Shakespeare Survey*,
    4 (1951), 56–68.

Woodbridge, Linda, 'Patchwork: Piecing the Early Modern in England's First
    Century of Print Culture', *English Literary Renaissance*, 23:1 (1993), 5–45.

Index